ONCE UPON A TIME THERE WAS A LITTLE GIRL

To ~~[name]~~,
I wish you a life
of love & peace.
With love & gratitude,
Marcella

ONCE UPON A TIME THERE WAS A LITTLE GIRL

the healing power of fairy tales in the lives of seven women

Marcella Hannon Shields, Ph.D.

iUniverse, Inc.
New York Bloomington Shanghai

once upon a time there was a little girl
the healing power of fairy tales in the lives of seven women

iUniverse books may be ordered through booksellers or by contacting:

iUniverse
1663 Liberty Drive
Bloomington, IN 47403
www.iuniverse.com
1-800-Authors (1-800-288-4677)

Because of the dynamic nature of the Internet, any Web addresses or links contained in this book may have changed since publication and may no longer be valid.

The information, ideas, and suggestions in this book are not intended as a substitute for professional advice. Before following any suggestions contained in this book, consult your physician or mental health professional. Neither the author nor the publisher shall be liable or responsible for any loss or damage allegedly arising as a consequence of your use or application of any information or suggestions in this book.

ISBN: 978-0-595-46106-6 (pbk)
ISBN: 978-0-595-71054-6 (cloth)
ISBN: 978-0-595-90406-8 (ebk)

Printed in the United States of America

For the seven women
who share their stories
in these pages,
and for little girls
everywhere

... all sorrows can be borne,

if you put them

into a story ...

—Karen Blixen

CONTENTS

ACKNOWLEDGMENTS

My heartfelt thanks go first to the seven women who trusted me to accompany them on the paths of their healing journeys. Witnessing their courage as they reclaimed their lives was a profound privilege.

I am deeply grateful to Marion Woodman, Jungian analyst, guide, and mentor, whose encouragement motivated me to share the stories of these seven women.

My special thanks go to all those who generously, patiently, and graciously helped with the many revisions of the manuscript that has become this book: Susan Clough, Deanna Lagroix, Maryian Milsom, and Leanne Kloppenborg.

I am also greatly indebted to Teri Degler, author, for her critique of the initial draft. She asked the hard questions that forced me to prune the work and to focus with greater clarity on the message I wanted to convey. I am also very grateful to the other readers of the manuscript in its many phases, who critiqued the work and offered suggestions for its development: Mary Jane Brustman, Marilyn Daniels, Donna Mahoney Lynch, Mark Nachmias, and Paulette Peterson.

My thanks to Diane Fassel and Moira MacDougall, for gracious permission to include their unpublished poems in this book.

I am also extremely grateful to Deborah Corcoran and her staff at the Hawley Public Library, for their patience with my many questions and for their untiring willingness to locate the resources I needed.

I particularly want to thank my two sisters: Mary Hannon Williams and Ann Hannon Carden for their invaluable support and their willingness to share their expertise in preparing the manuscript for publication. My special thanks to Mary for patiently teaching me the basic computer skills I needed to finish the book, and for assisting me in formatting the work for presentation to the publisher. I am extremely grateful to Ann for her exceptional work in editing these pages, and for her continued enthusiasm and encouragement.

My deep gratitude to our three daughters: Anna, Jennifer, and Nicole, whose loving kindness motivated me to keep going. They continually asked the encouraging question, "Is it finished yet?"

Our five granddaughters: Kristen, Brittany, Jessica, Bethany, and Grace inspired me to dedicate this book to little girls everywhere. Their presence in my life is a gift beyond measure. May they always know the love with which I hold each of them in my heart.

Finally, I want to acknowledge my immense gratitude to my husband, Eldon, a prince in the most profound meaning of the word! He attended computer courses at night so that he could work on the final draft of the manuscript. He believed in the message of this book and continued to encourage me to finish the work I had begun. He brought meals to my writing loft so that I could keep working. His love and compassion never cease to amaze and sustain me.

PROLOGUE

Once upon a time, there were seven little girls who had no mothers.

The first little girl's mother died when the girl was two years old. Her mother went to the hospital to have a baby and never came home again.

The second little girl's mother left her when she was nine months old. She never saw her mother again until she was sixteen, and, once again, she was rejected.

The third little girl had a mother who was hoping for a boy. When she was very young, she felt that she did not belong to her mother. At first, she wondered if she had been adopted. But later, she came to the realization that if her mother had been given a choice, she would have selected a boy.

The fourth little girl had a mother who was too busy with her own life to take time to be present for the little girl when she needed her most.

The fifth little girl had a mother who was anxious and overwhelmed with motherhood. She needed her little girl to reflect well on her as a mother and show signs of a good upbringing.

The sixth little girl had a mother who was in an unhappy and emotionally abusive marriage. She needed the little girl to take care of her and make her happy.

The seventh little girl had a mother whose *own* mother had committed suicide and was never spoken of in the family again. This little girl's mother married a man like her own father, trying to make her own loss right again, and living with her own feeling of unworthiness to be alive. The sad and shameful family secret hung like a pall over the little girl, who struggled to prove that she, too, was worthy of life.

Although they were born on four different continents, the seven little girls grew up to be women living in the same city. One day they met one another and shared their experiences of loss.

This book is the story of the transformation of these seven little girls into seven powerful, wise women, who claimed their right to spin the patterns of their lives anew.

INTRODUCTION

What would happen if one woman told the truth about her life?
The world would split open.
—Muriel Rukeyser

This book is the story of *seven* women who had the courage to tell the truth about their lives. What they shared in common was the loss of their mothers when they were young, either through death or physical and emotional abandonment. Working with the seven women whose lives unfold throughout the chapters of this book was like sitting on a diamond mine with no awareness of the magnificent treasure buried below. As each woman's hidden story rose to the surface to be heard and honored, miraculous shards of light rose with it from the deep.

Kathrin Asper calls this hidden story our *mute biography*.[1] The intense emotions associated with early childhood experiences are often buried deep within our unconscious, and thus, have no words. This is why the trauma of emotional abandonment in early life, regardless of the reason for the loss, is so difficult to unearth. To free ourselves from the isolation, fear, and grief of such a profound loss, we need a compassionate witness, someone to mourn with us, to support and encourage our efforts to find the words to tell our hidden story. Through their openness to listen to and honor one another's losses, these seven women escorted each other to the healing well within.

The inspiration for this book came from a seminar by Kathrin Asper, entitled "The Tale of Rumpelstilskin: The Voice of the Patriarchy," which she presented at a Jungian conference in Einsiedlin, Switzerland, where I was studying in the summer of 1994. In her seminar, Dr Asper explored the use of the Grimm's fairy tale, "Rumpelstilskin," in psychoanalytic work. She led us through the tale as if it were our personal dream, and invited us to engage in active imagination work with the various images in the story. Suddenly, an entire decade of my life became clear. I could barely contain the emotional response it evoked. I sat there stunned. In that moment, I realized for the first time why I had suffered a ruptured ovarian tumor just as I was completing the final chapter of my doctoral dissertation. That rupture cost me my right ovary, and, because of ensuing peritonitis, came close to costing me my life.

The images in the tale of "Rumpelstilskin" held a key to a part of myself that I had not yet discovered in my own personal work in Jungian analysis. I realized in that moment that my ovary, a part of my feminine generative life, had been sacrificed to the father/king patriarchal world of academia. I became aware that I had obtained my doctorate so that my father, long since deceased, would be proud of me. I had sacrificed my feminine nature, just as the miller's daughter had felt compelled to do in the tale of "Rumpelstilskin." I was deeply shaken and moved by the power of this experience. I decided then to bring the opportunity of working with fairy tales to seven women who had been doing their psychotherapeutic work with me for several years. They all had grown up, like the miller's daughter in the tale of "Rumpelstilskin," without a motherly feminine presence in their lives. Although they had made progress in their personal work, they continued to carry the heavy burden of the early loss of their mothers.

When I returned home from Switzerland, I went to the children's section of the main public library and asked the librarian to show me where the fairy tales were for children aged five through nine. This is the time period in which children generally confirm their conclusions about how they are going to survive in life. I thumbed through the books the librarian identified until I found a tale in which the daughter had no mothering presence. I decided to include the tale of "Rumpelstilskin" because of my own personal experience in Switzerland. I selected six additional tales with the help of some of the women who were clients in my psychological practice. I then invited seven women to be part of a group to explore fairy tales as an adjunct to their ongoing psychotherapy. I clarified with the women that our work together was intended to be an opportunity to use the resources of the group to reflect on what the tales had to say about our own life stories. I also indicated that I hoped that our work together would culminate in a book about exploring fairy tales as part of the psychotherapeutic process, and would provide an opportunity for us to share what we had learned with others.

We met weekly for seven months, from November 1994 through May 1995, working with a particular tale until it appeared evident that each woman had gleaned what was valuable for her from the experience. Usually, we spent three or more sessions focusing on a given tale. We approached each story as if it were a dream, making associations and doing active imagination dialogues with the images and characters in the tale. Between sessions, the women were encouraged to express any reactions they had to these images in words, art, or movement. This was intended to help them connect more deeply with the images. They were also encouraged to record their own dreams before and after our work on the tales.

As I had expected, certain fairy tales had a more powerful effect on some women than on others. Some were able to readily identify with a given tale as an expression of their own life stories. The power of the process was evident right from the first session. Several women experienced physical reactions to the stories, even when they were not able to consciously connect to the images in the tales.

We began our weekly sessions with the tale of "Rumpelstilskin," followed by "The Handless Maiden," "Mother Hulda," "Briar Rose" (also known as "Sleeping Beauty"), "The Raven," "Clever Beauty" (a variation of the tale of "The Three Spinners"), and finally, "Snow White." To avoid getting trapped in an intellectual interpretation of the fairy tales, and to ensure that their responses to the stories would be their own, I encouraged the women to refrain from reading any commentaries or interpretations of the tales that explained their meaning. This was important to ensure that each woman's responses would be her own conscious and unconscious reactions to the tales. I also avoided reading any related material so that I would not be looking for a particular response and unconsciously guide the group in that direction. I had no agenda or set of expectations. Indeed, the process provided many surprises for all of us!

We worked with a tale for as long as a response to the story emerged from each woman's dreams and reflections. When this seemed complete (with the realization that additional material related to the story might emerge later), we moved on to the next tale.

After completing the work on all seven tales, the group met in October of 1995 for an intensive weeklong experience. At this gathering, I invited each woman to share the life experiences that had brought her into psychotherapy, and to describe what she had learned in the process of working with the fairy tales. Each woman ritualized her experience at the end of her presentation, including the other members of the group in the process.

Witnessing the courage of these seven women was a profound privilege. They bonded with one another through the sharing of their pain, their joy, and their creative responses to life. We sang, danced, made bread, listened to music and poetry, and viewed beautiful paintings, all of which celebrated the lives of each of these brave women.

The group members continued to meet annually to share and celebrate what was happening in their lives.

Four years after completing their initial work, the women gathered to revisit the fairy tales, and to explore what each tale now said to them. The new insights the women had four years later were striking! Fairy tales that had had no particular energy for them in our initial work were now charged with meaning. New realizations and deeper personal insights emerged.

The power of fairy tales lies in the fact that they are timeless stories of the struggles of the child who feels abandoned and alone. The seven tales, chosen because they included no nurturing maternal presence, provided a place for each of these seven women to begin to focus her energy on alternatives to despair in the face of abandonment. In each tale, the heroine finds a way, beyond what appears to be an overwhelming obstacle, to reach her true potential. All the tales we explored are many centuries old. It was a powerful source of consolation for each of the women to hear a variation of her life story told with a happy ending. It was also hopeful for her to know that girl children throughout the ages have encountered some of the same issues she has been forced to face and have survived to tell the tale.

There are three ways of viewing fairy tales: the literal story, as it is usually shared with children who need no interpretation; the personal story, which involves viewing the tale from that place in the story where we find ourselves; and the collective, or archetypal, story, which explores what the tale means in relation to the overall communal or cosmic story of humankind.[2]

Our focus as a group was on the personal story. In each group session, and in her own individual work, each woman entered into the tale from the perspective of her own life story. I encouraged the women to approach each fairy tale as a collective dream into which she could insert herself as if it were her own dream. The effects of this process were profound. As an experienced psychologist, I was amazed at how consistently the process accelerated the awakening of personal consciousness in each woman.

"Archetypes are universal images that have existed throughout the ages and are found across different languages and cultures."[3] These "primordial images" (as Jung called them) arise spontaneously out of the unconscious and are found in dreams, fairy tales, and other experiences of the imagination. Examples of archetypal images include the wise old woman, the king or queen, and the divine child.

Fairy tales are related to archetypal dreams of the unconscious. They differ from folk tales in which the hero or heroine has a numinous experience through an encounter with an archetypal image. Generally, in a folk tale, the hero or heroine decides to cross a threshold into the "other world," but he or she is free to run back anytime into the "real world."[4] In a fairy tale, archetypal images meet one another and there is no "other world" to which they can retreat. When we encounter such archetypal images in our dreams, we must either work through the conflicts and dilemmas they present, or wake up.

Each of the women in the group had powerful archetypal experiences with different images in the tales. This was evidenced both in her dreams, and in the life choices she made in claiming her own uniqueness and wisdom as a woman.

Feminists have long debated the dangerous potential of fairy tales to reinforce cultural norms of patriarchal dominance.[5] There is ample evidence of this in the

Disney versions of classic fairy tales, and in the adaptations the Grimm brothers made in order to support cultural norms for good girls and boys.[6] However, the essence of the tales we explored as a group was the triumph of the daughter/heroine over the obstacles she had to face in order to survive. We used the tales in their original purpose: to convey, in symbolic language, a life story of victory over difficulties that appear to be insurmountable.

The symbolic language of fairy tales is also the language of our dreams. The tales we explored were the opening script for each woman as she began to identify the symbolic language of her own life story and to access unconscious creative energy for her healing.

For the sake of the reader who is not accustomed to terms generally used in Jungian analytic work, I have attempted to use common language throughout this book. Whenever a term that may not be familiar first appears in the text, I provide a definition. In addition, a glossary of terms is available at the end of the book for the times when I may have neglected to fully explain a word or phrase.

One of the challenges of using terms that have their origin in another language is making their meaning clear. For example, the use of the terms *masculine* and *feminine*, have a particular meaning in a Jungian approach to understanding dreams. When a masculine image appears in a dream or fairy tale it can carry either positive or negative energy (e.g., the prince or the devil). A positive masculine image in the dream of either a man or a woman is generally connected with energy that is focused, purposeful, and moving toward one's destiny. A negative masculine image, on the other hand, is usually associated with energy that derails us from our life purpose, negates our efforts to discover our own life paths, and impedes our progress. A positive feminine image in the dreams of either a man or a woman is generally connected with energy that is creative, generative, and committed to relationships with others, our body, and the natural world. A negative feminine image carries the opposite energy. It is usually associated with the devouring, rejecting, and/or negating of one's creative life. The dreamer decides if the energy is positive or negative.

As women and men, we have both masculine and feminine aspects of ourselves that seek a *yin-yang* balance on the path of healing. Jung referred to this process as the *path of individuation*, the choice to become truly oneself that brings one to the realization of the greatest possible fulfillment of one's innate potential. It is not about "egotistical self-realization," but rather an appreciation of one's life as an ongoing journey of conscious development.[7] Each of the women in the group understood that she was on the path to individuation. Each declared her willingness to commit her life energy to reclaiming the self she lost when she lost her mother.

This book is divided into eight chapters. Chapter 1 provides a context for the exploration of the tales and introduces each of the seven women to the reader. Chapters 2 through 7 explore each fairy tale and the responses of the women to the tale. Because the tale of "Rumpelstilskin" and the tale of "Clever Beauty" (a variation of the tale of "The Three Spinners") are related to one another, they are explored together in one chapter. Otherwise, the chapters follow the sequence in which the group explored the tales. Each chapter begins with an introduction and a synopsis of the tale. The themes in the tale are then examined, along with the dreams, active imagination work, and reflections of the women related to that theme. Each chapter ends with the responses of the women when we revisited the tale four years later. Chapter 8 is a summary of the learning of each woman over the period of our work together. Following each chapter, the reader will find a list of reflection questions. Additional reflection questions for mothers, stepmothers, grandmothers, and fathers raising daughters without a consistent maternal presence are included in the appendix. A companion guide is available, upon request, for psychologists and psychotherapists interested in using the process in their practice.

Throughout the book, I have attempted to be faithful to each woman's story by reporting her dreams, active imagination work, and reflections related to each tale, in her own words.

The active imagination process, which is explained in greater detail in Chapter 1, involves setting up an imaginary dialogue (generally recorded in writing) between the images in a dream or fairy tale in order to uncover the unconscious meaning of the images. Because I believe that the body is an essential messenger for the unconscious, I encouraged each woman to record and report any physical symptoms or reactions she experienced during or after working with the images in the tale.

Each of the women in the group has a pseudonym, which she chose. To maintain her privacy, some details of her life that were not central to her story have been changed.

This book is *not* about blaming mothers, who have endured enough recrimination from psychological circles. It is about healing the mother-daughter relationship through conscious understanding and development of the greatest feminine virtue: compassion, for oneself and others. In fact, through the process of our work together on the seven fairy tales, remarkable healing took place between the women and their mothers across thousands of miles, and in some cases, even across the chasm of death.

In Einsiedlin, Switzerland, where the idea for this book was born, there is an ancient monastery in which an image of the Black Madonna is prominently displayed. Her image is considered a source of healing for women who are barren and want to become mothers. The Black Madonna is associated with Isis, the Egyptian goddess of motherly love and the regeneration of life from death.[8] There was a simple replica of the Black Madonna in the chapel of the retreat house where the Jungian seminar was being held. I went several times to the little chapel just to sit before the powerful ebony simplicity of that image. Here was a maternal energy that transcended the ages. She became a symbol for me of the healing power of love through suffering.

In the summer of 2004, I began a sabbatical year to focus my energy on completing the manuscript that I had begun ten years earlier. As I sorted through the volumes and volumes of notes and material I had accumulated through those years, I felt overwhelmed by the task before me. While I was struggling to recapture my energy to write again, I came across J. D. Salinger's advice to his fictional character, Buddy, "Write what you would like to read."[9] When I asked *myself* the question, it became very clear that what I needed to write about was the courage of seven women who significantly altered their lives, who claimed their own potential despite the odds of their familial and environmental histories, who declared a sisterhood with one another, and who moved beyond their own personal losses to lead meaningful lives that have made a difference in the world.

This book is the story of seven women who discovered the treasure of womanhood without the love and attention of a mother; who, despite, or perhaps even because of, their early loss, fought to stay alive and to claim their own power. They are seven women whose contributions to their worlds will be remembered long after they are gone. They stood up to be counted among the courageous heart-full women who had experienced heartbreak in their lives and yet continued to believe in the possibility of healing in relationships. They are seven women who, through their own experiences of being wounded, became healers for others, carriers and midwives of the creative life of other women.

On the day in August 1995 when I began this book, I wrote in my journal:

> As I begin this work of recording the remarkable transformation I have witnessed in the lives of seven women, I am sitting beside the lake, my feet in the cooling water and my beach chair perched on the edge of a magnificent rock carved into crevices and curves by ancient glaciers. Above me are the layers of stone formations etched by the wind and the persistent water rising and falling throughout the seasons of snow, ice, sun, and rain. Below me, the water swirls and hurls itself in a chaotic rhythm against the rock, caressing my feet like liquid silk as it continues

to wear away the surface of the stone. It reminds me of the song about drops of water gradually wearing away what otherwise seems impossible to move or change.[10]

This book is my "drop of water" and those of the seven women who courageously share their stories in these chapters. May the water that has flowed from our mingling tears of suffering and joy leave a new trace of hope for women everywhere who lost their mothers when they were young.

CHAPTER I

SPINNING THREADS THAT HOLD

Sophia whispered:
You have to keep on spinning
'Til you find the place that holds
Your story strong.

Every woman is a weaver
Spinning life against destruction
It is hunger, yes, and hope that
Moves us on.

My stories are the spinning
Fragile threads from deep inside me
How I longed to spin them out
And have them hold.

"But that makes no sense," he told me
Each husband, doctor, teacher
And the web was broken.
Stories left untold.

Sophia, you keep on spinning
Threads of love out of aloneness
And you long to have them hold
Upon the earth.

Spin within me, through me, with me
Hold me close against the storming
For I have stories
Yet to birth.

(Claire, *untitled poem*)

One evening, after we had been meeting weekly for about four months, Claire taught us all how to spin. She borrowed spindles from friends and brought scraps of cotton and wool for each of us to spin into threads. Most of us felt very awkward rotating the spindles. It took practice and patience to work the fragments into a thread that would hold. This was essential to the process. If the thread was weak, it would not hold and would break when it was used for weaving. If the thread did not hold, nothing more could happen. It could not be used to create a new pattern.

Each of the women in the group understood that the ability to spin symbolized her opportunity to reconstitute what had unraveled in her life into a strong thread that could be rewoven into a new life pattern. That night the women named themselves the Spinsters.

The motivation to learn to spin came out of the first four fairy tales we had explored: "Rumpelstilskin," "The Handless Maiden," "Mother Hulda," and "Briar Rose" (also known as "Sleeping Beauty").[11] In the tale of "Rumpelstilskin," the daughter is required to spin straw into gold. The handless maiden has no hands and is unable to spin. She, therefore, remains dependent on others for her survival. In the tale of "Mother Hulda," the daughter loses her spindle down the well and is ordered by her stepmother to jump into the dark pit to retrieve it. In "Briar Rose" ("Sleeping Beauty"), the thirteenth fairy predicts that the princess will prick her finger on a spindle and die, but the twelfth fairy modifies the curse to falling asleep for a hundred years. The king has all the spindles banished in an attempt to save his daughter. As a result, all spinning stopped in the kingdom, and nothing new was woven into existence.

Spinners of Threads and Tales

Historically, the spinster was associated with the storyteller, a woman who was able to spin tales as she spun the fragments of wool into threads for weaving. The distaff, or spindle, side of one's family was considered one's maternal heritage. "Swearing on Berthe's distaff," according to Jacob Grimm, meant swearing on the honor of one's grandmother or maternal ancestors.[12] Berthe's father was reported to be the king of Hungary and her mother, the legendary Blancheflor, the daughter of the Byzantine emperor. She was, therefore, a daughter of the East and the West—that is, in her the opposites came together. The traditional beginning of fairy tales, "Once upon a time" has an alternate in Italian that translates, "In the time when Berthe spun."[13]

Berthe, whose name means *bright* or *light*, was the mother of the great king Charlemagne and the sister of St. Martin of Tours. She was said to have large feet from working the spinning wheel with her foot. There is some question about the accuracy of this assumption, because there is no evidence of the spinning wheel being used in Europe before the fourteenth century. The other noble-women of Berthe's time had small feet, which were considered more appropriate for women.

Berthe's large feet were associated with the splayed foot of the storyteller Mother Goose. To have a splayed foot was considered suspicious because it was connected to one's animal nature. The woman who developed her capacity to spin and weave and tell tales in the process could stand on her own feet and earn her own living independent of her husband, father, or brothers. Perhaps Berthe was associated with a saintly son and brother to give her credibility. To be a spinner of threads and tales was considered potentially dangerous. Such a woman did not hold her tongue, a virtue considered essential in a good wife.[14] Over time, the title *spinster* became a derogatory term referring to an old maid, a woman who could not find a husband, or one who was not chosen in marriage. The unmarried woman was viewed by society as having little value. Interestingly, after the women decided to call themselves the Spinsters, negative reactions arose from their male partners, who expressed concerns about what was happening in the group. It seems that just the title was threatening!

There is historical evidence of a connection between the sexual initiation rites of young girls and spinning. In some rites of puberty, girls were taught, amidst rituals of song and dance, the feminine skills of spinning and weaving. The moon was connected to spinning and weaving human life, as it was associated with the menstrual cycle and the conception and birth of children.[15] Fertility was seen as a process of spinning and weaving, and therefore, closely connected to the image of the mother who spins and weaves us into life. The threads of the daughter's relationship with her mother are intricately connected to the patterns of life relationships that the daughter spins and weaves for herself.

For each of the seven women in the group, the thread of the mother-daughter relationship had been broken, either through death or physical and/or emotional abandonment. When she began her psychological work, each woman was strug-gling to re-spin the threads of her own feminine existence from the fragments of her relationship with her mother. Each was faced with transforming the fragments of her life into strong threads that would hold as she rewove a new life pattern.

Carl Jung observed that a woman with a negative relationship to her mother, which he referred to as a *negative mother complex*, might actually have a greater chance of achieving higher consciousness. He reasoned that the loss of her mother forces the woman to fundamentally reappraise her feminine nature. She is not able to become a woman unless she becomes conscious.[16] Such women, according to Jung, live closer than others to the unconscious world. However, they may only be willing to surrender to becoming conscious when they are in a state of desperation and desolation. This was evident in the lives of all seven women. They did not seek help until, no longer able to defend themselves from the pain of their loss, they succumbed to depression. Asking for guidance through their pain from a woman-therapist required considerable courage. In doing so, they risked being rejected again by another mother.

Who Are the Seven Spinners?

Spinning is a symbolic expression of the work of the unconscious. It involves putting pieces that have been separated from our consciousness together and making a thread connection from the fragments. Through the process of associating images from dreams, the threads of the message struggling to be revealed begin to hold, and the fabric of the message can be woven and deciphered. Dreams are the product of the Great Mother spinning her fantasies. The thread she spins can be traced to reveal the coded message.[17] Indeed, a powerful dream had pushed each of the seven women into psychotherapy.

Claire began psychotherapy after she had a serious accident while bicycling through India. The accident forced her to confront the fragility of her life in the face of death. In one of her dreams, she was swimming underwater, while torpedoes passed her on all sides. The power surrounding her was overwhelming and frightening. Then, Claire realized that the torpedoes were an image of her own power! She could claim this power if she touched the passing torpedoes with her foot. Claire began to recognize that she did not need to be afraid of the power of her emotions, which, for the most part, she had previously suppressed. She had felt herself powerless in the face of the demands of others, even when her own life was at risk.

After her accident, Claire came to realize that she would actually prefer death to continuing to live according to her partner's agenda. She recognized that she could no longer follow someone else's itinerary for her life. However, she was not yet clear about her own direction. In severe pain, with no one to help her, Claire found a quiet place in a meadow. She was startled to realize that she could "be still and still be alive." All her life she had been actively moving and attending to others. Whatever she gave was never enough. She had lived for and through men who always seemed to expect more and more from her. When she began her psycho-therapeutic journey, Claire found herself so angry that at times she was speechless, unable to take a breath. She decided to learn to play the flute so that she could make a sound that could be heard.

In Claire's birth family, neither her mother nor her father had been able to express love. Her mother began a career that took her away most of the time when Claire was very young. Her father was generally depressed but controlling. Little Claire took on the role of peacemaker, a little mother to her parents and siblings. She carried this familiar role into her adult life. During her psychotherapeutic work, Claire came to realize that she had a choice. She stated, "I don't want to be a mother anymore to all those in my life that demand my time and energy." She was increasingly fatigued and experiencing tinnitus (ringing in her ears). Then she declared, "I want my hearing back; I have no tolerance for whining, complaining, and unexpressed anger." Claire yearned to be a rooted, solid person. She resolved to come to the place where she could trust and honor herself.

The dream image that brought **Jessica** to do her inner work was a cataclysmic scene of a major earthquake in which the earth opened up beneath her. There was desolation everywhere, as the quake became more expansive and the ground under her became more and more tenuous. Finally, she had no safe place on which to stand. This was her dream:

> I was in a place that looked similar to the part of the country in which I was born and raised. There had just been a major earthquake, and there were giant crevices where there once had been houses. I was on a part of the earth that had not quite fully collapsed. But I could tell that it was shaky, and that I could easily slide into the abyss.

Then, a few days later, Jessica had the following dream:

> I was back in my hometown again and went for a walk across a field. I did not realize how muddy it was. My boots sank into the mud, and I could not move.

In her associations with the images in her dream, Jessica recognized the opening of Mother Earth as an invitation to examine the depths of her tenuous relationship with her own mother and the history of her maternal heritage.

The earth is a metaphor for mother, that which supports and nourishes our life. There was a dark secret in Jessica's family about her maternal family. When she reflected on the images in her dreams, Jessica realized that what had been kept a secret so long was now being unearthed. Trying to keep the story hidden was no longer possible. Jessica also realized how the history of depression in her family was keeping her stuck, literally mired in the mud of the earth mother. Using the process of active imagination, Jessica changed the ending of the dream by step-ping out of the boots to let the mud ooze through her toes. To escape from the fear of the dark secret and how it might contaminate her, she let herself feel the mud so that it could cleanse her.

Just before we began our work with the seven fairy tales, Jessica found the story of "Peter Rabbit," which had been one of her favorites as a child. Jessica saw Peter's dilemma as not knowing how to get his mother to love him, and so, he hid under baskets to avoid her. Jessica decided that she no longer wanted to hide who she was or to keep the family secret, even though she feared her mother's wrath and that of her siblings if she spoke the truth.

The loss of a significant relationship brought **Michaela** into psychotherapy. Several dreams precipitated her decision to do her inner work. The first was within days of her moving into a university dormitory. She dreamed:

> I was in my room and heard a lot of noise in the corridor. It was late at night. I thought I was awake. I was curious about what was going on but also wondered if someone needed help. I tried to get up, but couldn't, and I kept telling myself that I should. Then, I dreamed that I fell asleep again, and the noise in the cor-ridor awakened me again, and I went through the same thoughts and immobility.

In the morning Michaela asked other people in the dorm if they had heard the noise. They said that nothing had happened in the corridor that night. Then, a week later, the day before her first psychotherapy session, she had the following dream:

> A person (a man?) wrapped like a mummy and in chains was in a big foyer. He (or she) was being thrown out the front door by a group of men. The chains were either removed or fell off as the person was thrown out, but the wrappings remained.

Reflecting on the dream, Michaela realized that she was the one being thrown out the door in the dream. Part of her was wrapped up like a mummy, paralyzed by the binding and unable to speak. She reported that she was indeed fearful that her depressive symptoms would prevent her from participating at the university and that she would be "thrown out" (this did happen six months later). However, in the dream, even though she still felt bound and helpless, she was no longer in chains. Through the process of her psychotherapeutic work, Michaela gradually released herself from the sense she felt of being bound by others' expectations of her, and by her own expectations of herself. Through her continued exploration of her dreams and work with the other women in the group, the origin of her fear of the noise in the corridor gradually revealed itself, and she was no longer paralyzed.

A mummy is a dead body preserved by binding. *Mummy* is also a Canadian term of endearment for mother. Michaela had been estranged from her mother for years, as well as from a sense of the value of her own femininity. She grew up feeling unattractive and apart from other women. She felt the deep loss of being cut off from the feminine in her own body. Michaela recognized that she was caught between her yearning for and her fear and avoidance of intimate relationships. She knew that she needed to give herself over to love, which she both longed for and resisted.

Michaela reported that her early dream images as she grew up had been of wounded children. Just before we began our work in the group, she dreamed:

> I saw a mother dog by the side of the road. Its abdomen had been split open and the teats turned inward. The puppies were trying to suckle from the dead mother, but they could not reach the teats to get the milk.

What motivated **Alexis** to begin the psychotherapeutic process was her fear of being responsible for someone else's pain and suffering. She was terrified of the unconscious and of dark archetypal images, which she feared would take over her life if she dared explore them. She associated these images with primitive black magic and images of the devil into whose power she was told as child she would be taken if she were not a good girl. Being good, for Alexis, meant being as pure, quiet, and unassuming as a lily of the valley (her favorite flower).

Alexis made the decision that she could no longer live in the state of anxiety and sadness that had kept her isolated and silent so long. Relying on the gift of her richly creative interior life, she wrote a fairy tale about a bird kept in a golden cage that was too frightened to sing. Her inner realization was, "What good is all this, if the song dies?" Alexis knew that she had to find her own voice if her soul was to survive.

Alexis's mother had also had no voice of her own. She too had felt the constant pressure of always having to do "the right thing." The touch of her anxious mother had not been reassuring to young Alexis. As a child Alexis had feared that she would be given to the gypsy who sold vegetables in the town square if she was not a good girl. She both longed to be a gypsy and out from under the controlling environment of her home and, at the same time, feared being abandoned by her mother because she was not the good little girl her mother expected her to be.

The dream images in Alexis's early psychotherapeutic work included tidal waves, which swept her out to sea to drown and over which she felt she had no control. In another image she found herself hanging from a tower, trying to hold onto a child. These dream images brought Alexis face to face with her perception that she was helpless in the face of powerful external forces. Her emotional life overwhelmed her in a tidal wave, and her fear kept her silent and reluctant to trust her own creative work.

The dream image that brought **Rita** into psychotherapy was a strange, monk-like figure that invited her to choose life for herself and claim her own right to exist. Rita had struggled with feelings of low self-worth and even self-hatred since childhood. After her mother died suddenly when Rita was just two years old, she was placed in the care of a hostile stepmother, who did everything she could to diminish little Rita. Her stepmother told her that she did not want her. Rita heard the clear message: "don't *be*," "disappear." As a child, she had always felt scared and walked with her head down. She survived by retreating into her own interior fantasy world where she felt safe. The life experience that saved her from ultimate despair was her relationship with her dead mother's family, who loved her and showed her all the affection they could. But even these visits were under her stepmother's control. Her father felt intimidated by her stepmother and did not defend Rita in the face of his wife's emotional abuse. In spite of all this, Rita idealized her father. When she began her psychotherapy, he was dying. She was grateful that she had a chance to tell him how much she loved him before he died. Her psychotherapy work focused on how she could claim her own power and free herself from the internalized messages of her stepmother.

One of the dreams that highlighted these negative messages came to Rita in her early work:

> It was morning and I received a card in the mail. The card indicated that I had been appointed a director of the Royal Bank. I did not go and said later that I could not come because I did not get the notice. But that was only a pretense; I could have gone.

Rita was able to make the association with the Royal Bank as a place where money (a metaphor for energy) is held in trust. Because it is a "royal" place, it is associated with worthiness, honor, distinction, and prestige. She had been invited to this place of power and honor (images that are related to positive self-worth).

She pretended not to get the invitation, although she knew she could have gone. Here we can clearly see the painful ambivalence of Rita's wounded spirit.

Rita associated the monk-like figure in her initial dream with a spiritual power within her that was inviting her to a new choice. He represented a positive masculine image of possibility and hope. Rita realized that it was within her power to accept or refuse the invitation. She decided to accept it.

Feelings of depression in the face of family discord brought **Estelle** into the psychotherapeutic process. She had grown up in an extended family with a cold, dominating grandmother, a loving, creative aunt, and an anxious, depressed mother. Her father was emotionally abusive to her mother and controlled little Estelle and her siblings through his dark moods and unpredictable, explosive anger.

Her mother depended on Estelle to be her confidante and comforter, effectively thrusting Estelle into a role of pretend mother at a very early age. Estelle learned that this role was expected of her and would be rewarded with praise from her mother and others in her family. She wanted to study music in university, as her aunt had, but her father rejected this plan. Instead, he insisted she do something useful that would not be wasted when she got married. So, Estelle became a nurse and sought a career as a healer, hoping that it would also bring her healing.

She married, hoping that her husband would care for her and allow her to express her feelings. After her first child was born and needed almost constant care, Estelle was deeply distressed. She wondered how she could feel love and anger at the same time. Years later, she came into psychotherapy feeling distressed and confused. After all that she had given to her children, she felt that her "wounds were being pierced with poisoned arrows."

The following dream came to Estelle just after she began her psychotherapeutic work:

> I was in the old house where I grew up. All of a sudden, a motorcycle gang rode up and surrounded the house. I was very frightened; they looked as if they were planning to invade the house, and I was alone.

Estelle associated the motorcycle gang in her dream with a shadow side of herself that is in anarchy, determined to destroy the old established order. She realized that she could no longer exist alone in the "old house" (or way of responding to life) as she had when she was growing up. Estelle was then able to see that the invaders might actually be liberators from a way of life that was no longer in her best interest. A few days later, she dreamed: "I meet an old woman who is

homeless. She has painted her own bench red." Estelle realized that she needed
to clearly mark her own space in life. She joined a group of musicians. After our
work on the fairy tales, she left her nursing career to become a musician.

What brought **Emily** into psychotherapy was her need to sort through the
unfinished issues in her relationships with the mother who abandoned her when
she was only nine months old and the father who physically and emotionally
abused her because she was "that woman's daughter." To emphasize his disdain, he
tore up of a photograph of her mother in front of little Emily.

Her father remarried a much younger woman and left Emily in her care. Her
new stepmother was kind to her at first, but, after her own daughter was born,
she shunned Emily and favored her own daughter. Her father and her stepmother
both tried to suppress Emily's creativity, denying her books and paper for her art
and creative writing. Little Emily was forced into the choice of either surrendering
to death or choosing life. She chose life. She continued her creative work in secret,
although she received repeated physical punishment for these transgressions from
her father, who expected absolute obedience.

Emily ran away from home several times, but each time she was returned and
punished. When she was sixteen, at her birth mother's encouragement, she went
to another city to visit her. Once again, she was rejected, as there was no room
for her in her mother's new family. A less determined young woman might have
collapsed under such repeated losses. But Emily kept herself alive with her determination not to be defeated by her mother's abandonment and her father and
stepmother's negative assessments of her.

Eventually, Emily married and had two beautiful daughters. She learned, on
her own, what it meant to be a faithful mother and to love and cherish her children. Through her work with the fairy tales and the images in her dreams, Emily
reclaimed her life and found relief from the most profound pain a child can experience, deliberate abandonment by her own mother.

The Curse and Blessing of Depression

All seven women began psychotherapy because they were depressed. Some were at
the point of contemplating suicide, while others came with the heaviness of heart
and body that generally accompanies depression.

Depressive feelings (that are not purely a bodily chemical reaction) are usually
a signal that we are on the wrong path or taking a negative direction in our lives
that is depleting rather than restoring our life energy. When we are on a path
that is truly our own, and not one determined for us by others, our energy keeps
renewing itself no matter how hard we work. Depression generally is a sign from
our bodies and psyches that we are not living our own lives.

Research has indicated that while low self-esteem is associated with a higher risk for depression, other factors, such as the loss of her mother before puberty, increase this risk for a woman.[18] Two other factors that significantly increase a woman's vulnerability to depression are dependence on others, and an expectation that she meet others' needs. Accompanying these expectations are a host of rewards or punishments that are contingent on her compliance. Women who are more interpersonally sensitive have a greater risk of depression in the face of the potential loss of a relationship. Just because a woman is more oriented toward taking care of others does not necessarily increase her risk of depression. Other factors must also be considered, such as a perception that she is helpless in the face of life circumstances, or the expectation that she cannot avoid a negative outcome. Abramson called this *hopelessness depression.*[19]

Women appear to be more vulnerable than men to relationship problems within marriage and report feeling "isolated and lonely within relationships of inequality or emotional distance." Unhappily married women experience more depressive symptoms than any other group of women.[20]

One highly significant predictor of depression in women is the experience of victimization in interpersonal relationships. Sometimes, the experience of depression may actually be a long-standing post-traumatic stress reaction to sexual or physical abuse in childhood or to sexual harassment within families or at work. All seven women reported childhood trauma in the form of experiencing and/ or witnessing physical or psychological abuse. Two of the women had suffered severe emotional and psychological abuse from stepmothers and fathers. Several women reported early trauma related to sexually inappropriate behavior. Through the process of our work in the group, one woman discovered an incident of early childhood sexual abuse that she had repressed in her memory.

While women who have experienced early loss and trauma have a higher risk for depression, they also have potentially the highest motivation to move beyond their depressive symptoms because they realize that, if they don't, they will not survive.

Carl Jung referred to depression as a gift that forces persons to decide between doing their own inner work or ending up in the daily grind of despair. He indicated that this was particularly true for women who had lost their mothers, or who had not experienced positive mothering. He contended that if they did not become conscious, they would never understand what it meant to be women.[21]

Four factors protect a woman from the ravages of depression that lead to despair. The first is the capacity to experience and to express her feelings (including sadness) in the face of loss. The second is the ability to be open to receiving the support of others. The third protective factor is the development of a sense of competence, that is, the capacity to experience mastery in the face of life's challenges. And the fourth factor is the ability to express compassion for herself and for others.[22] Compassion is a conscious recognition of being one with another. It is reflected in a willingness to be in communion with and to express concern for others while not attempting to rescue them from their pain or distress.

All four of these factors were central to our work in the group. Each woman was encouraged to express her own feelings as she chose, through the voice of one of the daughter-heroines in the fairy tales. Being part of a group of women in which all had felt the loss of positive mothering provided a common base of support. The only information the women had about one another when they began their work in the group was that they were invited because they shared this common experience. Each one was encouraged to participate in the reflection on the tales in any way and to whatever extent she chose. Norms of deep respect for one another were established early, so that each woman could feel safe in the group. There was no confrontation of one another around a shared reflection on the tale. Each contribution was considered a gift to the group. While the women would comment on how another's reflection might have touched them, there was no judgment of another's work. Any attempts to rescue or give one another unsolicited advice were intercepted and redirected.

As a consequence, an atmosphere of compassion developed and prevailed. Each woman's competence in addressing the issues presented by the tale was affirmed by the other women in the group.

The perception of our competence in dealing with life challenges includes an assessment of our ability to confidently confront difficult problems and to choose resolutions that will be favorably supported by others. This includes having our achievements acknowledged and affirmed by others. Depression is a logical emotional consequence of feeling incompetent. Thus, when a "husband, doctor, teacher" in our life tells us that what we think "makes no sense" (or is nonsense), the web of the fragile threads of our lives unravel and our stories are "left untold."[23]

Psychological research suggests that when we feel competent, experiences of success are a source of encouragement for resolving future difficult situations, and failure does not get in the way of our willingness to deal with a problem. When we feel competent, we are able to attribute success to our efforts and abilities and failure to the difficulties in the situation. On the other hand, if we do not perceive ourselves as competent, we attribute failure to our lack of personal ability and not to the difficulty or complexity of the problem. When we do not feel competent, we are not able to honor our successes and are, thus, less likely to be able to face the next (inevitable) conflict in our lives with any degree of confidence.[24]

Some women who experience a loss or disappointment have a tendency to ruminate over their situation, sorting through potential explanations of why it happened and searching for ways they might have prevented it. They go within themselves and replay the event over and over, looking for an explanation. This inner searching often accentuates and prolongs depressive feelings, particularly when the woman comes to the conclusion that she was/is powerless.[25] All of the women in the group had this tendency, some to a greater degree than others. That is why it was so important in structuring the reflection on the fairy tales that rumination on the plight of the heroine was discouraged. Instead, alternative responses, using the process of *active imagination,* were used.

Active imagination is a conscious process using the power of imagination to discover elements of our unconscious that are seeking a way to be heard. It was developed by Carl Jung, early in the twentieth century, as a tool to more deeply explore our inner worlds. In its essence, active imagination is a dialogue between different parts of ourselves in order to open a window of awareness to access our unconscious while in a conscious state. It is like participating in a dialogue within a dream except that we are awake. It differs from guided imagery in that it does not involve a script or specified path and does not include passive fantasy or day-dreaming.[26] Our use of the active imagination process involved each woman taking on the role of the heroine-daughter in the tale. In this role, she engaged with the other characters in the tale in order to give expression to her thoughts and feelings, and to explore a new ending or conclusion to the story. Each woman was also encouraged to envision alternative next steps in her own life, and to move beyond feelings of passive helplessness to active mastery over her own destiny.

As our work in the group progressed, positive responses were evident in the changes in the images in each woman's dreams, in the shifts in her choices to more positive relationships, and in her willingness to express her creativity in ways that bought her affirmation from others. These were all signs of a developing sense of personal autonomy and competence.[27]

Fairy Tales: Spinning and Healing

Seven fairy tales were selected for reflection in the weekly group meetings. They were chosen randomly from those available in the children's section of the public library. The women in the group suggested two of the tales. The only criteria for selection was that the tales be about daughters who either were abandoned by their mothers or for whom there was no positive mothering in the tale.

Abandonment is a repeated theme in many fairy tales read to children. Bettlehiem, who has done extensive work as a psychoanalyst on the interpretation of fairy tales, concluded that the purpose of the tales is to help children deal with the negative side of their relationships with their mothers.[28] Fairy tales describe the trauma so that the child listening to the story can come to see that she is not alone in her experience and that she will survive. The heroine in the tales is often presented as not perfect, and capable of making mistakes, which is consoling to the child.

"Fairy tales are stories spun by the same Great Mother that spins dreams. In the last analysis, they are products of the unconscious, not of the human ego."[29] They are actually timeless manifestations of the power of the human imagination.

Robert Johnson pictures "two conduits that run from the unconscious to the conscious mind. The first is the faculty of dreaming, and the second is the faculty of imagination. Dreaming and imagination have one special quality in common: their power to convert the invisible forms of the unconscious into images that are perceptible to the conscious mind. This is why we sometimes feel as though dreaming is the imagination at work during sleep and the imagination is the dream world flowing through us while we are awake."[30]

Working with both her active imagination dialogues with the images in the fairy tales as well as the images in her own dreams appeared to have a profound effect on the depth to which each woman was able to go to discover the obstacles to claiming her life more fully.

The process of exploring the fairy tales allowed each woman to see reflections of her own life story in a broader, timeless tale that has touched other women over the ages. Having the opportunity to clearly see these reflections converts the isolation and shame that characterizes profound personal trauma into an awareness of the shared experience of loss, from which others have emerged with hope and a renewed appreciation of their personal power. As the women in the group listened to one another's different perspectives on a given tale, they became increasingly more open to new ways of viewing the messages of the story. Even when one or two of the women felt they could not relate to a particular tale, they contributed insights that were useful for the others. Having a common story to use as a base for exploration and reflection allowed each woman to share only what she chose of her own life story, in her own time.

We worked with a particular fairy tale for several hours on consecutive Wednesday evenings until the women in the group decided that they had completed their work with that tale. Consequently, some tales would be the focus of five sessions, while others would only require two. The tales provided the context for exploring the personal traumas each woman in the group had experienced, particularly those that involved the loss of her mother. The story with which we worked the longest was the tale of "The Handless Maiden."

The trauma of the loss of one's mother and the experience of being inadequately mothered is profound. As Adrienne Rich expresses it in her book *Of Woman Born*, "The loss of the daughter to her mother and the mother to her daughter is the essential female tragedy." She describes the connection between mother and daughter as "beyond the verbally transmitted core of female survival, a knowledge flowing between two like bodies, one of which has spent nine months inside the other."[31]

The first goal of psychological healing for those who have experienced a profound loss, such as the loss of one's mother, is to provide a process of empowerment through which the person is able to bring to consciousness the experience of the trauma and address it repeatedly until it is robbed of its power.[32] The series of fairy tales provided the opportunity to repeatedly view the loss of the mother from a broader perspective, without potentially re-traumatizing each woman by requiring that she report the details of her own story to the group. It gave each one a context beyond herself from which to view her story. Because the tales are timeless, each woman was able to appreciate that she was not alone as she viewed how the daughter/heroine dealt with a similar loss.

The process of each woman's healing also included acknowledging and working through her emotional responses to her loss, including feelings of anger, helplessness, anxiety, guilt, and sadness. This involved allowing herself to experience the loss in her own body. Although each woman could relate to parts of each of the fairy tales, she could identify more strongly with some tales than with others. The evidence for this was in her physical symptoms. Those fairy tales that most closely touched the theme of her own life story awakened the most powerful bodily reactions. The strength of those responses surprised her. Experience has taught me that our bodies never lie. To release tensions in the body evoked by the tale, movement and a brief ritual were part of each weekly session.

The individuation process that Jung proposed is essentially about discovering who we truly are, developing a sense of autonomy, and clarifying and pursuing goals that give our life meaning. These characteristics are identical to the instrumentality dimension that McGrath and others refer to in their research on women and depression.[33]

The Abandoned Child

The women in the group had experienced different forms of abandonment by their mothers, both physical and emotional. As adults, many had insulated themselves from their own inner world so that they would not have to feel. Kathrin Asper refers to this state as *self abandonment.*[34]

For the woman with an abandonment wound, working on her shadow (what she attributes to be negative within herself) is neither helpful nor healthy until a basic sense of self is established. To introduce or promote reflection on her negative side is to potentially feed into an unconscious preoccupation with passing judgment on herself, with which she is all too familiar. The woman wounded by early abandonment must first discover self-love and develop her capacity to move beyond self-estrangement. For this reason, each woman was encouraged to use the process of active imagination, taking on the role of the heroine/daughter in each of the tales, so that a new resolution could emerge.

Working with fairy tale dramas can be compared to the therapeutic process of sand play, in that we unconsciously put the figures in the tale in the places that are reflective of our own inner world. We interpret the tale by fitting it into our own life stories. This is especially evident when we do an active imagination dialogue with the characters in the tale. In this process, we use our imaginations to enter the story so that it becomes our own. Working with the images in the tales enabled the women in the group to begin to give voice to and emotionally express what they might not have been able to directly express in their own life stories. Each woman appeared to be functioning well in the outside world, successful in her profession, and engaged in relationships within and outside her family. In other words, each had a highly developed persona or way of presenting herself to others that covered the pain of self-estrangement that she carried just beneath the surface.

Through the process of working with the group on the fairy tales and continuing to analyze the messages from her dreams, each woman gradually came to discover and honor her own uniqueness. She was then able to develop a sense of autonomy and to articulate and pursue goals that gave her life meaning. As we progressed through an exploration of each of the tales this became more and more evident. Residual feelings of self-doubt and self-estrangement sometimes arose with each new story, but, over time, these periods of self-doubt became shorter and shorter. When the healing of the self-estrangement of abandonment occurs, it is not as if the wound disappears. It remains a tender scar in a woman's psyche, making it imperative that she is able to acknowledge and express compassion for herself.

Children who are abandoned are not consciously able to acknowledge their loss. The pain goes underground, and the child/woman is shaped by the loss, which, although it remains unspoken, strongly influences how she will respond and function in life. The child avoids expressing her grief for fear that she will be ignored or that her pain will be discounted. Her traumatic feelings may become frozen and submerged only to re-emerge when she becomes a woman, often when she is least prepared to deal with them.[35]

Emotional abandonment can occur whenever there is not-good-enough mothering. This is not about having a perfect mother (which is not humanly possible) but about having a mother who is a good-enough fit to meet our needs as children. Not-good-enough mothering occurs when the child's feelings or needs are not noticed or taken seriously by her mother.[36] As a consequence, the child may experience herself as bad or not good enough to receive her mother's love.

One of the women discovered, near the end of her work in the group, that the deep shame she felt in her body was related to a memory she recalled of her mother spanking her and calling her a "wicked, wicked little girl." This occurred after her mother discovered her, at age three, engaged in some exploratory sexual play with a neighbor boy. The pain of the experience was buried deep within this woman's psyche for more than forty years only to be uncovered after her work in the group. She reported that, as a woman, she had always been afraid of her sexuality and had felt unworthy of being in a mutually satisfying sexual relationship with a man.

Another woman indicated that she felt as if something was wrong with her because she couldn't feel any other emotion but sadness. Even in situations in which she saw herself exploited by others' unreasonable demands, she could not feel anger. Consequently, she also could not feel deep joy. For the most part she felt sad, but she knew how "to put on a good face." There had been so much emotional turmoil in her early life that she felt overwhelmed and shut down. She was particularly afraid of anger, which she associated with the destructive rages of her father. Very few people knew how much she was hurting underneath her smiling facade.

The child who experiences herself as abandoned by her mother often does not learn how to experience her feelings or how to trust those feelings if/when they do emerge. When a woman cannot feel, she is in a state of self-estrangement and abandonment. Her perception that emotions are dangerous leads her to suppress any feelings that are trying to emerge. She cannot, therefore, come to know who she truly is and to experience a sense of autonomy. She is also tentative in identifying and pursuing goals that would give her life meaning, since she is not really sure if they are her own goals or someone else's goals for her life.

A third woman in the group felt overwhelmed by what she perceived was her obligation to serve the needs of others. It was difficult for her to give voice to (or even perceive clearly) what *she* wanted. She reported that, in her early years, her mother frequently dismissed her needs and feelings. Her mother's needs came first. As a little girl, this woman had been required to buy and bring home groceries that were actually too heavy for her to carry. As an adult, she continued to shoulder the heavy burdens of others and to deny the anger and rage she felt for having complied with their unreasonable expectations. When her anger finally emerged, she was startled by its power.

The process of abandoning her own feelings allows the abandoned child/woman to deny the feelings of her own abandonment. The woman who is so wounded needs to be able to acknowledge her loss so that she can more deeply understand and mourn it. Only then can she allow herself to feel again and to see new possibilities for her future beyond the pessimistic patterns of the past. This is evident in Rita's dream in which she is invited to be a director of the Royal Bank. She pretends, in her dream, that she did not receive the invitation, although she knew that she could have gone.

Jessica shared the feelings of terror that enveloped her when she realized there could be a positive outcome to what she desired. It seemed so impossible that it was frightening. In her later work, Jessica came to realize that feelings of joy were foreign to her. She was more at home with a quiet sadness, passed down through the generations of her maternal ancestors, who expected life to be difficult and burdensome.

Women who carry the wound of maternal deprivation may appear very reserved and distant. Their words may be tentative. They use the words *perhaps* and *possibly* as a way of not fully committing themselves. They may even hold their hands over their mouths when they speak, to partially silence themselves. One of the women in the group would press her lips firmly together to keep herself quiet. Pictures from her early childhood showed her in the same pose, her lips sealed, and her eyes sad. It was not considered appropriate in her family to speak one's needs or concerns. "Grin and bear it" was the family motto.

One of the women in the group carried the wound of her mother deprivation by covering her loss with pseudo-vitality. She always tried to be cheerful, as a way of being in control over what often seemed to her to be a bottomless pit of despair into which she dared not fall for fear of being annihilated in the darkness.

Early hospitalization of a child may precipitate the trauma of loss of her mother. This was the experience of two of the women in the group. While their parents and caretakers may have meant well, these two women had, as young children, been isolated from family members because of the perceived risk of contagion. An event such as this gives the young child the message that something is so wrong with her that she has to be put away. In the case of one of these women, even her doll was taken from her and destroyed when she left the hospital. Her mother never acknowledged her mourning for her doll. Instead, she was given a new doll, which was considered adequate compensation for what her mother perceived as a trivial loss.

When we are able to consciously acknowledge and mourn our early losses, we can move on to new ways of dealing with them. Feelings of anger and powerlessness were addressed throughout our work on each of the tales, so that each woman could claim a sense of personal worth and establish a connection to the other women in the group. This was a very important part of the healing process. The common wound of the seven women was the loss of their mother, the primary feminine connection with our lives as women. Feelings of isolation from other women were transformed as the work of the group progressed. They became sisters to one another and advocates of one another's healthy choices.

Throughout the first year, the women continued their individual psychotherapy on a bi-weekly basis. They brought their dreams to their individual sessions for analysis and reflection. At the weekly meetings of the group, they focused on their active imagination work, dialogues between the heroine/daughter and the characters in the tale, and their personal reactions to the tale we were working on at the time. By the end of the first year, the women began to bring their own work on their dreams to the group. This was an indication that they now felt safe enough with one another to share the deeper parts of their unconscious.

When we had completed the first full year of our work as a group, we decided to gather for a weeklong intensive experience. At this gathering, each woman was invited to share why she had come into psychotherapy, the dreams and images that had been important for her inner work, and the insights she had gained over the year of our work together. Each woman was encouraged (if she chose) to celebrate what had been transformed in her life by inviting the group to share in a ritual of personal celebration with her. It was a power-filled experience for all of us!

Through this experience, each woman had the opportunity to create meaning out of her trauma, to integrate it into her life and understanding of her world, to clarify her own new identity, and to renew her commitment to continue to grow personally and interpersonally in a healthy way. She also had the opportunity to share that meaning, understanding, and commitment with others and to experience their compassion and affirmation. The powerful impact of this experience was evident when we revisited the tales four years later.

The psychotherapeutic literature suggests that moving beyond a traumatic loss involves:

- developing healthy, trusting relationships,
- sharing information about the effects of loss, grief, and mourning,
- recalling the trauma in a safe environment, dealing with the feelings that are evoked, and

- restructuring one's thinking, so that the trauma can be integrated with meaning into one's life and view of the world.[37]

The Seven Fairy Tales

Every one of the seven fairy tales selected for reflection by the group contained the theme of the daughter's abandonment wound. We did not attempt to interpret the tales in an analytic process. Instead, we used them as examples of collective dreams with historical connections and potential personal significance.

The first tale we explored was "**Rumpelstilskin**,"[38] a poignant story of a young girl without a mother, who, as a result of her father's boasting, is forced by the king to try to spin straw into gold. Since she does not have the skills to do so, she is in danger of losing her life, until a little dwarf appears and agrees to accomplish the task for her, at a price. Although he saves her from death, the dwarf is stunted, an image of immature development. The lesson of the tale is that if we try to survive through an immature approach to life, we are at high risk of losing what is most precious to us.

The tale of "**Clever Beauty**"[39] is similar in its theme to "Rumpelstilskin," except that, in this story, it is the bragging mother who turns the young girl over to a greedy queen. The abandoned daughter is required to make fine wine from thistle juice, bake fine bread from thistle stalks, and spin fine silk from thistledown. Three old spinners save the young girl. They are visibly deformed women to whom she had previously shown compassion despite their repulsive appearance. They complete the onerous tasks required by the queen. As a reward, Clever Beauty marries the prince. She invites the three ugly spinners to her wedding as her godmothers. These strangers are her saviors. In contrast, both the mother and the queen in the tale are insensitive to the daughter's needs and use her to meet their own.

In the tale of "**The Handless Maiden**,"[40] the daughter is left unprotected by her powerless mother while her father cuts off her hands, as a result of his pact with the devil. She leaves home defenseless and goes out into the world with her arms and dismembered hands tied behind her back. She has no spindle of her own and no hands to spin and weave her own destiny. She is doubly handicapped. She has been victimized by her father's greed and her mother's silence. She goes through a series of painful trials through which her hands grow back again.

In the tale of "**Mother Hulda**,"[41] the daughter/heroine loses her spindle down a well. She is forced by her mother (who the Grimm brothers turned into a stepmother) to dive into the depths of darkness to retrieve it. This is a story of two sisters—one favored, and the other rejected by their mother—and of the consequences of this relationship for each of them. Mother Hulda, an image of the Great Mother, is the teacher who provides the lessons necessary for the transformation of the abandoned daughter from a place of despair to one of hope.

In the tale of "**Briar Rose**,"[42] an overprotective father and negligent mother deny the favored daughter a spindle for creating the thread of her own life. For her own good, her father banishes all spindles from the kingdom so that no woman can continue the ancient craft of spinning. This has serious consequences for all of the feminine energy in the kingdom and results in a one-hundred-year period of sterility and lifelessness. After pricking her finger on a spindle that had been hidden from her father, the young daughter falls asleep for one hundred years. She awakens when the time is right, and the prince appears—a metaphor for her finally claiming her own autonomy and power over her own life.

The daughter/heroine in the tale of "**The Raven**"[43] is snatched from a mother who, overburdened by the needs of her child, allows her to be taken from her. The infant girl turns into a raven with claws (metaphorically, a regressed state). In the tale, the daughter/raven tries to engage a young man in her rescue. However, he repeatedly falls asleep. The child who is abandoned and deprived of her mother's affection and protection when she is very young faces a long process of recovering her sense of self-worth. It may take her years to reclaim the threads of her own existence and, thereby, avoid sinking into a pit of despair. Generally, a relationship with a nurturing woman (or women) is needed so that she can have the experience of "good-enough mothering."

In the tale of "**Snow White**,"[44] the heroine escapes the murderous jealousy of her narcissistic mother by hiding in the house of the seven dwarfs. There she is required to spin, clean, and cook for her hosts in exchange for protection from her mother's rage. But the dwarf energy, a metaphor for a stunted, naive approach to life, is not able to protect her. It keeps disappearing and going underground when what is needed is constant vigilance. Only after she dies at the hand of her jealous mother do the dwarfs take turns guarding her coffin (a sign of too-little focused, purposeful energy that comes too late). However, the stumbling servants of the persistent prince restore her to life again.

In each of the seven fairy tales, the daughter/heroine finds her way through the grief of her abandonment. Her persistence through her trials breaks apart what appears at first to be a fate from which she cannot escape. In each of the tales, some helper or advocate emerges, sometimes in the form of a prince or a wise woman. Each of these helpers/advocates is a symbol of her own inner resources of competence and mastery over her own destiny. These precious resources will become available to her if she stays faithful to the process and does not succumb to despair. This is a very delicate balance point for the woman with an abandonment wound. Sometimes, it may actually feel easier to fall into the numbness of addictions or to avoid relationships so that she can disappear into her fate. At times, it may feel too heavy a burden to make another choice. When we live out our lives as if they are our fate, we believe we have no choice. What is clear in the seven fairy tales is that each time she is confronted with another trial, the daughter/heroine faces the choice to live or die.

In two of the tales, "Briar Rose" and "Snow White," it appears that the heroine has died at the hands of evil forces. However, other aspects of herself are then activated to raise her out of her sleepy, unconscious state and restore her to health. In the other five tales, as well, there are dark forces. The greedy dwarf, the wicked stepmother, the devil, and the dark sorcerer are all intent on destroying the heroine or keeping her captive and a slave to their wishes.

As I worked with these seven courageous women, I became ever more deeply aware that psychotherapy—which means walking with or beside the psyche (soul) of another—is essentially a process of allowing the other to discover her capacity to suffer and to move through the suffering to claim her own resources for healing. The earlier and deeper the wound, the more consistent, loving accompaniment she needs in order to claim her own life.

All of the seven fairy tales are about confronting the darkness, discovering our capacity to suffer, and mobilizing the resources within ourselves that we previously did not know existed. The messages of the tales are clear; there is no easy way!

The Path of No Return

When each of the women began her psychotherapeutic work with me, part of our first session was devoted to what I refer to as the "informed consent of the psyche." Beyond the usual confirmation of the boundaries of confidentiality, it is essential that the woman understand that, once she decides to take the path of exploring her unconscious and allowing what may have been dormant to wake up into consciousness, there is no turning back.

Each of the daughters/heroines in the tales, once she set out, could not turn back. She had to live through the stages of suffering and encounters with darkness, usually three times, before the resources she needed to claim her own destiny were revealed.

The unraveling of the fabric of her life, as painful as it is for the woman with an abandonment wound, provides her with a new opportunity to more clearly identify who she is and to discern the purpose of her life. It involves detaching herself from the fabric of the identity and role prescribed for her by others, or that she had interpreted as her fate.

Spinning and unraveling are opposite functions. It is the circular clockwise movement of the spindle that binds the fragments into a thread. This same movement is associated with the coming of the sun's light. To unravel means that we unwind, disengage, undo, and therefore, also set free. The counterclockwise movement of unraveling is associated with darkness, a prelude to death. However, it also can be viewed as an opportunity for liberation from old life patterns and a coming to a new appreciation of who we truly are. Unraveling provides the possibility of disentangling ourselves from conclusions set at an early age about how we were to survive in an uncertain world.

During the process of our work together, Claire wove an image from one of her dreams into a beautiful reversible pattern. On one side of the fabric, the dominant colors were red, yellow, and orange, colors she associated with passion, warmth, and fire. On the other side, the cooler colors of green, blue, and purple were dominant. The dream image, however, was visible on both sides. It was important for Claire to experience both sides of herself as beautiful. She felt cut off from her feminine body, which had never been honored by her own mother. She longed to be more grounded in her commitment to her own passion and what gave her energy and spark, and not in what others said she ought to be or do. In the past, she had primarily focused on her introspective side and been self-critical. She now longed to enjoy her warmer, brighter side and to acknowledge both aspects of herself as worthy of honor.

The threads of the fabric of our life are like strands of the DNA inherited from our ancestral mother's womb. They have been woven together into patterns by past generations who determined and passed on a code of how to live and survive, which we unconsciously accept as our own reality. Those threads that are woven too tightly in an attempt to create an illusion of safety eventually need to be examined. Once we begin the unraveling of old ways of thinking, feeling, and behaving, we can also begin the sorting of the fragments. In the unraveling, the fragments or filaments of our lives remain. Some of the threads of our histories that are no longer useful, or are particularly destructive, need to be discarded. It is important for the process of transformation and individuation that this is done consciously. If not, we will find ourselves reweaving the same patterns of fate and passing them on to our children. Whatever remains unconscious within us will be lived out as fate with no perception of choice. In each of the fairy tales, the daughter/heroine had to make a series of decisions in order to remain alive and engaged in life, even when the outcome was uncertain.

Just as this book began to take shape, a friend who was in the midst of a life-and-death struggle, sent me the following poem, which she wrote after a powerful dream.

I was in the middle of a
Struggle for my life
when I had a dream,

Shook me
burst me out
of the gray softness of numb.

An old woman and a young
child are rushing through
a tunnel. Each accompanied
by a woman.
Oblivion waits at the end
as certain as nightfall.

One will be lost, one
will be saved
and the child goes first
I sicken with dread
The young one will die,
some failure of mine
to nurture this tender bud.
The wizened will survive.

Midway in the inevitable
hurtling downward
the escort encircles the child
slips her into the tiniest
crevice of the wall, but a shadow space
a blithe stepping aside. And whoosh!
The hag is hurried by
disappears into gone.

The child surges forward
as I surface, panting, sweating
night dripping off me.

That day, my friend, the poet, calls.
She says, "I thought of you this morning
Your story's been told
Your healing's satisfactory
And it's not enough
to save your life. [45]

Here we see the destruction of an old way of living (the wizened old woman) and the birth of a new young feminine (the girl child). My friend fears she has neglected the child, and now she will die. It could have gone either way in the dream, an indication of the fragility of life.

How does the young feminine soul survive when the energy of the wizened, dried-up feminine of the negative mother could so easily overtake and destroy her? How close it is, this stepping aside to let the negative energy pass by!

The poem also expresses the reality that it is not enough to save our own lives. Once we have accepted the gift of the choice to move out of the self-deprecating wound of abandonment, we must, as women seeking to live from a place of competence and compassion, share our experience with others.

Before we began our work as a group, the seven women knew that—while we respected each one's confidentiality—our experience together was intended for publication. They understood that the purpose of the book would be to encourage other women carrying a similar wound to see that it is possible to sweep the old negative mother images into oblivion and allow what is new and full of promise within them to find its way into the light. Each woman recognized that she was part of a sisterhood in a life-and-death struggle with feelings of depression. From the beginning of our work together, each one also recognized her own fragility. She opened herself to the possibility of the new, while, at the same time, holding in reserve her own doubts and fears. She entered into the exploration of the fairy tales, open to the possibilities this might offer, but knowing full well that it was not magic. There would be hard work involved—of this each one was certain. Perhaps the process of exploring fairy tales would be like the "blithe stepping aside" that my friend mentions in her poem. To outsiders, it may have seemed trivial to be spending time on fairy tales. Yet, each of these women trusted her relationship with me and with the others and stepped into the tunnel of transformation. It was a very moving experience to witness the young feminine soul emerging on the other side.

For each woman in the group, the process of unraveling led to an inner freedom that allowed her to sort the fragments of her life in the company of other women she grew to trust. In the process, she also grew to trust herself and to honor the strands of her own life spun around slim filaments of courage. Each woman expressed the desire to weave a new tale of hope and promise from "threads of love out of aloneness."[46]

The following chapters are the stories of their rewoven lives.

Reflection questions:

Chapter I—Spinning Threads that Hold

1. Where do I find my own life patterns unraveling?

2. Are there old ways of responding to life circumstances that are keeping me estranged from myself?

3. Are there strands of my life story that I need to discard?

4. Are there new threads that need to be spun?

5. Where and how will I begin?

CHAPTER II

IN THE NAME OF THE FATHER: THE TALE OF RUMPELSTILSKIN

My soul cannot be sold,
I will not spin straw into gold.
—Estelle

Before she left on a trip abroad with her parents, both of whom generally demanded that she be attentive and responsive to their needs, Estelle composed a humorous lyrical song to remind herself of her intention to clearly maintain her boundaries with each of them. Determined to not get entangled in the web of their neediness, Estelle made a commitment to remain compassionate toward them and herself. Whenever she felt she was getting close to being consumed by their demands, she would sing the song to herself. She used the chorus as a mantra to stay clearly conscious of her intention. The song renewed her sense of humor and helped her to change the mood from one that was often deadly serious into one that was simply human. Humming the chorus helped her maintain her balance in the face of a series of family conflicts involving her siblings. The trip went very well, and both her parents thanked her. They all agreed that it was the most enjoyable trip they had ever shared.

The theme of Estelle's song came out of our work on the tale of "Rumpelstilskin," the first fairy tale we explored as a group.

Before our first session, I distributed copies of the tale to the seven women who agreed to be part of the group. The first evening we reflected on their reactions and responses to the tale. I did not share any interpretation of the story and encouraged each of the women not to read books or other commentaries that explained or analyzed the tale. It was important for each of them to view the tale as if it were her own dream and to allow it to speak to her through the metaphors and images it presented.

At the end of the first session, I offered several questions for dialogue between the characters in the tale, using the process of active imagination. As described in Chapter 1, active imagination is a traditional Jungian approach to uncovering the meaning of dream images. An individual using the active imagination process begins by first observing the dream or fairy tale image. She then engages in a written dialogue with those images. Each woman was familiar with this process, since each had experience using it with her own dreams in her individual psychotherapy sessions. I also invited each woman to draw any images or symbols that came to her in response to the tale and to explore any bodily movement it evoked. My purpose was to encourage her to take the tale into her body and not merely treat the reflection as an intellectual exercise.

The second and third group sessions included opportunities for sharing the active imagination dialogues and any other responses the women had to the tale. Four years later we revisited the story to see if their responses had changed and what, in retrospect, each had learned.

For our reflection, we used the version of the tale of "Rumpelstilskin" from the Grimms' collection. Its original name was "*Rumpenstunzchen*," which means to make a noise and to be on stilts. The Grimm brothers first published the story in 1810–1812, in *Childhood and Household Tales*.[47] In the second edition, published in 1819, the tale changed to one that was compiled from four versions. It is interesting to note that the tale existed under different names across many countries. Rumpelstilskin was known as Trit-a-Trot in Ireland, Tom Tit Tot in Britain, Terrytop Terrytop-top in Cornwall, Whuppety Stoorie in Scotland, and Ricdin-Ricdon in France. Rumpelstilskin's name and his story date back to a publication in German in 1575.[48]

The heroine of the tale is a motherless daughter who finds herself having to live out a destiny not of her own choosing because of her father's pride. In his name, for his sake, she forfeits her future and nearly loses her life.

A Synopsis of the Tale of Rumpelstilskin

Once upon a time, in a land far away, there lives a miller with a beautiful daughter. One day, when he is with the king, he boasts that his daughter is so clever that she can spin straw into gold. The king is very impressed. He asks the miller to bring his daughter to the castle so that he can meet her. When she arrives, the king takes the girl to a large room filled with straw. He orders her to spin the straw into gold if she values her life. Then he locks her in the room.

The poor girl has no idea how to spin straw into gold. She begins to weep. Just then, a little man appears. He asks, "Mistress Miller, why are you weeping?" When she tells him about her plight, he agrees to spin the straw into gold for a price. "What will you give me, if I spin the straw into gold for you?" he asks. She offers him her necklace. Then, while she is sleeping, he spins all the straw into gold. When she awakes in the morning, the whole room is filled with gold. When the king unlocks the door, he is overjoyed with the gold that fills the room. But he wishes for more. So, the next night, he locks the miller's daughter into a larger room filled with straw. As she still has no idea how to spin straw into gold, she once again dissolves into tears, and again the little man appears This time, when he asks what she will give him if he spins the straw into gold, she offers him her ring. Once again, the miller's daughter falls asleep, and when she awakes the room is full of gold. When the king opens the door and sees all the gold, he is overcome with greed. He decides to lock the miller's daughter into an even larger room filled with straw. Then he says to himself, "If she is able to turn the straw in this room into gold, I will marry her. Even though she is only a miller's daughter, I will not find a richer woman anywhere." And so, for the third time, the king locks the miller's daughter into a room full of straw. But this time, he promises her that if she can turn this straw into gold, she will become his queen. At her wit's end, the miller's daughter once more begins to weep, and once more the little man appears. "What will you give me this time?" he asks. The poor girl is in deep distress, because she has nothing more to give. "If I turn this straw into gold for you, will you give me your first child when you become queen?" Thinking that she has no choice, and fearing for her life, the miller's daughter agrees. Then, once again, while she sleeps, the little man turns the large room full of straw into gold. When the king comes the third time, he is so delighted with the sight of all the gold, that, true to his promise, he makes the miller's daughter his queen.

A year later, the queen is filled with joy when she gives birth to a beautiful baby boy. Then the little man appears to take what she had promised. The queen is deeply distressed. She offers him all the riches of the kingdom if he will let her keep her son, but he refuses, saying, "I would rather have a living being than all the riches of the world." Once again, the miller's daughter breaks down in tears. The little man finally agrees that if she can guess his name in three days, she can keep her child. The queen collects all the names she can find. When the little man appears on the first day, she asks him, "Is your name Matthew?" "No," he replies. "Is it Luke?" "No," he replies. "Is it John?" "You have not guessed my name," he answers. On the second day, she asks him, "Is your name Bandy-legs, Hunch-back or Crook-shanks?" Again, he denies that any of these are his name. On the third day, a messenger of the queen returns, saying: "I haven't heard any new names, although I have searched far and wide. But last evening, when I was on the other side of the hill, in the place where the fox and the hare bid each other good night, I saw a little man dancing around a fire, singing, 'Little does my lady dream, Rumpelstilskin is my name!'" The queen is overjoyed to hear this news. When the little man comes the third time, she asks him, "Is your name Henry?" "No," he replies. "Is it Charles?" "No," he responds. "Could it be Rumpelstilskin?" "Some witch told you that, some witch told you that," he cries. In his rage, he stamps his foot so hard into the ground that when he tries to pull it out he tears himself in two.[49]

Exploring the tale of "Rumpelstilskin" was a challenging, as well as an enriching, experience for the women in the group. Initially, several of the women, who did not have a father who would boast of their accomplishments, felt that they could not relate to the tale. However, when they explored their dreams and active imagination dialogues with the images in the tale, new and surprising aspects of their own stories were revealed.

Each woman had a story that she alone knew. Working with the tale of the miller's daughter provided an opening to a deeper understanding of each story. Healing only begins, according to Jung, when one's personal story can be told. "It is [her] secret, the rock against which [she] has been shattered."[50] One's story reveals the human background and suffering that is the foundation for therapeutic healing to occur.

Each woman in the group had heard versions of the tale of "Rumpelstilskin" when she was young. To open herself to the meaning of the tale for her now, each one recorded her dreams and addressed the following questions in her active imagination with the images in the tale:

- What conversation did the miller's daughter have with her father at her wedding?
- What did the daughter say to her missing mother?

I also encouraged each woman to record in her journal any other reactions or responses she had to the story.

Who Is the Miller's Daughter?

Are there ways we recognize her in ourselves and other women? How does she come to be caught spinning straw into gold?

The miller's daughter has no name of her own; her identity is through her relationship to her father. The miller was considered an entrepreneur at the time the fairy tale was written, an early industrialist who took the work of others and used it for his own gain. He transformed the farmer's harvest into flour by harnessing the power of nature for the grinding wheel. The miller was not engaged directly in producing food. While others did the hard work, he reaped the benefit. We see his greed in his readiness to sacrifice his daughter to the king with his boastful lies. She, then, is forced to produce for his benefit, in order to save her own life.

The miller's daughter feels isolated in the community of women. She has no mother, no positive feminine image to reflect to her what it means to be valued as a woman. Generally, only men would come to the mill. The daughter lives on the edge of town with her father. She primarily cares for him, prepares his meals, spins and weaves for him, and sweeps up the straw from the mill. She lives alone with her thoughts and feelings. She is an industrious and intelligent young woman. Her father is proud of her and boasts of her cleverness and, as a consequence, endangers her life.

Forced to her wits' end by the king's demand for gold from straw, she breaks down in tears. Often, women who are millers' daughters cry, not because they are sad but because they are angry. They discover when they are young that expressing anger, which is simmering just below the surface of their existence, is dangerous and unwise. When they are angry, they weep. Usually (although not always) this is not a conscious deceit. With the release of their tears, they often find another way out of their dilemma.

A colleague remarked to me once that he noticed that many women cover their anger with sadness and tears, and that many men cover their sadness and tears with anger. Millers' daughters, however, rarely let anyone see their tears. Neither the king nor her father saw her cry. Millers' daughters generally do not visibly express their emotions. They do not weep or express anger publicly. They shed tears in public only when they are at their wits' end or when their true feelings surprise them and they don't have time to get them under control.

In isolation, locked in by the king's hands, the miller's daughter weeps, and little Rumpelstilskin appears. He is a part of her she has never seen before, an aspect of herself that, while she's unconscious (sleeping), does what is needed to save her from death.

The miller's daughter colludes to save the pride of her father and strives to continue to be the daughter of whom he is proud. The ultimate price for her is the loss of her sense of self, her own creative identity.

Millers' daughters do not want to believe they are sacrificing their creativity in the name of their fathers. They think they are doing what their own hearts desire. They go to school, achieve, and earn degrees to make their fathers proud of them. Or, they may feel driven to achieve in order to disprove the negative assessments of them. They will become important or famous people to show their fathers that they were wrong.

All manner of potential creative gifts are sacrificed in the father's name. These women do not want to be like their mothers, who they secretly loathe as ineffectual and powerless. They believe that power is to be found only in the world of the father/king.

Once they are turned over to the king, they cannot disgrace their fathers and lose their lives. They must perform, perform, perform! They are put to the test within themselves. They do not believe they are creative. They sacrifice their necklaces, a metaphor for their voices, the mediator between their rational and emotional worlds. They sacrifice their rings, symbols of their ability to be committed to relationships beyond their fathers. And, finally, they even sacrifice their children, a metaphor for their souls. For some, the years of school, then graduate school, then a professional career, takes its toll on the availability of their time to be creative. They do not know themselves in ways other than how the fathers, who bestow degrees and provide professional promotions, name them or how their husbands/partners expect them to be. Each room of straw gets larger and larger as the king becomes greedy for more and more gold. The little dwarfs spin for their lives, but not without a price. "What will you give me?" they demand.

Always, there is a price. Put to the test, millers' daughters see themselves as having no choice. They may even believe that their fathers meant well. Promise them anything they want! In order to stay alive in the demanding corporate, academic, or professional world, they have to do as the father/king asks. What he asks of them is to make more and more gold for him!

The miller's daughter lives on in all women who feel caught in trying to survive in the patriarchal world of the father/king. We may recognize her in ourselves as the one who continues to try to become someone of value in life situations where the rewards are few and the demands are many.

The Demanding Father: Doing What Daddy Wants

When Estelle did an active imagination dialogue between the miller and his daughter, she asked: "Why do *I* have to be *your* achievement? You think that everything I do and everything I am belongs to you."

Estelle remembered a time in her adolescent years when her father boasted to his business colleagues about what an accomplished pianist she was. When she declined his request to play for them after dinner while they had their coffee, he went into a rage and told her she was a "slut" and that she could live on the street if she couldn't do what *he* wanted in *his* house. Stunned, she ran and hid in the garden and wept. No one came for her, and he never apologized.

For Estelle, the negative images evoked by the tale of "Rumpelstilskin" were words that she associated with own father speaking to her, "Your only value is in what you can produce, and in the ways you can feed *my* self-esteem and *my* self-worth."

Estelle realized that she only felt valued by her father for her achievements. She was important to him if she was behaving in a quiet, respectful manner, and not expressing her feelings. As a consequence, Estelle feared making any decisions for herself or allowing herself to express her emotions.

The day after we explored the tale of "Rumpelstilskin" in the group, Estelle dreamed:

> I rode my father's bicycle downtown and stopped at a pub in a rundown part of town to get something to eat and drink. I took the wheels off the bike and brought them in with me so it wouldn't get stolen. I placed them under the table and had my meal. I forgot I had the bicycle with me and made my way home some other way. When I got home, my father was packing the car for a trip. I suddenly realized that I had left the bike downtown. I didn't know what to do. I was afraid because I knew he would be angry, since it was *his* bike. I couldn't go back downtown as we were leaving soon, and I couldn't remember the name of the restaurant. I rationalized that given the part of town it was in, the wheels had probably already been stolen. I decided to tell him that the bike had been stolen from the garage. I feared that if I told him the truth, he would be angry with me and tell me I was stupid and irresponsible and say, "Where is your head?"

Estelle associated the bicycle in the dream with a metaphor for her own individuation process, her commitment to becoming more conscious of her own self. To ride a bicycle requires balance, rhythm, and the energy of the rider to move it forward. It is significant that, in her dream, Estelle rode her *father's* bicycle. In other words, she used his way of moving in the world. Then she left the bicycle in a part of town where it was stolen and feared telling him the truth. Like the miller's daughter in the tale, who felt forced to tell a lie and pretend she had spun straw into gold, Estelle also protected herself with a lie. The good news of her dream is that her father's bicycle, the vehicle for his life's journey, was no longer available for her to borrow for *her* life. She now needed to find her own way.

Two days later, in her dream, Estelle found herself on foot. She dreamed:

> I was in a forest, walking along an unpaved road. I told my father to leave me there, as I wanted to walk home. I walked and walked. I came out of the forest and found myself walking along a road beside the ocean. I didn't know how long it would take

me to get home. As I walked and walked, I began to feel a little concerned, as I had no identification papers with me, no money, and no keys. I kept walking and started to feel tired. I finally came to a beach kiosk, and there I met my brother. I was pleased and relieved to see him. He offered me a ride home.

In this dream, Estelle found her own way through the forest (which she associates with a place of transformation). Her own energy moved her with no help or direction from her father. She went just as she was, with no signs of external power (that is, identification, money, or keys). As she persisted on her journey home, the road opened out beside the ocean (a place she connected with peace and happy childhood memories). Her brother, who Estelle views as representing her own positive, caring, masculine energy, was waiting at the end of the road, ready to accompany her the rest of the way home. During this time, Estelle became increasingly aware of her need to separate from her father, to claim her own spindle, and to weave her own life. As painful as this was, she persisted in setting boundaries around her father's demands on her. She learned to respond to his requests in ways that were both truthful and compassionate. She then made the conscious choice to no longer be caught in lies to protect him or herself.

Many millers' daughters feel that they have no choice but to "do what daddy wants." In her active imagination dialogue between the miller and his daughter at her wedding, Jessica reported the father saying:

You have a good man. Take care of him and he will look after you. I am no longer responsible for you. I've done my best. Look at all you have, thanks to me! You have everything and a wonderful husband to take care of you. All you need to make life complete is a family to care for.
The miller's daughter responded: "Oh, Daddy. I don't want to get married, I am afraid. I don't know what to expect. I don't want to live in his house. I like your house better."
He replied: "Every respectable girl gets married. What will you do if you don't? Who will look after you? You *must* get married."
The daughter answered: "But, Daddy, I want to see the world, have fun, be carefree, and find my own way!"
The miller-father responded: "You can't go traipsing off by yourself into the world. What will the neighbors think? What will I tell them? No, it is better to settle down and marry this fellow while you have the chance."

The daughter responded: "But, Daddy, it's not right for me ..."
The father replied: "You'll see, my child. Everything will be all right. Once you have children you will be happy."
The daughter answered, with submission: "Oh, all right, Daddy. If it makes you happy."

In this dialogue we hear the resignation of the miller's daughter caught in the patriarchal view that she can only survive "under a man or behind a wall," an axiom of the Middle Ages. If a woman didn't marry, her only alternative was to go into a convent, "behind a wall," where the fathers of the church were then responsible for her.

In our present day Western world, women aren't usually forced into marriages or convents. However, such arrangements still exist in many parts of the world. Even in the West, unmarried women still experience pressure from family and friends to "make up their minds" and have children before it is "too late."

When Estelle did an active imagination dialogue between the miller and his daughter at her wedding, the father said:

I am so proud of you. I don't know how you did it; somehow you spun that straw into gold. Now you are queen. You will be rich and won't have to worry about money. People will respect you. I also hope that you will be in a position to help your father and pass some of your wealth on to me.

In Estelle's words, the daughter replied:

You had no right to tell the king that I could spin straw into gold. You had totally unrealistic expectations of me and actually put me in a life-threatening situation. If I hadn't achieved what the king wanted, I would have been put to death. But, on the other hand, I have to thank you because otherwise I would not have seen what I was capable of achieving. I learned that when I am really pushed far enough someone will come to my rescue— and it's not you! You never really helped me at all. You expected a great deal from me. But you didn't really show me how to achieve what you expected or how to be self-sufficient in life.

Shortly after doing this active imagination dialogue, Estelle had the following dream:

> I was in a high-rise building. It was a bank building in the middle of the city. For some reason, I had to spend the night in one of the offices. I kept thinking that this was a strange situation to be in. Then I was in a writing class. The teacher was Katherine. The process was very exciting, but she wasn't explaining clearly what she was doing or how she achieved the end product. This was frustrating. Alexis was also there. Someone swore in French, saying, "*Merde.*" Another person wanted to know what it meant, and I replied, "It means *shit.*" Alexis said, "Yes, it's about eliminating toxins from the body, a release of frustration." Then, I was showing a male friend around our new house. He really liked it. He said that we would probably find a change in attitude in all the members of the family because of this new space. I agreed with him. I had already noticed that the children seemed happier and more content.

After this dream, Estelle appreciated that something was shifting in her own inner state of being. She associated the image of Katherine with an enthusiastic, less anxious part of herself that was open to play and did not take herself so seriously. She saw the dream as an invitation to trust the process, even if it felt frustrating, unfamiliar, or strange. Estelle associated being caught in an upper-story office of a bank building with the place her banker father spent most of his time.

On the last evening of our reflection on the tale of "Rumpelstilskin," Estelle dreamed:

> A woman, who was highly competent, completed a very complex painting and won the competition. As part of the competition, the participants had to skate and complete a series of precise figure skating moves on which they were judged. After that, they had to paint a still life in watercolor. I was impressed with how talented this woman was. She could both paint and skate. Her name was Katrina de Witt. She was staying with me in my home. I asked her what it was like to be so famous. She said she had previously felt a lot of pressure, because it was so important for her father that she win and be the best. Now, she enjoys what she is doing because she does it for herself.

In this dream, Estelle discovered a positive aspect of herself she hadn't previously known, one who is now staying in her home. The name of this competent, well-balanced side of Estelle—who no longer achieves to please her father—is Katrina de Witt (which Estelle translates as *Katherine, the Wise One*). She is witty, clever, intelligent, and no longer dependent on her father. She knows how to skate, which requires the ability to maintain her balance, *and* she also excels in the arts! Estelle found this dream very affirming of her efforts to separate herself from her father's demands and expectations.

Emily experienced the tale of "Rumpelstilskin" as physically and emotionally disturbing. Her body reacted to the story with abdominal pain. Her mother, also named Emily, had abandoned her when she was nine months old. She was then marked as "that woman's child." Emily still experienced deep rage at her father, who did everything he could to squelch her creative soul. She wrote:

> I still have a great deal of difficulty with images of the masculine. I recall, as a child, thinking about this fairy tale. What if the king asks her to fill a fourth or fifth room with gold? What if she can't do it? This forces me to look at all the expectations my father placed on me. Am I still running to please him? Is that why I sit obediently in my office doing something I don't like to do? Is that why I haven't chosen to do what I desire—because I remember him telling me that I would never amount to anything?

When she reflected on what the miller said to his daughter at her wedding, Emily experienced feelings of shame and degradation. His remarks were full of negative sexual connotations: "You have the body of a woman but the mind of a child. Now, go and do your duty, and do it well."

Emily's response from the daughter to her father was very direct: "Well, Father, I'm sorry. When I was a child I had no choice but to listen to all you said. You said so many degrading things so often that I believed them. Well, now you see I am a queen. Come to think of it, I could have your head." Emily associated this image with her own need to "behead" the internalized voice of her father that continued to hold her captive. She recalled the story of Judith in the Hebrew Scriptures, who saved her people by beheading Holophernes.[51]

Taking on the role of the daughter in the tale, Emily continued:

> So, Father, now that I am queen, I can answer you back. I am not a tramp, nor was I ever one. I was a child full of wonder, beauty, and innocence. You were not around for the first six years of my life. You were away at war. If you had connected to me as your daughter, even in the slightest way, when you returned,

you would not have handed me over to the king. You let me go through an ordeal of three nights and days that could have cost me my life. You did not think of me at all. I was just a commodity for your aggrandizement. What if I hadn't succeeded? Why don't you answer me? Don't you have a voice?

"Eat your dinner, it will get cold." Emily remembered, with pain, her father's abuse. He forced her to eat the fat from the meat, even though she choked on it. While exploring this tale, she experienced the symptoms of a gallbladder attack. She could taste bile. The daughter who has no mother, and who is treated as an object by her father, lives with the taste of bitterness on her tongue.

The Greedy King: Produce Gold or Die

The king is very pleased with the gold that the miller's daughter has spun from the room of straw. What was considered of no value, to be swept away, has been transformed into treasure. The miller's daughter is relieved to see the transformation when she awakens the first morning from her sleep. Through the intervention of the mysterious dwarf, Rumpelstilskin, she has survived. But her relief is short-lived, because the sight of all that gold makes the king greedy for more. On the second night, the king locks her in a larger room filled with straw, with the threat that it must be spun into gold by daylight or she will die. Once again, she weeps and the dwarf appears. This time, when he asks, "What will you give me?" she offers her ring, since it is the only thing she has left. Rings are associated with choices to commit oneself in relationships, links to family, and signs of belonging. In giving away her ring in order to save her life, the miller's daughter symbolically cut herself off from a connection to her past and to relationships that may have been more fulfilling than her life with the greedy king.

The king was overjoyed at the sight of so much gold after the second room of straw was changed into treasure. However, his appetite for gold was not yet satisfied. He then brought the miller's daughter to an even larger room full of straw. He promised her that, if she were able to spin this straw into gold, she would become queen. "I know she's only a miller's daughter," he said to himself, "but I'll never find a richer woman anywhere."[52]

When she was alone, the dwarf came for the third time. He asked, "What will you give me this time?" She replied, "I have nothing more to give." He then made her promise to give him her first child if she became queen. Believing she had no choice, she consented. In the morning, when he saw the third room full of spun gold, the king made good his promise and married her. The miller's daughter became a queen. She now had the power to call on her own resources.

Often millers' daughters swallow the message of the king. They believe that it has to be gold, and nothing less, or they will die. A harassing voice (now within) demands that they do more, be more, win the gold medal, make more money, and achieve greater status. They feel that they must continue to give of themselves, even when they know they have nothing more to give. Then, in their desperation, they promise their children, symbols of their own souls. The effects of this bargain will be felt in their bodies. They exhaust themselves with their striving and fall victim to diseases (such as chronic fatigue) or find themselves in the pit of depression.

The miller's daughter has to produce gold; she can't do anything less. She is in a state of terror that the king won't be pleased and feels that her life is on the line. However, in her heart she knows that what she has produced is not *really* gold, just straw in disguise. Her unspoken fear is, "What if they see beyond the disguise; where will I be then?" Her father will be disgraced for his boasting. The king will be angry at being cheated out of what he desired, a wife who would make him wealthy. She struggles with the question, "Who will love me if my performance doesn't turn to gold and bring wealth, status, and pride to my family?" Her family includes her missing mother, the absence of the positive feminine (a caring support for her unique self). Her mother may also have been caught in performing for the king, ensnared in patriarchal values of productivity's gold. Her mother's ambition to be pleasing to the world of the king may now be assigned to her daughter.

In this tale, the greedy king's message is clear: "Produce gold or you will die." Each woman reflected on the tale as if it were her own dream, in which each of the images had a message waiting to become conscious within her. Each one asked herself the question, "Who is the greedy king within me whose message I have swallowed, so that I feel forced to drive myself to 'get the gold,' no matter what the cost?"

Bargaining for Our Lives

Many fairy tales have a motif of three torture nights, through which the heroine can be redeemed.[53] The three nights of torture begin for the miller's daughter when the king locks her in a room full of straw so that she can fulfill her father's boastful lie that she can spin straw into gold. As she has no idea how to spin straw into gold, she falls into a state of despair.

In this moment of profound powerlessness, a little dwarf appears. The appearance of Rumpelstilskin seems initially to be a positive one for the miller's daughter. He comes as soon as she dissolves into tears. He provides a creative alternative. He will spin the straw into gold, for a price. "What will you give me?" he demands.

She offers her necklace, which is associated with the energy of the voice. It is worn around the neck, the bridge between our emotional and rational worlds, between our thoughts and our feelings. When the feminine voice is suppressed, feelings are repressed and a woman loses her capacity to articulate her needs.

After working with this tale, Estelle had the following dream:

> I was in a car with Daniel, who was driving up a narrow, curving mountain pass. I was afraid that we might go over the edge. At the top of the pass, he stopped at a small hospital, the Princess Margaret Cancer Hospital. He went in to visit one of his patients. I saw a small store across the street with trinkets and amulets scattered around. No one seemed to be attending the shop; it seemed like a place of chaos. I looked at the necklaces. I really liked them but couldn't decide which one I wanted. The store-keeper came out, a young man, and showed me a necklace of a clown. I didn't want it, as I thought it was too big. He asked me where my necklace was. I told him I had lost it. I said I would have to come back later as I was running out of time. Then, I went back to the car.

When Estelle explored the meaning of the dream, she associated Daniel with a controlling, negative masculine side of herself that drove her on a dangerous road, from which she could "go over the edge." He stops at a cancer hospital to visit some part of her where things have gotten out of control (cancer). The shop-keeper offers her a necklace with a clown image, but she thinks it's too big for her. In the dream, she reports that she has lost her necklace, which Estelle associated with her ability to articulate and give voice to what she wants for herself.

When Estelle reflected on the image of the clown necklace, she saw the clown as an aspect of herself with which she was not comfortable. She admitted that she usually felt she had to "keep everything under control." She saw the clown as "the fool who can simply and directly tell it like it is." Estelle recognized that having to maintain the pretense that she had everything under control was the same trap in which the miller's daughter in the tale had been caught.

Our voices are associated with our capacity to achieve harmonious resonance in our lives, if we use them to speak the truth. This realization reminded Estelle of an earlier dream she had had of a wise old Japanese man, who had looked like a Buddha and showed her how to play temple bells. This was her dream:

When I shook the bells in a certain rhythm, the music was soothing, calming, and healing. If the rhythm were slightly off, the music was jarring. The wise old man was guiding me as I played. I thought it would be a good idea to use these glass bells as a healing tool with some of my patients who had had strokes and were in wheelchairs and could no longer speak. The hospital orderlies wheeled in two female patients. I was going to show them how to use the bells.

In her active imagination dialogue, the image of the wise old man gave Estelle the following instructions:

Follow me, follow my rhythm; go slowly, methodically, don't rush; move both hands simultaneously. Touch the ground, then lift the bells and shake them slowly, gently, then touch the ground again. It is important to follow the rhythm. Trust the process. Trust me to lead you, and then follow my pattern and rhythm. I will show you the path. You just have to trust.

Getting in touch with her own music, her own voice, the healing rhythm of her own life, required considerable courage of Estelle. She had great difficulty giving voice to her feelings. Her early life experience had taught her that to do so in front of her father was potentially dangerous. The wise old man who looked like a Buddha (one who invited spiritual awakening) offered her sacred healing bells. To heal the parts of herself that are paralyzed and in wheelchairs (that is, do not have the capacity to stand on their own), Estelle must play the bells in a gentle rhythm, touching the ground as part of the healing ritual. This requires claiming her relationship to her own body more consciously and allowing the rhythm of her life to be directed from her own inner spiritual center.

Just after beginning work in the group on the tale of "Rumpelstilskin," Claire also had a dream about claiming her voice and speaking the truth. She dreamed:

A huge, tornado-like wind came up. There were many young children camping outside. I manage to get inside with some of my friends, but a few were left outside. Their tent was almost flattened by the wind. Then, I was watching a street show. The singers were all dressed up in disguise. One had fishing boots on. There were three of them dressed like clowns. One guy took his outfit off except for the boots. He was really an opera singer, well

trained, out for fun. I was told to come to a place like Carnegie
Hall that night. They told me they needed "someone to fill in."
Then I was with the Lowen family. They were oddly quiet with
me. I was confused. Should I go to this show and sing? I didn't
know the words yet. The men didn't say what time to come, but
they said to be there. Then I went for a walk with Mrs. Lowen.
She said, "There was no contract; you aren't responsible for being
there just because someone said so." They hadn't provided a car
to pick me up, and I hadn't signed any agreement. I feel relieved
not to have to go to perform.

Claire awoke in tears from this dream, feeling that she'd never know what was
right, and thinking of herself as maimed, mute, and defective. In working with the
images in the dream, Claire acknowledged the ways in which she allowed herself
to be blown away and overwhelmed. She was relieved to hear the words of Mrs.
Lowen (a positive mother figure in her life). Claire realized that she didn't have to
do something just because some articulate men expected it and then gave her no
support to carry it out. She associated the three masculine figures in her dream
with men who made demands on her time and energy. Claire recognized that she
often assumed she had no choice but to meet their expectations. Like the miller's
daughter in the tale of "Rumpelstilskin," she didn't speak the truth. Instead, she
attempted to do what she knew she could not do. Then she found herself trapped
in continually meeting the needs of the greedy king, who always wanted more.

On the other hand, when Claire looked at the dream from the perspective of
her own inner world, she saw that one of the masculine figures was a trained opera
singer. He represented a part of her that could give voice to the story. However,
Claire acknowledged in the dream, "I don't know the words yet."

Claire realized that it was important for her to avoid becoming overwhelmed
and overly involved in meeting the demands of others, or she would end up in a
state of collapse.

During the time of our work on the tale of "Rumpelstilskin," Claire had severe
menstrual pain, which she hadn't experienced since she was an adolescent (when
the family physician prescribed whiskey to deaden the pain). Then, her young
feminine body was drugged. Now, she experienced dizziness and fluctuations in
her energy. She also felt pain in her left arm, which she associated with her heart.
When the pain began to shift, Claire was able to do her creative work again.

The second night, when the miller's daughter was, once again, faced with having to spin straw into gold, the dwarf asks her what she will give him if he spins it
for her. This time, she offers him her ring. A ring of commitment to a relationship

is generally worn on the fourth finger of the left hand (which is connected to the energy of the heart). Giving up our rings involves letting go of heart choices. When we hand over our rings, we are left feeling that choices about our lives belong to others. They choose us, as the king chose the miller's daughter in the tale. She did not freely choose him. Millers' daughters often find themselves bargaining away what is precious to them because they perceive that they have no choice.

Who Is Rumpelstilskin?

Where does Rumpelstilskin come from? Why is he so demanding? If we take each of the images from the tale as if it were our own dream, then each image has a message for us about ourselves. Who is this aspect of ourselves that comes to our aid and then turns against us?

According to Von Franz, dwarfs often come into women's dreams, and generally carry images of early creative responses to life.[54] Rumpelstilskin certainly demonstrated creative energy in spinning straw into gold to save the miller's daughter's life. Her dilemma was, "How can I survive?" Initially, Rumpelstilskin provided what was needed for her survival. Over time, however, his demands became greater and greater.

One of the clues to his identity is in his name, *Rumpel* (to make noise) and *stilskin* (to be on stilts).[55] In other words, he manifests an aspect of our inner selves that makes an unintelligible sound and that is not fully grounded in our human reality. Could he be an expression of our early defensive position about how to survive in an uncertain world?

According to human development research, between the ages of six months and three years,[56] we come to conclusions about if, and how, we are going to live, and whom we can trust in order to survive. These survival conclusions generally become set by about age seven. Early strategies of how we respond in situations of trust, particularly in times of crisis, continue to influence us into our adult lives. Until we become conscious of and name these early precognitive survival strategies, they will continue to interfere with our adult decision-making processes, particularly when we are in crisis. While the survival strategy may initially appear useful, in the long run it turns destructive, because it prevents us from consciously choosing to use our adult resources.

All children develop survival strategies that they take into their adult lives. These strategies are simply their ways of dealing with the uncertain external world in which they find themselves. When the girl child is deprived of adequate mothering, she may, as an adult, form insecure relationships, which leave her feeling anxious and dependent on others for survival. Or, on the other hand, she may decide that she doesn't need relationships with others. She may develop an atti-tude of "I'll go it alone," which manifests itself as a false self-sufficiency.[57]

In the early version of the Grimm's tale of "Rumpelstilskin," the miller's daugh-ter is described as clever. Her father boasts of her accomplishments, exaggerating that she can spin straw into gold. He may have meant it as a metaphor for her capacity to turn what is ordinary into the extraordinary. Nonetheless, he turns her over to the king. When his daughter protests that she cannot do what he has promised, the miller ignores her and does not come to her rescue.

The child/woman who uses cleverness as a defensive position for survival is often expected to achieve beyond her capabilities. She may find herself in the dilemma of taking on unreasonable expectations of others, which she feels she cannot meet, and yet must, in order to stay alive. The more she accomplishes, the more she's expected to accomplish.

The child/woman who uses being helpful and accommodating as a defensive position for survival may believe that she must meet the need of others regardless of the cost to herself, in order to maintain the relationships that she perceives she needs to stay alive. She may even pretend that being available to meet others' needs and accommodating herself to others' desires fulfills what *she* wants and desires. Her basic defensive stance (which may or may not be fully conscious) is, "I need my relationship with you in order to survive. Please don't leave me."

Our survival conclusions are reflections of early stages of our personal develop-ment.[58] These survival messages operate (primarily unconsciously) as if we are still in those childhood stages. In crisis situations, these survival strategies are often activated and produce heightened feelings of fear and anxiety that are out of pro-portion to the situation in which we find ourselves. If I were to come to the early conclusion that I am dependent on my relationships for my survival and my identity, who I see myself to be might become fused with my relationships. This could also be stated as: I do not create my relationships—they create me. On the other hand, if I were to come to the early conclusion that I am dependent on my achievements for my survival and my identity, then who I see myself to be might become fused with my accomplishments. I do not create my accomplishments; they create and define me. Either way, the child/woman feels trapped. If she iden-tifies with her relationships, she believes her survival depends on maintaining and nourishing those relationships, even if her life is jeopardized in the process. If she defines herself by her achievements, she is compelled to keep achieving, even if she is exhausted and becomes ill as a consequence. Regardless of which defensive survival position the child/woman takes, whether she surrenders her identity to her relationships or to her accomplishments, she feels isolated and alone.

Rumpelstilskin is an illusion, a drive toward survival that keeps us going in circles rather than leading us to the place of claiming our own personal power. He is an illusion of safety, which has no solid ground on which to stand. He is the compulsive clinging to relationships that are no longer healthy because we fear we won't survive without them. He is the controlling drive for achievement to meet the requirements of belonging to the world of the father/king.

The tale of "Rumpelstilskin" is about naming what unconsciously holds our souls captive. The Rumpelstilskin within us destroys all possibility of having our own voices (associated in the tale with giving up our necklaces). As long as he continues to control us from within, he gets in the way of our developing healthy relationships (associated in the tale with handing over our rings). While he is in control, he prevents us from honoring our own souls (associated in the tale with his desire to consume our first-born child).

Rumpelstilskin is that stunted, immature part of our thinking that defines and restricts us. In effect, he will devour our souls, if we don't become conscious and discover his name. Once named, the illusion of power he offers self-destructs (like any illusion which disintegrates when we hold it up to the light of consciousness). Rumpelstilskin is that part of us that believes we have to join the father/king world to survive, because the world of the mother is powerless and unpredictable.

Our beliefs are the precursors of our feelings and our behaviors. If we want to change the way we act in the world, we need to examine the beliefs that drive our choices to respond in particular ways. Otherwise, we do not have Rumpelstilskin—he has us! As long as Rumpelstilskin is operative, we are under his power. We are caught in living a lie and will do anything not to be found out.

But the lie itself is a lie. If I believe "I am my relationships," and that I must fulfill the demands of others or die, that is, in itself, a lie. If I believe "I am my achievements," and that I must force myself to achieve to stay alive, that, also, is a lie. Both these beliefs are illusions that can destroy who I truly am. Regardless of whether our survival conclusions are primarily focused on our relationships or our achievements, the effect is the same. We are not free. Furthermore, the cost of *living the lie* increases over time.

There is a third, potentially more dangerous, fusion, which I refer to as a fusion with death. It manifests itself as a pull away from life, into despair, toward which women with early mother abandonment wounds may be especially drawn. Jung referred to these women as "in life as if on parole,"[59] choosing daily to stay or go, get sick and die, or commit suicide. These women believe not only that they are not loved but also that they are not lovable. This is another lie that may force them into super-performing or putting themselves into relationships where they are exploited, which then reconfirms their lack of worth.

When our relationships are the primary way we define who we are, then acceptance by others and meeting their needs and expectations may be ruling our life choices. We may feel that it is dangerous to express our own needs or to set boundaries in our relationships. On the other hand, when our achievements define who we are, our sense of power may be in our need for performance. We may then have a tendency to defend against relationships and to primarily define ourselves based on our accomplishments.

In the tale of "Rumpelstilskin," the miller's daughter is in a dilemma of survival. In the external world, others see her as dedicated to caring for her father. In her world, there is no maternal feminine presence. She has to figure it out for herself. She only knows her father's world and all that it demands. How can she refuse to silence her own voice (not give up her necklace), choose healthy relationships (not hand over her ring), and refuse to allow her feminine soul to be devoured (not relinquish her child)?

The Missing Mother: Redeeming the Abandoned Feminine

The message of the tale of "Rumpelstilskin" is deeply ingrained in the negative patriarchal values of the primacy of status and money and the devaluing of the feminine values of relationship, creativity, and the capacity to be generative. The miller's daughter has no mother or feminine presence in her life. In addition, her father has literally abandoned her in order to fulfill his boastful lie to the king. In her active imagination dialogue between the miller's daughter and her absent mother, Jessica pleaded:

> Where are you, Mother? I am lost and alone. I feel as if I'm doing the wrong thing, but I don't know how to change it. Life just happens, and I follow. I'm not a participant in my own life. I feel like a pretender. Maybe it will get better. But I feel as if I have no choice. I need a man to make me whole, to take me out, to make life exciting for me, to make me laugh. But I don't want him to decide what makes me happy. He doesn't know. How could he, when I don't know myself? Oh well, this seems to be the only way; I will work hard to make him happy.
> (There was no answer from her mother. She was silent. Perhaps she had also handed over her necklace in exchange for survival.)

Emily was overwhelmed with grief when she dialogued with the absent mother in the fairy tale. She wrote: "There is so much pain, Mother, and sadness. What comes from my inner heart is longing—longing to belong."

The child tastes paradise when she has a satisfactory relationship with her mother. The trauma of abandonment does not destroy her longing for the taste of paradise. She yearns for the experience of being loved and valued for her own unique self. She searches for someone worthy of her love and to whom she can belong.[60] The woman who has been abandoned by her mother longs for affirmation. She seeks to find her own home, her place of belonging where she can discover her true self.

The abandoned child/woman often believes that she should be perfect. She finds it very difficult to accept herself as she is. She may believe that if she had been perfect she would not have been abandoned.

After we began exploring the tale of "Rumpelstilskin," Rita, whose mother died suddenly when she was very young, had the following dream:

> I was outdoors with a young girl. I wouldn't let her have a flower. She wanted the yellow one, which had blemishes on it. Then I saw that they were all ringing; the flowers were vibrating with life.

Rita associated the color yellow with the gold of the sun and with having the courage to take action for her own life. But the flowers in her dream were blemished. Rita didn't want to give them to her young feminine dream image. Then she saw that they were ringing and vibrating with life. Rita recognized that she needed to take the necessary steps to live her own life. She realized that her blossoming didn't have to be perfect to be of value. She was now free to make healthy choices for herself that she previously did not have the courage to make.

When we are driven by perfection, we think (as Rita did) that we have to always "get it right." This belief may paralyze us and leave us unable to make the healthy decisions for a truly fruitful life.

If our identity is fused with our achievements to prove to the father-world that we are worthy of affirmation and recognition, we can fail to recognize our own blossoming as beautiful, even when it is blemished by our everyday human struggles. The Rumpelstilskin in us demands that we hand over our soul/child because we don't *really* know how to spin straw into gold (even though those around us think we do and keep demanding more and more proof of our being worthy of their praise and admiration). There comes a time when, as millers' daughters, we have to honestly face our human limitations and to let go of meeting the inflated expectations of others and of ourselves.

The girl child may believe that she has to prove she's as good as a son. She may abandon her own feminine nature and strive to demonstrate that a daughter can be as worthy of love and affirmation as a son. While she was growing up, Michaela believed that she must have been adopted because she felt so different from her siblings. She finally decided by the age of seven that she couldn't have been adopted, because if her mother *had* selected a child, she would have chosen a boy.

In Michaela, we see the wound of the abandoned feminine spirit in the child. For her, to be feminine was to be handicapped, of less value than a masculine child. She was driven to try harder in order to prove that she too deserved her mother's praise and admiration.

A few nights after exploring the tale of "Rumpelstilskin," Michaela dreamed: "I saw a young adolescent male shackled to a wall. He was wild with rage." When she looked at her dream from the perspective of her own inner world, Michaela saw her young life energy shackled to a wall. When she explored the "walls" in her life, Michaela appreciated how she held herself back and felt unable to move forward in the way her heart desired. She could not get on with her own life in a focused, purposeful way. Instead, she felt bound in shackles. This dream was reminiscent for Michaela of the dream that had originally brought her into psychotherapy. In her earlier dream, she had been bound, shackled, and thrown out the door by a group of men.

After the first evening we explored this tale, Michaela became very angry. She experienced irregular heartbeats, which frightened her. The arrhythmia disappeared, however, when she reached the doctor's office. She wasn't sure if she would be able to continue in the group.

It is not unusual to experience symptoms in our bodies when our survival conclusions are tapped. These conclusions are a safety valve on our early perceptions of our ability to survive and to avoid despair and death. When that valve is touched, warning signals travel through our bodies. For Michaela, the early wound against which she had to defend herself in order to live was a broken heart. She felt cast aside from her mother's love in favor of her younger brother.

After the first evening of our work on the tale, Michaela dreamed she saw an orca whale rise up out of the sea between two mountains. She drew the image from her dream and associated it with a black and white phallus between two breasts. Her unconscious gave her a powerful metaphor for what she was experiencing. A black and white (negative and positive) masculine image was operating below the surface between her breasts, in the area of her heart. The orca is known as a killer whale. Michaela recognized that the tale was evoking a message for her that there was an unconscious killer in her heart.

Michaela had had a very close relationship with her father, who died when she was still young. He took the time to read her stories and tell her tales of his adventures around the world, while her mother did not have time for her. She felt, at times, as if she were still grieving his death. She had not been able to find a satisfying mutual relationship with a male partner, although she had attempted several times to do so. Each time, he was not able to sustain or commit to the relationship over time. She felt she had experienced, several times over, what it meant to have a broken heart.

Just after working with the tale of "Rumpelstilskin," Michaela had the following dream:

> I was with a young man in a room. I was sitting at the side of the bed. He was sitting at the bottom of the bed. I don't think there was anyone in the bed. I was telling him a story about a woman as if it were an opera. As I told the story, the young man had an erection. I could see his penis rising up at the end of the bed. Then he moved toward me, and I felt threatened. I wanted to get out of there. I found it very difficult to move. It took tremendous willpower to get off that chair (as I thought about this when awake, I thought it was because I felt responsible for his erection). As I left the room, he seemed angry. In my hasty retreat, I left my purse in the room. I felt annoyed, but I was determined to get it back. I went back and knocked on the door, and when he opened it, I said, "I want my purse." I felt fearful. He handed me my purse and then apologized for his behavior. I said, "I never saw anyone have such a reaction to an opera story." He replied, "Do you know any more?" We both laughed and started to hug and kiss. He turned into a black man with a black beard. As he did this, I was quite fascinated and kept kissing him. Then I thought, "This guy is too young for me," and I left. I don't know whether that meant that I was too old for him or it meant I could do better. But it was fun. My relationship with both the white and black man felt very positive.

There were some very interesting images in Michaela's dream: the opera story that evoked a sexual response, the lost and reclaimed purse, and the embrace of the young man (who was white and then black, like the image of the orca whale in her other dream). Early in her psychotherapy, Michaela had a dream of a young girl who had lost her purse. She associated the loss with her hospitalization as a child and with the devastating effects that experience had on her young psyche. (Years later, she connected the image of losing her purse with an experience of sexual assault while she was in that hospital.) Michaela saw the image of the purse in her dream as an expression of her feminine identity. What was interesting for Michaela was her determination to get her purse back, even though she was afraid.

Michaela noted that she felt responsible for the man's sexual advances, although there doesn't appear to be any reason why she would assume this responsibility. This is a common response of children and even adult women who have been sexually exploited. Often they feel they are the cause of their own trauma.

When Michaela reclaimed her purse (the feminine identity that she had left behind) from the potential rapist, the energy in the dream changed. Now, she has a *choice* to be with both the positive and negative aspects of the masculine image in her dream, a choice that had been frightening when it came in the form of the black and white killer whale in her previous dream. She can now choose to come or go. She has reclaimed her own personal freedom as a woman. Early in her psychotherapy, when asked what she thought was valuable about being a woman, Michaela could not answer. She could not think of anything!

The power of Rumpelstilskin for Michaela was connected to her early survival belief that she "had to go it alone." Her redemption from his power came when she was able to reclaim the positive side of her mother, her own feminine nature, and the feminine face of God. After this dream, Michaela wrote in her journal: "Oh God, help me to believe the truth about myself, no matter how *beautiful it is.* The message that I'm not alone and that I am deeply loved is finally penetrating my body. I weep, because it is too good to be true."

The tale of "Rumpelstilskin" is a story of the feminine quest for redemption, a journey of a motherless daughter who finds her own life and lives it. She becomes empowered, despite a father who uses her to save himself and a king who exploits her.

Emily's words expressed it well, "My glory is that I have claimed my own child and my motherhood as my greatest treasure."

Enter the Messenger: Claiming Our Personal Power

The positive counterbalancing force in the tale to the destructive energy of Rumpelstilskin is called "the messenger." We explored as a group how this messenger was manifested within ourselves.

When the miller's daughter becomes queen, she can claim the resources she needs to make decisions about her own life. She calls on her messenger to help her save her child (a metaphor for her own soul). In the early versions of this tale the message is clear that the dwarf plans to feast on the queen's child.[61] The messenger (not designated in the tale as either masculine or feminine) is an image of her adult conscious self who explores and subsequently recognizes the unconscious devouring force that lives on "the other side of the hill."

The queen's messenger discovers Rumpelstilskin's name in the place where the "fox and the hare bid each other good night." In other words, the answer lies in the place where the opposites come together; where what was once in conflict is now in harmony; where aspects of ourselves that were once destructive and devouring now coexist in peace. In each of us, the messenger provides the possibility of discovering a new way to live our lives more freely and without fear.

A year after the wedding, the dwarf comes to claim the newborn child of the miller's daughter, who is now queen. She has forgotten all about her bargain to give him her first child. She promises him all the riches of the kingdom if he will let her keep her son, but he refuses. Once again, she weeps, and he takes pity on her. He gives her three days in which to discover his name or she will have to hand over her child.

This is the final test for the miller's daughter. There is always a cost, which increases over time, if we stay in the primitive stage of our early survival conclusions. What the miller's daughter now needs is a mature messenger (androgynous in the tale) who can assist her in moving beyond the dwarfed way she has approached her life decisions. Whenever we find ourselves in a major life dilemma, our original survival conclusions will rise to the surface, no matter how many years we have spent focusing on becoming more conscious of who we truly are. However, as we develop our mature messenger and claim our own power to direct our lives, we are able to name the dwarf and not sacrifice our souls for the sake of survival. As we become more conscious of our personal power, we develop a deeper appreciation of our choices. We can then exercise those choices and no longer have to respond in the way we did when we were young and simply needed to survive.

An example of this struggle is found in Alexis's dream:

> I was climbing a steep hill, in an old car borrowed from someone. Meanwhile, another car (driven by a man) was behind me, also trying to climb the hill. I was driving slowly. I finally got to the top. The man who was following me also stopped at the top of the hill and asked if he could help me. I had, in a baby carriage, an old man whom I was taking home with me. All I could see of him was his blotchy and wrinkled face. The man from the car said he would take care of it, and I looked at his badge. He was a policeman. The man in the carriage had something I needed; that is why I was taking him home.

In this dream, Alexis used a *borrowed car*, not her own vehicle, for moving up the hill. However, she was driving. A man of authority, a policeman in her dream, drove his own car. He is a part of Alexis that is patient with her ego and its limitations. He is in contrast with the shriveled, dwarf image in the baby carriage that Alexis recognizes as Rumpelstilskin. Alexis sees this image of Rumpelstilskin as an undeveloped aspect of herself that has regressed to an infantile stage and cannot walk or stand on its own (a graphic image of her early survival conclusion that she needed to be dependent on others in order to survive).

The day after this dream, Alexis was at the library. She was very frustrated and feeling helpless because she could not find a book that she needed for her class. She went over to another shelf and immediately discovered what she needed. Alexis recognized that her messenger had come to her rescue!

A few days later, Alexis reported that she felt she had really started her quest and that she was going to need discipline to proceed on the path to claiming her own creative life. She was struggling with her early survival conclusion around not trusting herself and needing to find others to trust. She declared, "I *can* trust myself; at my center is the self that can be trusted." She made the decision that she no longer needed to carry around the old survival conclusions of helplessness, personified in her dream image as Rumpelstilskin in a baby carriage.

Alexis also remembered an earlier dream that she recognized revealed an important message for her related to this tale. It concerned the ways in which she allowed her creative power to be taken from her. This was her dream:

> A thief was prowling in the neighborhood. I went to the neighbor's house and talked to Vivian. A few hours later, William told me that he had found a thief sitting on the bed in Vivian's room. My house had also been invaded. I saw where the thief (a girl) had climbed a ladder to a small patio. My bedroom window was left open and she had come right in. I had gone to William to find out what the strange-looking white stuff was that was growing in their backyard and that was now burning. It looked like a patch of old snow, but organic. It was also growing in my own garden. The gardener was thoughtful as he admitted that he was the one who had set fire to it.

When Alexis worked with the images in this dream, she recognized that the thief was about thirteen years old. She had come to challenge Alexis. When Alexis did an active imagination dialogue with the girl thief, she realized that the thief had come to steal a precious stone with hidden power that belonged to Alexis.

The potential could be released from the stone if Alexis invested it with meaning. Alexis wrote: "I need to guard my treasure and protect it. It was easy to get into my space; the window was left open and the ladder accessible."

Alexis reflected on the ways in which she allowed what is precious to her to be stolen. As a teenager, she felt very inadequate. Her father, who thought artistic studies were a waste of time and that she should focus her time on mathematics, denied her the opportunity to develop her creative gifts. The young thief in her dream came carrying the remembrance of her early loss and the insecurity she felt. Alexis recognized the young thief as a part of herself inviting her to wake up and to not allow what is precious within her to be stolen.

When Alexis did an active imagination dialogue with the image of the gardener who set fire to the "old white stuff in the garden" (which she named "old manna"), she discovered that he was transforming what could no longer nourish her. He burned the "old manna" so that it will be available to enrich the soil for the new planting of what her soul needs now. Alexis recognized the messenger of the tale in the dream image of the focused gardener.

In order to name the Rumpelstilskin side of ourselves, we have to go to the other side of the hill, that is, get a new perspective on our lives and see our dilemma from another vantage point. This place is found where opposites come together, where the fox and the hare (natural enemies) bid each other good night. In other words, we have to let go of dualistic thinking and see our lives from a more integrated perspective. We never lose our survival conclusions, but we can name them and break apart their power over us.

Exploring this tale led several of the women in the group to a new understanding of the ways in which they could claim their own powerful energy and their own messenger within. Just as we began our work on the tale, Claire dreamed:

> I was in a new subdivision, a new house. My partner was there. I went for a walk over rough and rocky terrain. There were deep holes that I had to walk around, and many rocks and crevices. When my shadow passed over these holes, snakes awakened. There were dozens of them! I was horrified. "Get me out of here!" I headed back toward the house, but one snake, very persistent and large, followed me. I tried to ward it off with an Irish knit sweater my father had owned. I killed the snake. I got its head and the flesh hollowed out, and I put it between the pages of a book because I didn't want to see it. While I was walking back, I saw big earth-moving machines. My book opened, and the head of the snake flew away, blown by the wind. When I got

back to the house, my friend Matthew was taking a photograph
of what a room looks like after children have played.

Claire associated the Irish knit sweater that had belonged to her father with
the one she had worn when she was pregnant with her first child. She saw the
snakes as primitive energy unearthed by her shadow, energy within herself, of
which she is afraid. She killed the snake, robbing this primitive instinctual energy
of its power, with her dead father's sweater, a garment she associated with her
Celtic heritage. (Irish knit sweaters have designs that indicate the wearer's family,
so that if a person were drowned while at sea he/she could be identified.) Claire
took the head of the snake for a trophy but then hid it away because she "didn't
want to see it." The earth was being moved, and things that had been buried were
now emerging, but her snake head trophy blew away in the wind. Her friend was
back at the house taking a photograph of a room after children had played there,
which she associated with a place of creative chaos.

Claire acknowledged that she is fearful of the powerful instinctual energy within
herself. In her dream, she used her father's persona (the image of his sweater which
she has worn) to kill this awakened surge of energy. Claire's father led a rather
reclusive life. He was chronically depressed and died of a heart attack when she
was still in her teens.

The kundalini energy of the Hindu tradition (with which Claire was familiar)
is depicted as a snake, coiled at the base of the spine, waiting to be awakened by the
spiritual process of enlightenment. The trophy of the decapitated primal energy
of the snake is of no value to Claire hidden away in a book. Her interior process is
about to be dug up to allow what has been buried to come to the surface.

In the second part of her dream, Claire associated Matthew with a positive,
creative masculine side of herself. The dream reassured Claire that she had a place
of creative chaos or child energy at play within her. This is the energy that was
photographed, preserved so that it could be remembered. It reminded Claire of
her own creative, playful child within, to whom she had not been attentive.

Claire associated the snake she killed in the dream with the "passionate and
alive part" of herself, her own creative energy. She realized that with the death of
the snake, her passion for life was gone. Claire's connection to her father's world
destroyed what was vital and alive within her. She had hidden the passionate part
of herself so that she did not have to see it. And then, her creative, vital energy
blew away!

In their work with their dream images, many of the women were surprised at
the powerful aspects of themselves that they had shut out of their consciousness.
What surprised them the most was their *fear* of their own potency and creative

energy. If we don't know our own potency (that is, our potential for claiming our own true selves), we are easily held captive by old patterns of thinking, feeling, and behaving in which we felt safe. A part of us resists the consciousness that would set us free. A highly skilled saboteur of knowing exists within each of us.[62] To be redeemed from the captivity of our early survival conclusions (the hold of Rumpelstilskin) requires claiming our personal power, honoring our own inner messengers, and responding with the courageous and consistent intention to become conscious.

Redemption from Living a Lie

I had chosen a fifth fairy tale for the group; it was called, "Clever Beauty." It was among those I randomly selected at the children's library because it met the criteria of having an unengaged mother. I did not realize at the time that some folklorists considered it a sequel to the tale of "Rumpelstilskin."[63]

The tale of "Clever Beauty" brings an end to the queen's dilemma, so that she can never again be commanded to turn straw into gold and be faced with the lie she had been living. In the tale of "Clever Beauty" (known in the Grimm's version as "The Three Spinners"),[64] the mother endangers her young daughter by boasting to the queen about her daughter's skills. The daughter is then tested three times by the queen to see if she is worthy to be a suitable bride for her son. Three ugly old women come to the daughter's rescue. But their demands in exchange for their labor are simply public acknowledgment and kindness. They ask only that the young girl introduce them at her wedding as her godmothers. In return, they complete the tasks that the queen demanded: spinning and weaving fine silk from thistledown, baking fine bread from thistle stalks, and making fine wine from thistle juice. In the tale of "Rumpelstilskin," that which is considered useless (straw) is transformed into something valuable (gold). In the tale of "Clever Beauty," that which is considered useless (a remnant of thistles) is also transformed into something valuable (clothing, bread, and wine).

At the wedding, the young girl warmly greets the three ugly old women and seats them between herself and the prince. They tell him that they are so ugly because of their work of making wine, spinning thread, and baking bread (the tests the young girl had endured to please the queen). The prince vows that his young bride will never again be asked to do such work; for fear that she would also become ugly. Consequently, the daughter is relieved from having to face the lie in the future that all the work that was done had come from her own hands. The tale ends with the assurance that Beauty would never again be asked to spin or weave or bake or make wine, and that no one would ever know that she really could not make bread, and wine, and silk out of thistles!

Michaela loved this tale because Beauty was not caught in having to live in shame. She was struck by the fact that the daughter/heroine was able to be compassionate, and that this was what saved her. What delighted Michaela most was that the three wise women redeem the daughter from "having to live a lie."

The three wise women, who manifest themselves in the form of hags, are representations of powerful feminine energy disguised in a misshapen, ugly form. The message of this tale is that it is important to honor even the ugly messengers in our lives, as they may have wisdom to share with us. Jessica commented, "We often assume that the bearers of good news should be fair of face." Messengers come in many forms. What is important is that we are able to be open to all the messengers that come to us so that we can hear their messages with an open mind and not restrict ourselves to viewing life events through the limited lens of our expectations.

Because the tale of "Clever Beauty" was so closely related to the tale of "Rumpelstilskin," we treated both as variations of the same story. Therefore, there is not a separate chapter on this tale. One of the striking differences between the two tales is that in "Rumpelstilskin" there are primarily masculine images (other than the miller's daughter): the father, the king, the dwarf, and her son. In the tale of "Clever Beauty," the characters are all feminine, with the exception of the prince. In the first tale, it is the father who brags and brings a life-threatening situation down on his daughter, and the father and the king use the daughter for their own needs. In the second tale, it is the mother who boasts about her daughter, and the mother and the queen exploit the daughter for their own gain.

Women who are unredeemed or unconscious millers' daughters are caught in the dilemma of continuing to pretend to be what they are not, in order to be good enough, and therefore, safe from abandonment. This is an intolerable burden, which becomes heavier and heavier over time, with the initial pretence leading to another and then to another. All the while, these women are afraid that they will be found not to be as smart, clever, or beautiful as the father/king believes. No wonder millers' daughters are depressed! When are they allowed to be just themselves? Do they know who they are separate from the deceptions? Do they have a name of their own that is not a lie?

Two main themes emerged in response to the tale of "Rumpelstilskin" from the dreams and active imagination work of each of the women in the group:

- the recognition that she had a *choice* to reclaim her own personal power as a woman, and
- the importance of refusing to live a lie in order to survive.

Recognizing that she could choose to reclaim her own personal power encouraged each woman in the group to find her own voice, to speak the truth of her own experience, and express her thoughts and feelings in ways that were constructive for herself and others.

Acknowledging the importance of refusing to live a lie in order to survive, each woman examined and named her own early survival conclusions. Once she had done this, she could be free of Rumpelstilskin's hold on her. This did not mean, however, that she would not revert to old patterns of responding in her attempts to deal with a crisis in the future. But, once Rumpelstilskin is named and she is conscious, she would now be able to recognize if Rumpelstilskin had returned. Then, she could *choose* how she wanted to respond. She was no longer trapped into allowing him to eat her soul alive.

Four Years Later

We revisited the tale of "Rumpelstilskin" four years later, exploring how it had affected each woman over time. The women in the group shared several very interesting insights.

Michaela acknowledged the ways in which she had always gotten trapped when she ignored her own limitations in order to impress someone else. She now recognizes her early survival strategies and makes another choice. She declared, "I now ask myself the question, am I making this choice out of love or to impress the other?"

Claire had dream images of turkey vultures coming to rid her of whatever needed purifying in her life. She indicated that she no longer felt regretful about her past relationships. In this tale, she saw bargaining as the basis for relationships, and, as a consequence, everyone acted out of fear. Claire wrote:

> When I get caught in my own ego, I experience fear and anxiety and I cannot breathe. I've sent out my messenger and let go of needing to analyze everything to feel safe. I can go into the unknown now, with a deep compassion for myself.

Jessica responded to the tale four years later by declaring that she had now "taken the bull by the horns." She recalled a dream she had had when we first worked with the tale, which had helped her recognize her fear of her own creative potential. In that dream, she and her son were at the Winter Fair when a bull broke loose. In her reflections on this dream, Jessica recognized the powerful energy within her that she was keeping "penned up." When we reviewed the tale four years later, she dreamed of a large, dark figure in a doorway that was blocking her way through. Jessica declared, "I know now that I need to send my messenger out again to name and remove this obstacle in my way." She recognized the image as the "devil in the doorway." Once she named him, she knew she could cross the threshold and share her creative work with courage.

Estelle acknowledged four years later: "I am now able to let go of perfection and stay focused. Four years ago, my father and my husband made my decisions. Now, I make my own. I can see how a task can be completed, and I am able to take care of it myself."

For Alexis, the shift came in "trusting my own body, knowing my own voice, my own intuition. I have reclaimed my own spiritual child within, my own soul essence."

With her hand over her heart, Emily acknowledged: "The negative aspects of my father are no longer able to command me. There is an inner voice within me that speaks up against his remembered voice. Now that I know I am loved, I can love myself. Today I would say to him, 'You gave me an introduction to the beauty of the mountains, in that, you gave me the best mother.'"

What was clear from the reflections of the women in the group, four years after their first exploration of the tale, was that each had moved to a place of deeper consciousness of her own personal power and each felt a stronger determination not to get caught in living a lie.

Another way of viewing the daughter's dilemma of turning straw into gold is from the perspective of the ancient alchemists. Their efforts to make gold from dross (which was discarded as worthless) can be viewed symbolically as the life-long process of individuation, the journey of claiming one's own life and living it fully. The alchemical understanding of gold was consciousness of the *Self*, the sign of unity, and reclaiming the divine within. The *prima materia* of alchemy in the tale of "Rumpelstilskin" is the straw that is left over from what has been milled and discarded as waste to be swept away (that is, shadow material). In the tale of "Rumpelstilskin," we see the daughter/heroine struggling with the coming together of the opposites: the straw (shadow) becoming gold (light).

Those of us who are millers' daughters, women in a patriarchal industrial world, are daily put to the test. Can we make gold, which is considered precious, out of something that is generally viewed by the father/king as ordinary and of little value? How much of our day-to-day life as women is spent doing precisely that! I recall being newly married and in graduate school. My budget for groceries and all household supplies was twenty-five dollars a week. Now, as I look back on that time, I remember the delicious and creative meals that were the result of my dilemma. Women have created so many artistic ways of turning straw into gold, including beautiful quilt patterns made from scraps of old fabric, jewelry made from dried seeds, delicious bread puddings made from stale crumbs, soap made from scraps of candles, fabrics made from spinning wool, and colorful dyes made from wild roots and flowers.

Four years after our initial reflection on the tale of "Rumpelstilskin," when we again explored the life messages in the tale, it revealed to each woman a more profound meaning than it had on our first exploration. Each one came to a deeper, more heartfelt sense of recognition and reconciliation with her early survival conclusions and with the ways those conclusions had affected her relationships with herself and others. Emily was able to reconcile with the positive side of what her father had given her and to claim her own voice. Michaela was able to acknowledge her own beauty and the fact that she was deeply loved. Claire was able to look herself in the eye and tell the truth, acknowledging her own power to purify her relationships and release herself from self-imposed obligations. Jessica claimed her own potency and creative gifts. Alexis let go of ambivalence and focused on her own creative work. Estelle claimed her own creative life and released other women in her family to do the same. Rita made new life choices that were more healthy and satisfying.

Four years later, each woman was committed to centering herself in the reality of her own personal power as a woman, refusing to live a lie in order to survive. Giving voice to her truth, clearly and with conviction, each one was able to echo the words of Estelle's song:

"My soul cannot be sold,
I will not spin straw into gold."[65]

Reflection Questions:

Chapter II—In the Name of the Father: The Tale of Rumpelstilskin

1. Who is Rumpelstilskin in me?
   - When under stress, are my survival conclusions more related to a fusion in achievements or a fusion in relationships?
   - Is there a part of me that has a tendency to get caught in a fusion with death?

2. How do I see myself as a miller's daughter in a patriarchal, industrial, and corporate world?
   - When I feel under pressure to perform, do I hand over my necklace and allow myself to be silenced, or do I silence myself rather than speak the truth as I see it?
   - Are there ways in which I give up my ring, my power to make my own choices in relationships?
   - When I feel I have nothing more to give, do I promise my soul (my creative, generative, feminine potential) in order to be recognized and affirmed as special?

3. Are there ways in which I still find myself doing "what Daddy wants," living out his dream for me, perhaps one he himself was not able to achieve and, instead, passed on to me?

4. Is there a greedy king in me whose message I have swallowed, so that I feel forced to drive myself to "get the gold," no matter what the cost?

5. Who is my inner messenger, the part of me that:
   - sees what needs to be done,
   - is able to claim my own personal power by getting another perspective on the situation (going to the other side of the hill), and
   - works toward accomplishing what my heart desires, while at the same time honoring the relationships to which I have committed myself?

What are some examples in my own life of times that I have been aware of my own inner messenger?

EMANCIPATION FROM SERVITUDE: THE TALE OF THE HANDLESS MAIDEN

One day you finally knew
what you had to do, and began....
—Mary Oliver, "The Journey"

To be emancipated means to be freed from a state or place of bondage in which we are restrained and subject to the will of another.

Just after she began psychotherapy, Claire had the following dream:

> A little girl, about age three, was taken from her mother to be a prostitute. She lost her memory of home and didn't know her way back. When she was sixteen, her father came, pretending to need a prostitute, and he brought her home. Her mother hugged her, but the girl was rigid and unresponsive. The girl said, "I'm addicted to cocaine. You won't be able to live with me." The mother responded, "You can go for treatment." The daughter answered, "I need all three of us to go."

The dream indicated the state of bondage that Claire was experiencing in her life. At a crucial time in her development (age three), when she was beginning to experience her separateness from her mother and to sort out how she was going to survive, the little girl in her dream was taken to be a prostitute. Prostitution is a state of having to sell your soul for the service and pleasure of others in order to survive. This life of servitude and loss of soul left the girl numb, unable to feel, and addicted to cocaine (one of the earliest antidepressants used by humans). The father in the dream came to get the little girl under the pretence of needing a prostitute. He brought her home, but she could not respond to her mother's embrace. The resolution of the dream dilemma is clear. All three need healing: the negligent mother who did not protect her daughter from being taken into bondage, the weak father who rescued her through deception and came too late, and the girl child, now numb to life, who has been exploited by the patriarchal world for its own needs.

In the tale of "The Handless Maiden," we meet all three of the figures portrayed in Claire's dream. It is the story of a woman's journey from servitude to freedom, from loneliness and isolation to triumph in the face of suffering.

A Synopsis of the Tale of the Handless Maiden

Once upon a time, in a land far away, there lives a miller who finds himself growing poorer by the day. All he has left is his old mill and a beautiful apple tree that grows behind it. One day, when he is in the forest chopping firewood to keep his family warm for the winter, a dark stranger approaches him. The stranger offers him a continuous supply of gold in exchange for what is standing behind his mill. The miller agrees to the bargain, as he thinks he can easily sacrifice the old apple tree for the wealth of unlimited gold. The stranger says that he will come for what the miller promised in three years time.

When the miller returns home, his wife meets him with the news that all the chests in the house are filled with gold. The miller tells her of his bargain with the dark stranger. His wife turns pale in horror because their beautiful daughter had been sweeping behind the mill when the miller made his promise. When the daughter hears what her father has promised, she weeps and weeps. Three years later, when the dark stranger arrives, she has washed herself clean and drawn a circle of chalk around herself, and he cannot claim her. Then the dark stranger instructs her father to take all water away from her so that she cannot wash, because if she is clean he will have no power over her. When he returns the second time, he still cannot claim her, because she has washed herself with her tears. Then the angry dark stranger tells the miller, "If you do not chop off your daughter's hands before I return the third time, I will take you away, never to return." The miller fears for his life. When he tells his daughter what the stranger has threatened, she holds out her hands with the words, "I am your obedient daughter; do what you must do." With the mother standing by, the miller chops off his daughter's hands. When the dark stranger returns for the third time, the daughter has wept and wept on the stumps, and she is once again washed clean. This time, the dark stranger loses his claim over her. The daughter asks her mother and father to tie her arms behind her back so that she can go out into the world and find her own way. Her father pleads with her to stay, promising that he will care for her with the wealth he has received because of her. But, determined to leave, she replies, "I will rely on compassionate strangers to care for me."

The next day, as the sun is rising, she leaves her father's house and starts out into the wide world with her arms tied behind her back. By that evening, she has walked far and is hungry. She comes upon an orchard owned by the king, in which all the pears have been counted. She longs for the fruit, but she cannot reach the tree because a moat surrounds the orchard. Then, an angel comes and closes the moat so that she can cross over into the orchard. She grasps a ripe pear in her mouth, and finds it to be delicious. She then crosses back over the dry moat and hides in the trees.

The next day, when the king comes to inspect his orchard, he notices the missing pear. The guard, who had witnessed the angel closing the moat and a handless maiden crossing into the orchard, reports what he has seen. That night, the king hides in the orchard to see what will happen. Once again the angel closes the moat, and the handless maiden crosses into the orchard to get a pear. When the king sees how very beautiful she is, he falls in love with her. He brings her back to the palace to make her his queen and has silver hands fashioned for her.

Not long after their wedding, the king is called to go to war. He asks his mother to watch over his bride and to give her every care if she bears a child. Indeed, within the year, she gives birth to a beautiful baby boy. The queen mother's messenger goes to the battlefield to bring the good news to the king. However, the messenger falls asleep on the way, and the dark stranger changes the message so that the king thinks the child is a changeling (that is, a child born of an animal, or even the devil himself). Although disturbed by the news, the king sends a message back to his mother instructing her to care for his wife and son until he returns. On the way back to the palace the messenger falls asleep again, and, once again, the dark stranger changes the message. The altered message from the king orders the queen mother to kill the young queen and her child and to save their eyes and hearts as proof that she has fulfilled his wish. The queen mother, who can't bear to take their lives, tells the young queen what has happened. So, once again, the handless maiden sets out into the wide world, this time with her infant son tied to her back. As they journey through the dark forest, an angel holds the baby to his mother's breast to be nourished.

After seven years, the king returns from war and asks for his wife and son. His mother responds, "How could you be so cruel!" She shows him his message and the eyes and hearts that she has saved at his instructions. The king denies that he had sent the message and weeps bitterly. The queen mother then confesses that she has not killed the young queen and his son, and that the eyes and hearts are actually those of a doe and fawn. To save his wife and son, she has sent them into exile in the dark forest. The king vows to neither eat nor drink until he finds his wife and child. For seven years, the king fasts as he searches for them in the forest.

Then one day, the king comes upon a little house with an inscription over the door, "Welcome, all who enter here." He lies down outside the house and covers his face with a cloth to get some rest, as he is very weary. The angel goes into the house and tells the young queen that the king has come. When she comes out of the house, the young queen recognizes him. She tells her son (whom she had named One Rich in Sorrow) that this is his father. She instructs him to lift the cloth from his father's face. But her son responds, "My father is God in heaven, not this wild man!" When the king hears their voices, he sits up and asks: "Who are you?" She replies, "I am your wife, and this is your son." He does not recognize her, however, without her silver hands. The angel, who had been with them in the forest, goes into the house and brings out the silver hands for the king to see. The once-handless maiden explains that, through the grace of God, since she has been in the forest her hands have grown back again. The king is filled with joy that he has found his beautiful wife and son at last. He exclaims, "A heavy stone has fallen from my heart." The king and queen return to the palace and are married again. After their second wedding feast, they live and reign happily together.[66]

Hands are a part of our human body that have evolved over millions of years. They provide us with the capacity to grasp, to hold, to touch, to climb, to explore, to defend, and to creatively express ourselves. The tale of "The Handless Maiden" is a powerful story of a woman whose capacity to be creative and to embrace her own life was cut off by the patriarchal father-world to which she felt bound. When her father approached her, apologizing for having to cut off her hands to save his own life, she replied, "Dear father, I am your child, do with me what you will." Then she held out her hands and let him chop them off. [67]

The tale tells us that her mother is horrified but does nothing to intercede for her daughter. Her mother is likely another miller's daughter in bondage to the patriarchy, living as if she had no choice.

The miller's daughter goes out into the world with her maimed arms tied behind her back by both her mother and father. In the tale, she asks them to do this before she leaves at sunrise, a metaphor for the time of the beginning of consciousness. In an early version of the story, she asks her father to tie her severed hands to her back as well. This is a significant detail in the tale. The handless maidens among us generally live with the remnants of their potential creative capacity for life in their shadow. They still have their arms and hands, but they cannot see them because they are tied behind their backs. Healing for them involves reclaiming their personal gifts, which they are no longer able to see or acknowledge as their own.

The daughter's insistence on leaving home in this maimed state may seem strange, after her father promises her riches and comfort for what she has sacrificed for him.

Other versions of the story, discovered by the Grimm brothers after the first edition of *Nursery and Household Tales,* clear up the mystery of her quick departure. In those versions, the young girl flees her father, "who first demands her hand in marriage and then has her hands and breasts chopped off for refusing him."[68]

In exploring the tale of "The Handless Maiden" we used the same process as we did with the previous tale of "Rumpelstilskin." The active imagination questions proposed included:

- What did the daughter say to her father before she left her father's house with her hands tied behind her back?

- What did the daughter say to her mother, who did not come to her aid when her father mutilated her?

Each woman was also encouraged to explore other questions that occurred to her in her reflections on the tale, using the process of active imagination. I also stressed the importance of recording dreams as potential unconscious responses to the tale. Very powerful dreams came to many of the women in the group. Some saw this tale as clearly connected to their own life stories and could identify with it more readily than could others. As with the previous tale, none of the women read any commentaries or interpretations of the tale prior to our work, although several resources were discovered and shared after we had completed our exploration of the story.

What was most interesting was the depth to which each woman was able to go with the tale. The responses reflected in her dreams and active imagination dialogues were profound. While her work reflected the uniqueness of her own life story, the evidence is strong that handless maidens are still among twenty-first century women.

Who is the Handless Maiden?

Where have we met the girl/woman with the artificial silver hands? What message does she have for us as women now? She appeared in various forms in the women's dreams and active imagination dialogues.

After our initial exploration of the tale, Claire had the following dream:

> I was a man with another man on an airplane bound for Australia. I was originally from there. I told him that those white tents down below us, at the foot of a huge cliff and snow-covered mountain range, belonged to families where the daughters had killed their mothers in order to live with their fathers or stepfathers. That's why they lived in such an isolated area. If caught,

the daughters were brutally whipped and beaten. One daughter was at a window, talking to a priest. He was dressed in white and gold garb with a cross on the back. The girl was in white, and she had been beaten. Her clothes were in shreds. She appeared to be hanging in the window. She was holding onto the top of the window frame. Her hands were not visible. She was pleading, "I never killed my mother." It seemed to take all the energy she had to speak. The priest seemed unmoved, as if he were made of stone.

Claire associated the other man in the airplane with a friend who lives in Australia, a place "down under." Australia was a penal colony, a place to which the undesirables of the British Empire were exiled and imprisoned. Her Australian friend respected Claire's uniqueness, believed she had wisdom, and encouraged her to live her own life. In the dream, Claire is looking down at the place of imprisonment from another perspective. She (as a man in the dream) describes the injustices of the penal colony below, a prison for women who have engaged in incestuous father-daughter relationships. The image of the priest in the dream reminded Claire of her own father, who had studied for the priesthood but had left the seminary and married before being ordained. She often wondered if he regretted his decision, because he never seemed able to enter into the joy of being a father or husband.

The girl in the window frame in the dream, pleading her innocence, had no hands. She was "framed in the window," her white clothes in shreds from her beatings. The stone figure of one of the fathers of the church had no words of consolation. He appeared unmoved by her distress and by her pleas of innocence in the murder of her mother.

In an active imagination dialogue between the dream images of the girl and the priest, Claire recorded the following conversation:

> Girl: "We have been like this for eons: me, standing deflated, depressed; you, inflated and sitting complacently. We have not heard each other. 'I did not kill my mother' is what I said."
> Priest: "Then who did?"
> Claire as man in dream: "You two are both inside of me and I am ashamed to see this. All I see is that endless cycle of inflation/depression as you keep passing the energy back and forth between you. How can I honor you both? What do you need from me?"

Girl: "I am constantly afraid. I want to be able to move freely without the constant pain that comes from being beaten for something I did not do."
Priest: "I'm also afraid, so I eat. I've made myself solid, unmovable, heavy with being righteous."
Girl: "I am frantic with energy that I want to express."
Priest: "I am unable to move and don't want to."

Claire as man in dream: "Stop all this!" To the priest: "You, priest, live in an angry, hostile world, and I am really tired of trying to defend myself, feeling constantly judged by your relentless authority, demanding more and more of me. I constantly arm myself with activities just to justify my presence." To the girl:

And you, girl, your potential for play, all the unknown possibilities that dance through you are deadened by your shame. You question where all your insights come from as if you must prove them legitimate. Listen to your pleading words, 'I never killed my mother!' *You* know it is true. Live your own life. Stop hanging around expecting some outer masculine authority to set you free.

Claire recognized the split in herself manifested in the dream: the young feminine image within her, who is handless, a victim of shame, living in isolation, pleading for her release from punishment for the crime of matricide which she didn't commit; and the priest in her, who carries the concretized fear she associates with her father, the negative masculine image within her that constantly judges her as deficient and worthless.

Claire acknowledged that the concretized fear in herself (in the image of the priest in her dream) is inflated, not with grandiosity, but with expectations that she cannot meet. She realized that she has to stay conscious of not reverting to feelings of depression when she perceives herself as inadequate.

On her further reflections on the images in this dream, Claire realized that she had continued, as her mother and grandmother had, to subdue and then kill the feminine consciousness within herself. She chose a male partner who carried the shadow side of her father, and who fluctuated back and forth between dominance and depression. She recognized that in the presence of this negative masculine energy, she would be beaten, "framed," and left without hands if she tried to assert herself in her own life. Talking to the priest wouldn't help. He had also killed the feminine consciousness within.

Claire asked, "What would the young girl within me like for herself?" Through her active imagination, Claire saw the young girl lowering her arms to her sides so that her hands could be seen. Then the young girl gazed at the priest, knowing from a place deep within her that there would be no more pleading. She stepped out of the frame with the intention of not returning again to the life she had once led. She walked on in a meditative state, seeking an answer to the questions: "Who am *I*? What do *I* want?"

Continuing her active imagination work, Claire saw the priest of her dream staring into the empty frame and recognizing that he was alone. She wrote:

> There is no one observing him in his pretend grandeur. There are no crowds to listen to his preaching. They've all lost faith, and so has he. He sits for a long time and realizes he is hungry. Will he search for more addictive food? He is moved by the young girl's silent response. She just left. She knew what she needed to do. What purpose does *he* have now? He decides he will also go on a pilgrimage. He is not sure where he will go, but he will begin the journey.

The window frame was empty now. Both the pleading victim and the unmoved judge were gone.

Often, the father of the handless maiden, who does not follow the creative opportunities presented to him in times of adversity, sells his soul to the devil in exchange for safety and security. If the father does not live out his dream and develop his own creative potential, his daughter may find herself living in the shadow of his depression and sorrow. Marie Louise Von Franz writes:

> The way in which the father's unconscious fantasies affect, especially, the daughters, is well-known; it is evidenced when the man who does not come to terms with his anima problem parks his fantasies on his daughters, by expecting them to live what he did not or by incestuous desires, and so disturbs the daughters' natural development. [69]

In our exploration of the tale of "Rumpelstilskin," we observed what happens to the daughter when the father expects her to live out *his* expectations and accomplish *his* wishes. In his name, she finds herself having to risk her future to live a lie. In the tale of "The Handless Maiden," the daughter does not have a proud father who wants to live through her achievements. She has a weak father who wants to possess her and to keep her weak and helpless.

The handless maiden in the tale is forced to flee her father's house with her arms and hands tied behind her back. This handicap was manifested in several of Claire's dreams in images of being cut off at the knees, not able to stand on her own or make her own way in the world.

In a small country in Africa, women are required to approach men on their knees. Women literally serve the men kneeling, because no woman can ever be "above a man." A woman missionary who worked there told me that she was exempt from this requirement because her ordination to the ministry made her a man.

The handless maidens among us literally become handmaidens, serving others but never themselves. If they do something for themselves, they feel selfish and unworthy. These women feel powerless, and struggle with a deep sadness that is just below the surface. They wash themselves with their tears and feel orphaned and alienated from their parents and family. "Born of them, but not one of them," is how one of the women expressed it.

The handless millers' daughters of our twenty-first century face the world with trust in others, but little in themselves. They feel misunderstood and not fully appreciated for who they are. There is no boasting of their cleverness or beauty by their fathers who live in fear, which is the reason they are so easily seduced by the dark stranger (an image of the devil).

Carl Jung saw the essence of evil to be the denial, in fear, of the life force. The handless maiden lives on the edge of fear in the state of anxiety that she inherited from her father. Her mother is also handless, as evidenced by her willingness to stand by while her daughter's hands are sacrificed to save the father.

The dark stranger in the tale says: "Why do you slave away at cutting wood? I can make you wealthy beyond your dreams. All you have to do is promise me what is standing behind your mill."[70] Her father's fear and anxiety about the hard times in which he finds himself make him ready to take the easy way out. He promises the dark stranger whatever he wants without asking any questions.

The miller assumes that what he is being asked for is only the apple tree. He has no connection to nature. He makes his living by harnessing water to run his mill. He's not used to working hard. *Who cares?* he thinks. If he can be rich, what else matters? He never asks the stranger, "Who are you?" He does not clarify the reason for the bargain. He is likely depressed and feels he is a victim of life circumstances.

Fathers of handless maidens are often addicted to alcohol or to work. Some live in a dreamy state of denial. They *survive* life, but they never really *choose* it. If their handless daughters don't grow back their hands, find their own legs to stand on, and go out into the world as they are without the burden of his shadow, they will also remain depressed and just *survive*.

What both the weak father and his handless daughter in this tale share in common is their basic survival conclusion. Since he does not trust himself, he looks to others (the dark stranger) to save him. She, in turn, does not trust herself and seeks her salvation outside of herself. This is the nature of the incest, which may or may not be sexual in nature. The seeds of his fear contaminate her young feminine spirit. If she stays with him and accepts his comfort in the sacrifice of her hands for him, she will always remain trapped.

After beginning our work in the group on the tale of "The Handless Maiden," Claire had the following dream:

> I was kayaking on a river and came to a cross-river where there was a curved set of rapids. I took a look at the rapids and figured out the safest route: where there were places to pause, and where one just had to *go for it*. There was a group of older people there who were anticipating these rapids. Some were very afraid. I assured them that it was possible and that they could follow me, or at least they could "walk over the route" with me.

This dream is a direct affirmation that Claire has the ability to reclaim her hands. It is not possible to negotiate rapids in a kayak without two strong arms and hands. Here, the dream indicates that not only can she get through this cross-river current (crossroad) of her life, but she can also lead others through.

Two nights later another affirming message came at the end of Claire's dream: "I do not have to be afraid that I cannot escape past experience or history."

Then Claire dreamed a poisonous snake had been left in her cabin. She had an active imagination dialogue with the image of the snake. She asked, "Why are you here?" The snake replied, "I'm bringing you protection; my venom will boost your immunity in your hostile environment."

When she worked with the images in this dream, Claire recognized the snake as a messenger sent to awaken her to face the truth and to not cover it with sentimentality. The snake challenged her to recognize the way anxiety has ruled her life. She realized, as she reflected on the dream, that the snakebite was an anti-anxiety inoculation for the part of her that identified with the handless maiden.

Claire's encounter with the snake in her dream released a lot of energy within her, which she perceived as dark, negative, and searing. She connected this energy with her experience of being orally raped at age five, a "snake forced down my throat." Claire realized that when she became fearful she would eat and then feel like vomiting.

The research literature indicates that when young girls are orally sexually abused, they often later experience eating disorders, such as bulimia. They alternate between seeking comfort by stuffing themselves with food and then vomiting.[71] Claire saw the snakebite in her dream as an inoculation against having to vomit.

As we worked on this tale, Claire had another dream that she associated with the tale:

> My partner and I were walking and crawling through streams
> and mud over roots to get out to a clearing. When we arrived, I
> saw that his left arm and hand were gone from below the elbow.
> He did not notice. I have to point it out to him.

Then the next night, she dreamed:

> There were some young men in a boat out of control. I was going
> down to the beach to swim. It was not a place I knew. It didn't
> feel right; it was as if darkness was over everything. There was
> no bright, warm sun, and everything was shadowy. I didn't want
> to go swimming. I looked up and saw in a high window what
> looked like my father's face. I was startled. I did not want to see
> him, or have him see me. I crouched behind a tool shed. I could
> really only see his eyes, searching me out.

Claire realized that her father was looking at her from his high window as if to say, "Are you really going to leave me/us?" It had become increasingly clear to Claire that her relationship with her partner was a mirror image of her relationship with her father, who was also dependent, depressed, and demanding. In her dream, her partner had lost his left arm and hand, which Claire associated with the energy of the heart. The image of her father in the frame of the window reminded Claire of her earlier dream of the girl in the window frame. This image of her father, however, has no visible arms or hands, only a head with searching, needy, demanding eyes. But Claire knew there was only one soul she could save, and that was her own.[72] At that point, Claire decided to separate from her partner and leave, taking her child with her.

The handless maiden is never free unless she is able to leave her father's house and all that it means for her, both positively and negatively. Alone with her son in the house in the woods, she can re-grow her own hands. What her helpless father and men like him have chopped off can only be healed outside of her father's house, as risky and as frightening as that might seem to her.

When Claire confronted the image of her handless masculine partner in the dream, she asked through the process of active imagination, "How did you come to lose your hand?" He replied, "It fell away as if it were never really attached." Claire realized that this was both an image of her external masculine partner and of the internal wounded masculine part of herself. She began to appreciate more deeply how her hands (her own creative energy and capacity for love) could appear and disappear depending on how conscious she was of her own soul. Claire wrote, "I just keep losing a bit of myself, then regaining something new. My arm and hand have not been lost forever."

In Claire's active imagination dialogue with the dream image of her father in the window, he confessed: "Your liveliness was a bitter reminder of how dead I was even before you buried me in death. I hated you at times." Claire asked "Why?" He responded, "You were one more woman to take care of, like my mother. I was always responsible for her, until I finally married in my mid-thirties. Then she moved in with us, the miserable bitch. She died finally when you were five years old. I never knew until then how much I hated her."

Claire then understood how much her father despised the feminine and was disconnected from his own body and his creative life. She realized how the wound in her own feminine sense of herself was inherited from her father's wounded state.

Following this reflection, Claire dreamed:

> I was walking in an area I did not know. I went into a building like a hospital and give birth to an infant daughter, a baby girl, without medical intervention. I wrapped her, carried her, and left the building. I did not need anyone to check to see if I had done it right. I knew I had. Next, I was in a class. People noticed that I had lost weight. After class, I went to my room and checked my vagina and perineum. It looked healthy; nothing is torn. I did not need to be stitched.

Here the dream makes it clear to Claire that she can give birth to her own feminine soul without the intervention of others who are considered experts. The dream affirms that she knows how "to do it right." The young feminine child emerged from her easily without tearing her apart. Claire knows how to give birth to her own feminine soul and how to celebrate this new life within her. She feels released from the prying eyes of her father, who she fears will rob her of her soul. Her fear is, "If I am creative, he will see and feed on me."

The handless maiden who is emancipated from her servitude and feelings of powerlessness is the one who can take the steps she must take to leave her father's house and the patriarchal world of her mother. Her task is fraught with difficulties. How will she find food for her body? How will her soul be nourished? An angel, her spiritual guide, helps her once she has made the choice. No angel appears before she takes the step to leave the father-world to which she has been bound. Once she makes the decision to leave and to find her own destiny, an angel comes to accompany her.

Leaving our father's house may be more difficult than it might initially seem. As a child, Emily tried several times to run away from her abusive father, but she was always returned. Although he attempted to "cut off her hands" and stifle her creativity, she survived by writing stories in secret. He was never quite able to render her handless, although he attempted repeatedly to do so. Through her creativity, she drew a cleansing circle around herself (as did the handless maiden in the tale) to protect herself from his demands for obedience.

When Emily won a prize for her writing, the prize money was taken from her by her stepmother under the guise of needing to pay for all the paper she used. Yet, Emily refused to hand herself over and to have her creativity cut off.

Emily found it very difficult to work with the tale of "The Handless Maiden." She was drawn to explore why the girl allowed her father to chop off her hands. What else could she have done? She was powerless. In focusing on her own hands, Emily felt a tingling sensation in them, "as if the circulation was rushing through for the first time, as if God in his mercy was just allowing my hands to grow back. Yes, my hands were also chopped off, my creativity stifled. They were beaten when I tried to protect my body with them."

After reflecting on this tale, Emily dreamed:

> Two very large, angry dogs came racing across the field from a house far on the horizon. They were running at top speed toward me. I had just opened the door to get out of my car. A Doberman bit straight across my right hand. He bit hard and did not let go. He bit into my hand in a rhythm. He pressed, let go, pressed, let go. I sat and didn't move, trying to figure out how to get away without being torn to pieces. He finally let go of my hand. There was not a mark on it, and there was no more pain.

The dream reassured Emily that although her hands had been beaten in the conflicts she experienced in her relationship with her father, she had now been released. There was no mark on her hand, and she felt no pain. She no longer had to live as if she was maimed for life. Her hands were back, tingling with energy. She could now make the new life choices that she had been yearning to make.

In her early reflections on this tale, Emily had noted, "the pears in the king's orchard were all numbered." In other words, they were ready to be eaten, but counted, and, therefore, not available. Now, Emily was ready to take the fruit from the king's orchard and to claim it for herself. She saw the image of the pear as a metaphor for the ripening of her own feminine consciousness.

Emily struggled in her active imagination dialogue with the king in the tale. She wrote: "I do have such a king within me, but the devil, the predator, is trying and most often succeeding, in keeping me from recognizing him. The king has wandered more than seven years (and been in the war inside me for a very long time). My king, I long for our remarriage. It will be a splendid one."

After this reflection, the following dream came to Emily:

> I had come to the end of a particular road and wanted to turn onto the next one. A person was standing at the top of the road. I asked, "Is this the way to get to so-and-so?" "No, it is the other direction." Without hesitation, I turned around and went the right way. I was on a forest road. I began to run to get back faster. I had a lot of energy. I ran through a thick cloud of mosquitoes and moved my arms and hands to ward them off. I was not stung.

Emily was ready to follow the next path into the forest. She went without hesitation, and despite obstacles, she emerged unharmed. She went to meet the king, that aspect of her own masculinity that is focused and able to choose wisely. Then Emily had the following dream:

> I was standing on the shore watching a small wide-bellied boat with a sail-less mast coming toward shore. The boat was full, with four young men and two women (one older). We were greeting each other happily. As I began to rush toward them, I saw a very young, slim apple tree in the water. The boat crashed into it, but then bent itself around the tree and did not break up or tip. It straightened itself out and landed on the shore. The tree was bare except for a few dry leaves. It was not broken or knocked

over. Then the dream shifted. An older woman was now with me in the meadow (an image that Emily associated with Mother Earth). She had lain down very close beside me. I very gently and politely told her that I couldn't stand being crowded, that she was too close to me. I suggested that she place herself in another spot. She seemed sickly and in need of some care. She then sat in the grass, holding a dish with food, but she had no spoon. I felt remorse for having asked her to move away from me. I brought her a spoon and gave her loving attention.

According to Von Franz,[73] the apple tree is an archetypal image associated with consciousness. In the story of Adam and Eve, an apple is the fruit of the Tree of the Knowledge of Good and Evil and of becoming like God. In alchemy, the golden apple is also associated with consciousness. In the tale of "The Handless Maiden," the miller is willing to sacrifice the old apple tree in exchange for wealth. In other words, he is willing to sacrifice consciousness to satisfy his greed for money. How appropriate this is in the corporate patriarchal world, where remaining unconscious is often necessary in order to maintain the system of control through power, prestige, and possessions.

Through her dream of the apple tree in the harbor, Emily recognized the ways she had neglected her own inner feminine spirit, her wise crone, who requires Emily's help to be fed. Emily must provide a spoon so that this aspect of herself can be nourished.

Emily sees the God of the handless maiden in the tale as a negative God. "The handless maiden is not fully conscious of the divine because of her *fear* of God. She is obedient and, therefore, does not resist the cruel and inhumane demands of her unconscious devil-fearing father."

The handless maiden may look beautiful in her helplessness and her determination to live in spite of the handicap she suffers at the hands of her father. The king falls in love with her when she eats the pear, a metaphor for feminine fruitfulness. She can appear complacent and beautiful in her passivity, particularly to men. The king makes her silver hands, feminine but artificial. He takes care of her, and she conceives his child. But then, at a time when she needs him to support the new life emerging in her, he leaves to go to war and is gone for seven years.

Unlike the miller's daughter in the tale of "Rumpelstilskin," the handless maiden (now a queen) has a messenger who is "unconscious." The *conscious* messenger for the miller's daughter in "Rumpelstilskin" was the one who saved her child by finding out the dwarf's name. The messenger in the tale of "The Handless Maiden" becomes *unconscious* (that is, falls asleep on each part of the journey) and, consequently, carries messages between the king and the queen mother that have been altered by the dark stranger (the devil in disguise). The handless maiden hasn't completely left her father's world, because, at his invitation, she readily becomes dependent on the king. She goes from her father's house to her husband's. Now, she is forced to take the journey alone with her son, an image of her own newborn inner masculine.

The handless maiden often feels hesitant about moving into the unknown, unless she is pressed into doing so by the circumstances in her life. In the tale, she does not leave her father's house until she is forced to do so by her father's abuse of his power over her. She doesn't leave her husband's house until her own life and that of her child are threatened. It takes a significant event to move her into a new phase of exploration.

After we began our work on the tale, Rita had the following dream:

> I was at the edge of a forest. I saw a tall woman striding into the woods. I could see that her legs were strong. I was amazed that she didn't seem to hesitate when she entered the forest, although the area was very dark. I was thinking I was supposed to go with her, but I stood back and just observed.

Rita acknowledged that part of her hesitates to take the next step to enter the unknown. She recognized the forest as a metaphor for the place of transformation and believed that the dream was inviting her to move into the unknown and trust the process. Just being part of the group was difficult for Rita. It took courage for her to enter the forest of transformation. Her dream presents an aspect of herself as a tall woman with strong legs, who doesn't hesitate to move forward. This image encouraged Rita to trust herself and the other women in the group. It inspired her to move forward without hesitation, even though she doesn't know what she will discover on the other side of the forest.

Women who are handless maidens are often creatively gifted. They are frequently writers, poets, artists, musicians, or artisans. Their gifts have generally not been developed, because they are not valued by the father-world. They are not able to make money using their creativity because it is not considered prestigious enough. Handless maidens tend to enter professions approved for women by their fathers, such as nursing, teaching, or secretarial work. They report that they could never be good enough at the creative work of their hands to "amount to anything." Once they allow themselves to focus on and to express their creativity, their hands grow back again.

Estelle felt constrained by her father's demand that she choose a *useful* career in nursing rather than pursue her dream to be a musician. Just as we began our work on the tale of "The Handless Maiden," Estelle had the following dream:

> I was in some kind of class and painting intuitively, just express-
> ing feelings and not thinking too much. When I finished, the
> teacher, a wise and compassionate woman, took the painting
> and said she would finish it. What she did was amazing! She
> divided the painting into three panels. In the first panel a beauti-
> ful young woman was attempting to paint, but her hands were
> in shackles behind her back. The middle panel of the painting
> was a continuation of the shackles. The images were symbolic
> of being tied up, imprisoned, and handcuffed. The third panel
> was symbolic of freedom, of breaking out of the shackles and
> being able to express creativity. I thought this was very symbolic.
> I really liked it, and we put it up in one of the showcases.

When Estelle worked with the images in this dream, she realized how "tied up" her creative work had been in her concern for "always doing the right thing, in the right way."

In her work with the images in the tale of "The Handless Maiden," Estelle recognized that *fear* causes parents to cut off their children's hands. Where there is fear, there is no questioning of the possibility of alternatives. Intense fear leads to the vacuum of despair, and the denial of fear is expressed in pseudo acts of power. Estelle grew up in a home where there was emotional and psychological abuse. She recognized that where there is emotional abuse, physical abuse and violence easily follow.

When the feminine is devalued, women are treated as objects. They may see themselves as helpless and, therefore, dependent on men for their survival. They may not know themselves apart from the identity that their fathers and husbands assign to them. While we were working with this tale, Estelle dreamed:

> I was with my daughter. She was trying on clothes. She put on a
> baby-doll dress and shorts but decided that she didn't like it. She
> was concerned that she would never find anything to suit her.

Estelle recognized her struggle with being put in the role of a dependent young, naive woman. She made the decision that she would not wear the baby-doll per-sona of dependency, an image of not being alive or real. She will not be a plaything of others, without a life and voice of her own. However, she is not sure what other persona to wear. Will she ever find what *suits her*?

A woman who is a handless maiden is invited over and over to reclaim her own life and identity, but this choice takes courage. As we were reflecting on the tale, Alexis dreamed:

> A huge bat was swooping over our heads. I was scared and went inside what looked like a commercial building with high ceilings. The bat repeats its maneuver over and over again, this time attacking the building next door. I was in a small cabin outside the main complex with two small children (one was the son of Jessica and the other the son of my therapist). I planned our escape and told the boys we would run as fast as we could to the main house. I was afraid to remain isolated in the cabin. We ran and got into the main building without the bat noticing us. Later on, I went outside. The bat, which had become a giant black bird, attacked me. It had been stealing eggs. It grabbed my hands with its yellow beak. With calm and composure, I grabbed the bird by its head and forced it to let go. Then I took a large kitchen fork and stabbed it in several places. Blood started pouring out of its abdomen. My therapist told me to put black pepper on its head. I questioned this, but I did it, feeling squeamish because I didn't want the bird to suffer. Then, I went inside, feeling guilty for what I had done.

When Alexis reflected on this dream, she recognized the negative force within her that tries to capture her hands so that she cannot do her creative work. It steals her eggs, which she associated with her feminine creativity and the possibility of new life. When she faced this negative force, defended herself, and refused to lose her hands, she felt guilty. As she analyzed her dream, Alexis realized that it was inviting her to reclaim her creative potential. In the dream, she uses a kitchen fork to kill the bird. Then she is instructed to put pepper on the black bird to prepare it for consumption. The dream indicates that her powerful shadow energy needs to be integrated and assimilated.

In this dream, two young boys Alexis associated with creative masculine energy accompanied her. She was protective of this energy, as she realized she must reach the main house and leave the isolation of the cabin in which they were hiding. The woman who is a handless maiden often hides her own creative potential. She doesn't feel part of the mainstream of life. Instead, she feels isolated and alone.

What is significant in Alexis's dream is her determination to protect her young creative masculine energy from forces that could attack and destroy it. The bat flies in the dark, a part of her shadow-self that is expert at maneuvering in the dark, and remains unconscious within her.

The image of a bat is connected with a time of transition and initiation in one's life. The bat is associated with the process of facing one's greatest fears. Its appearance in a dream image may be an invitation to let go of some aspect of life that is no longer useful.[74]

In her dream, Alexis initially hid from the need for a transition in her life (the swooping bat). Later, when she thought she had evaded the invitation to face her greatest fears, the bat turned into a large black bird, which attacked her. We saw a radical shift in the way in which Alexis responded. Instead of running in fear, "with calm and composure" she grabbed the bird by the head and *forced* it to let go. She was no longer afraid. After stabbing the bird with a large kitchen fork, she put black pepper on its head. Alexis reported feeling "squeamish," as she didn't want this shadow side of herself to suffer. Here we saw her ambivalence. First, she was afraid, and didn't ask for what she needed, and stayed in hiding. Then, when she faced her shadow (the black bird), she found herself ambivalent. For her to take the step to integrate and transform the energy of her shadow (the bat/black bird) required a major shift in Alexis's life. She will never be the same again once she reclaims the parts of herself that had been lost to her consciousness. This includes reclaiming her hands (her creative potential, which has been tied behind her back) and her ability to give expression to her own wisdom (her creative work as an artist).

As she worked with the images of the tale, Alexis remembered another dream:

> I was looking after my handicapped little girl, who had no one
> to play with her. Then I saw that an artist was painting a wall of
> the entryway of my house. She had created a mural of a beautiful
> lion with his mouth wide open. It was as big as the wall.

Alexis recognized the contrast between the artist creating an image of a lion with a big roar and her child who was handicapped (that is, without hands). The artist uses her hands to bring the image of the lion to life. There is nothing handicapped about the lion. He has a voice and he uses it. Alexis acknowledged that she often experienced herself as a handicapped little girl, without a voice to express her own needs. The mural reminded her of the lion in *The Wizard of Oz* who comes seeking courage when he already has it but doesn't recognize it within himself.[75] Alexis associated the artist in her dream with a wise woman who is committed to her creative work, not afraid to be seen and heard, or to have the work of her hands acknowledged.

After our reflection as a group on the tale of "The Handless Maiden," Rita struggled with choices she needed to make around her job. She wanted time to write and paint but didn't feel she could do her creative work as long as she stayed in her corporate career. She then dreamed:

> I was going by a construction site downtown. I saw human hands that had been dissected from bodies. They were stuck together and still warm. The hands had been removed from people to be used for the construction of the building.

After this dream, Rita exclaimed in alarm, "They would chop my hands off too if they needed them for their project!" Then several nights later, she woke up frightened with the following dream: "I was going off to war. I was part of an army and needed to leave for the front line at 6:00 AM. Other women were there with me, ready to leave to go off to war."

This dream further clarified for Rita that she needed to make a change in her career. She associated the 6:00 AM front line with getting up early to get to work by subway. Several weeks later, she reported: "I've hit the wall. I can't continue; I feel used up."

Women who are handless maidens often find themselves "used up," their hands chopped off for someone else's project. They feel in the front line of combat, put there to protect others at the risk of their own lives. In this tale, the daughter offers her hands for her father to chop off so that he will be protected from the devil. She cannot stay and participate in the rewards her father promises for her sacrifice. She must leave the place of easy riches bestowed by the father-world, because the cost is too high. When she claims her own potency, after leaving the king's palace with her son, her hands grow back again. Only then can she claim her own creative life, symbolized by her new hands. Her father tied the hands he had chopped off to her arms, behind her back. The king gave her silver hands. But it took her own courage to let go of seeing herself as helpless and maimed for the transformation to occur.

In the original version of the tale of "The Handless Maiden," the daughter is exploited by the inappropriate sexual behaviour of her father. She leaves his house after being mutilated by his actions.[76] Many women who have been sexually exploited feel their hands have been dirtied and hide their secret with shame.

After working with this tale, one of the women had a dream that invited her to reclaim her own power and not let herself be victimized, particularly by men. This was her dream:

> There was one more room to decorate, but there was a leak. Water was bubbling up behind the wallpaper. There were large bubbles behind the blue paper. It looked like the wallpaper in my grandmother's house, in her dining room.

In her reflection on the dream image of the water leaking from behind the wallpaper in her grandmother's dining room, the woman became aware that she wanted to hide behind the wallpaper. "I don't want anyone to notice me." Then she remembered a time in her grandmother's house when she and her sister were dancing for the adults. She wrote:

> I didn't want to perform for them. After our dance, my uncle grabbed me and tickled me. He held my hands so that I wouldn't break free and then put his other hand between my legs. I was shocked and enraged. I elbowed him in the gut. I can still see their eyes on me, as I broke free. *What is wrong with her; doesn't she like to be tickled?* In front of everyone, he touched me, and they didn't even see! They wouldn't believe me even if I told them. Anyway, I don't want them to know.

In her active imagination dialogue with the images in her dream, the woman re-entered the scene:

> From behind the wallpaper, I point my finger across the room and in a loud voice I tell everyone that my uncle touched me, right here! I show them where he touched me. I hear everyone in the room gasp as the water pours into the room. They are horrified as the wallpaper curls up on the floor. I have their attention now. I walk over to my uncle and tell him he is an ignorant fool who should keep his hands to himself. I have had enough! I tell him I have hidden behind the wallpaper long enough, and I'm sick and tired of watching life, living in the shadows. I tell my grandmother I'm sorry I ruined her wallpaper, but she says, "It was due to come off anyway. Don't worry; the wallpaper can be replaced. It's you I'm concerned about." I stand waiting to be

thrown out for making a scene, but she merely shakes her head.
The old man slithers away.

The girl child who is sexually exploited experiences the trauma in her body. She often sees herself as a "wallflower," unable to speak the truth lest she be blamed for "making a scene." The withheld emotion finally peels layers off that which was being covered up with silence.

The handless maiden frequently carries the shame of her exploitation by her father or other men. She expects no help from her mother, who, in the original version of the tale, stands by while her daughter's hands and her breasts are cut off because she refuses her father's sexual advances. The handless maiden may feel her role in life is to sacrifice herself for others and that to express her own needs is to "make a fuss." She may even remain unconscious of the ways in which others victimize her. Burdened by shame, she may not recognize her opportunities to give voice to her own power and to declare her own boundaries.

Just after beginning our exploration of the tale of "The Handless Maiden," Michaela dreamed:

> I was in a cottage that was not familiar to me. There was a man there with me, but he was in the bathroom bathing or shaving. I looked out the window and saw a beautiful bird with rainbow-colored wings. The rainbow colors were in two or three strings of a bead-like substance. The colors were around its neck, over both shoulders, and then joined together down the back. The feathers on the head and wings were brown-gray and spike-like. The bird was soft and feminine in its appearance. I called to the man to come and see this beautiful bird. Then the bird sat on a table and flattened itself out by splitting down the middle as if it were jointed in the middle underneath.

Michaela's initial reaction to the image of the split bird was that it was some form of self-sacrifice, in which both sides were visible. When she awakened, Michaela was puzzled by the dream. It was a feminine-looking bird, yet it had bright feathers. She saw the bird as quite contradictory. From her reflection on the image, Michaela was reminded of a priest's sacred robes worn backwards.

The image of the sacred robes reminded Michaela of a dream she had when she first began psychotherapy. In that dream, a priest she knew, who was naked from the waist up, was standing behind an altar covered with a blue cloth. When Michaela examined the cloth, she realized that it was the fabric of her favorite dress from when she was about four to five years old, made into an altar cloth. It was covering the place of sacrifice.

When Michaela examined why the images of the rainbow-colored feathers and the altar cloth were significant, she recognized that the dream was reflecting the vulnerability and helplessness she felt. For Michaela, the manner in which the bird was split in two was reminiscent of biblical images of ancient Hebrew sacrifices. She pondered the questions: "What in me is being sacrificed? Is it an old way of thinking?" Michaela associated the rainbow with a sign of God's covenant, the faithful Divine Presence in her life, which is her source of hope.

Usually, to be split in two in a dream means to be forced to face the conflict in our lives so that a third possibility can emerge into consciousness. Michaela recognized that the dream was inviting her to become more conscious of her ability to hold the tension between all the contradictory parts of herself and her world. She realized that it was important for her to move beyond the *either/or* perspective in her thinking and to appreciate the *both/and* possibilities in her life. She didn't have to be either all-power*ful* or power*less*. Refusing to acknowledge her own vulnerability was Michaela's major defensive strategy for survival. Feelings of self-doubt or powerlessness precipitated a state of terror and despair for her. After reflecting on the powerlessness of the handless maiden, Michaela dreamed:

> I heard some noise outside. When I looked out, I saw a young man at the back of a school. He was tearing down walls and breaking things. He seemed to be enclosed in a big yard with a high fence. I phoned the police. They said they were aware of the situation and were watching him.

Reflecting on this dream, Michaela realized that her young acting-out masculine side needed to be befriended and not to be put under the control of the police. She had the choice of moving toward this aspect of herself, which was out of control, with the openness of love rather than the restrictions of the law. She then recalled a poem about the cedars that grow on the rock ledges of the Cambrian Shield. The lesson she learned from the poem was that what appears to be an obstacle needs to be embraced so that something new can manifest itself.

Michaela recognized that she needed to embrace that which threatened her most, namely, her own vulnerability. Just after having this dream, she passed a derelict beggar woman on the street. She was overwhelmed with the realization: "I am she, and she is me. Beggars display their helplessness and vulnerability for all the world to see, and I most hate to have my vulnerability be seen." The experience brought her tears of anger at feeling exposed and having her defenses swept away. Her tears also signified for her a conversion of heart, a willingness to both acknowledge and feel her own pain and that of others.

The young man in Michaela's dream was destroying a school, a place of learning. He was caged in, a part of her enslaved by outer restrictions. This dream image is similar to one she had when we were exploring the tale of "Rumpelstilskin." In the earlier dream, the young masculine image was shackled to the wall. In this dream, he was free of the wall but still imprisoned. Michaela was clear that the message of the dream was to embrace her vulnerability and be willing to honor those things that she cannot control.

Several years later, after we had finished our work with the fairy tales, Michaela remembered an experience of sexual assault at the age of five that she had repressed in her memory. This was her age when she wore her favorite blue dress, which became the cloth on the altar of sacrifice in her dream. She then understood her terror of being vulnerable to the demands of men, as was the handless maiden in the tale.

Uncovering the painful memory of her sexual assault helped Michaela more clearly understand many aspects of her life that had previously been a mystery to her. She realized that she did not have to be a victim on the altar of self-sacrifice. She did not have to live in shame as if she might have somehow caused the sexual assault. She was now free to grieve the innocence she had lost. She could honor the fact that she now had the opportunity to live from a place of choice and to claim her own life.

After working with this tale, Michaela had difficulty sleeping, and she picked up a book that described several feminine images of the Divine. She imagined herself as a dolphin in a vast sea, buoyed up by God's love for her. She felt relief and opened herself to celebrate her creativity, which was at this point being recognized by others. She acknowledged, "I am an artist," something she had never been able to publicly declare.

Breaking the Shell of Isolation

As we were working on the tale, Jessica and Claire had vivid images of turtles appearing in their dreams. They also had encounters with live turtles, which startled and surprised them.

The appearances of turtles, alive and in dream images, can be seen as a metaphor for the life of the handless maiden waking up to her own turtle existence. To defend the vulnerability of her heart from further mutilation at the hands of others, the handless maiden often develops a shell, an impenetrable persona of being a good and dutiful daughter (mother, wife) into which she can readily retreat. In her shell, she needs neither arms nor legs and can remain invisible to others. Feeling invisible is both her defense and a source of her pain. The handless maiden may also have a tendency to ruminate, to go inside her shell and reflect over and over on painful situations in her life, which then deepens her sense of isolation. Unless she looks beyond the sorrow of her loss, she may sink deeper and deeper into a depression.

A turtle came in Jessica's dream just after our work on this tale:

> I was at an initiation party. A woman was getting her fingernails cut. A man was also there. He was getting his black hair cut. Then I was climbing the side of a mountain. A turtle resting on a ledge moved in front of me, with his tongue hanging out. We all scrambled off the mountain. I left my purse hanging on a bush. Some one claimed it and returned it to me. Then I went on to Montreal.

This dream indicated to Jessica that she was in an initiation phase in her personal work. In her dream, the feminine image does not lose her hands but has her fingernails trimmed. The masculine needs his hair trimmed as well. There is no indication of any mutilation of the hands and hair, only that they are trimmed. Jessica associated long fingernails with leisure. Trimming one's fingernails, for Jessica, was about getting down to the work that needed to be done. Long fingernails need to be maintained, like silver hands, which are artificial and always need polishing. The image of a haircut held a similar message for Jessica: letting go of what gets in the way of getting down to work. Having her hair cut meant that she didn't have to "fuss with it." For Jessica this image was also about lightening her way of thinking so that she could give her energy to her writing.

After the initiation in her dream, Jessica found herself climbing a mountain, a metaphor for the place one meets the Divine, a place associated with spiritual transformation. On the path, Jessica met a turtle with his tongue hanging out. The sight of the turtle's tongue frightened Jessica, and she fled in terror leaving her purse, the source of her feminine identity and financial power, behind. An unidentified dream image claims her purse and returns it to her. Then, she is ready for her trip to Montreal, which translated means the Royal Mountain.

Turtles are not usually found on mountains, unless they are by a lake, which is not indicated in the dream. The turtle in the dream had his tongue hanging out. Tongues are for speaking or giving voice to what is true. The throat and mouth that house the tongue are the bridge between the heart and the head. Jessica realized that she needed to give voice to the story of her maternal heritage so that she could begin her journey to the Royal Mountain.

In ancient Eastern mythology, the turtle was considered a metaphor for the union of heaven and earth. Its appearance in one's life or dreams was associated with longevity and an awakening to life's opportunity. Turtles have amazing survival skills and strategies. If turned over on their backs, they can right themselves using the muscles of their necks and heads. Symbolically, if an image of a turtle appears, it may be an invitation to use one's head to gain a new perspective on life.[77]

After our work on this tale, Jessica had another dream of a turtle—this time it was floating in the water on its back. Her active imagination dialogue with the image of the turtle revealed that it was a part of herself whose vision was restricted to just seeing below and immediately around her, always on the alert for danger. When Jessica perceived what she thought might be a dangerous situation, she would snap and retreat into her shell or sink underwater into emotional isolation. When the turtle image in her dream was flipped onto its back, Jessica had a whole new perspective on her world. She finally saw the sky, the tops of trees, birds of different kinds, mountains and hills, the sun, moon, and stars. Previously she could only see these reflected in the water, but never directly. While the turtle part of her is excited about this new discovery, she fears that this vulnerable state could be dangerous.

Jessica recognized that she needed to move beyond feeling vulnerable, or she would never be able to complete her writing of her mother's story. She was so moved by the images of the turtle in her dreams that she wrote the following story as a way of amplifying the image and discovering its meaning for her life.

There once was a turtle that couldn't see beyond the end of his nose. He looked down on himself. By a stroke of nature, he appeared to be turned in on himself. For a long time, the turtle was satisfied with his existence. He would swim in the river and dive for food. His watery habitat was comfortable in summer, and in winter he curled up in the mud and went to sleep. As life went on, he became bored with his existence. He wanted more. From a distance, he could hear others frolicking on the muddy banks of the river. It would take him all day just to get up on the riverbank. He felt sorry for himself.

One day he dragged himself along the beach and crawled up onto a rock, where he could look into the river below him. He was feeling quite miserable, when he slipped and fell into the water. He was so stunned that he squeezed his eyes shut. When he opened them, he felt himself being carried along by the current. What perplexed him was that he could no longer see what was under him; he now could only see what was over him. He could see beyond the end of his nose. He was floating on his upside-down shell. He was frightened, his stomach was exposed, and he felt vulnerable. Bobbing along, he tried to forget his fear because of the beauty all around him: green forests, the bright light of the sun, cows grazing on the hills. He saw an eagle fly overhead and got so excited he kicked his arms and legs, and, plop, over he went. He hadn't meant to return to the watery darkness so soon. "Oh no!" cried the turtle. He wanted to see more of the great, wide world. "But how will I ever get back? It's lost to me forever." Then, in his memory, he saw the sky, and the leaves on the trees. That night he crawled into his shell full of joy.

After working with her image of the turtle, Jessica finished writing her mother's story. She sent it to her mother and several members of her family. It was a moment she dreaded. Instead of reacting in a critical or rejecting way, as Jessica had anticipated, her mother was very grateful and honored to have the story told. She welcomed the end of the family secret and was not ashamed to let the story be read by others. After this experience, Jessica dreamed:

I was on the shore of the ocean. When the tide went out, two children found a woman tied to a stake. They rescued her, untying her hands, which were tied behind her back on the stake, and her feet, which were tied together and then to the stake. If they hadn't seen her and rescued her, she would have drowned when the tide came back in. The woman who was released walked down the beach and rode away on a horse that was waiting for her.

Jessica was very moved by this dream. She recognized that it signified the release of her own feminine soul. Her hands had been tied behind her back and then to the stake of despair. The children were able to release her because they were close to life and not yet contaminated by hardness of heart. Death by drowning was an appropriate metaphor for the unexpressed emotions that typified the women in Jessica's family. Once they read the story Jessica had written, their tears began to flow.

Tears keep the handless maiden in the tale from being taken by the devil. They purify her stumps, where her hands have been cut off. They release her from the pact her father makes with the devil and free her from the dark force focused on greed and easy solutions.

When our hands are cut off as women, we lose our ability to hold and to embrace life. We feel outside of what is happening in the world around us. We cannot touch and feel life in a way that is real to us. We doubt our emotions and perceptions and find ourselves isolated and lonely, even in a crowd.

The Danger of the Dutiful Life

Once she can get a new perspective, a wider view of the world, the woman who is a handless maiden no longer needs to play hide-and-seek with the world. She can choose to give up her turtle life and join the human community. One danger she faces, however, is that she can overcompensate for feeling an outsider in this world by over-identifying with collective expectations. For example, she may feel she needs to be the perfect mother, wife, and/or daughter, to the detriment of her own needs.

Von Franz associates this dilemma of the handless maiden with the image in the tale of her marriage to the king, who represents the archetype of the dominant, collective standpoint. When the passive woman marries the king, she can adopt "all the prevailing ideas concerning religion, duty and behaviour, and live in accordance with collective standards."[78] As a result, she may find herself living a dutiful life without spontaneity and joy.

Several of the women in the group had been deeply wounded by their fathers going off to war and leaving them vulnerable at a young age. They questioned, "Why does the king have to go to war just when his queen is about to have a child?" For the handless maiden, it inevitably happens that the protection from the world that she expects from her husband or partner doesn't occur. Eventually, she is forced to claim her own power. Unfortunately, some handless maidens go from one partner to another seeking this protection and end up feeling more and more deeply depressed.

In the Western tradition of marriage, we use expressions such as "asking the father for the daughter's *hand* in marriage." In the wedding ceremony, the father *gives the bride away*. These expressions are echoes of the plight of the handless maiden. She especially needs to stay very conscious when selecting a male partner. Many men are attracted to handless maidens, out of their own need to have someone serve them. Often, these men are maimed themselves.

Liberation from a Sorrowful Soul

There is a poignant quality in the life of the woman who experiences herself as a handless maiden. While her association with her father names the miller's daughter in the tale of "Rumpelstilskin," the handless maiden is named by her wound, that is, by the loss of her hands.

Generally, women who name and/or experience themselves in relation to their wound or loss in life have a soul that is sorrowful. They often struggle with a lifelong depression that leaves them feeling isolated. Sometimes they look for a diagnostic label for their wound that can reassure them that they are part of the collective world to which they both strive to belong and yearn to move beyond.

This is illustrated in Estelle's dream, which occurred while we were exploring this tale:

> I was driving home; it was dark. The scene was unfamiliar There appeared to be a roadblock. There were many cars blocking my way, and I had to take a different road. I felt afraid. I went into the bank, and the teller announced that my psychiatrist had left a letter for me in my file. I felt embarrassed, as everyone in the bank could hear her. I went to get the letter. My psychiatrist, a man I didn't recognize, walked in and nodded at me, acknowledging me in a cool, aloof manner. I couldn't decipher the letter. Then I was with my therapist. I had a cloth over my head and face. She asked me to lift it up and tie it on top of my head to feel and experience the difference. It felt much better; I could see clearly again.

Estelle associated the image of the psychiatrist in her dream with a perception that "there is something wrong with me." But she couldn't make out the diagnosis. She had a cloth over her head and face (like the king in the tale who was seeking to find his wife and son). She was not quite conscious yet, but all that was required was for her young masculine "rich in sorrow" to remove the cloth. This was reminiscent for Estelle of the custom of covering a person's face when he/she dies. Estelle's therapist suggested that she tie the cloth on top of her head. She did not suggest that Estelle get rid of it, as she might not be ready to do so. When Estelle tied the cloth on top of her head, she attained a new perspective. Now she could see more clearly. In the second part of the dream, she was given a diagnosis she couldn't decipher. In the last part of the dream, she took the action herself, which is essential for the redemption of the handless maiden from a life of fate.

In her active imagination dialogue with the handless maiden, Jessica hears her say: "Of course I feel helpless! I never know what to do or what to say." Jessica responds: "Miller's daughter, you lost your hands, a part of yourself that is most precious. I am lost in feeling sorry for you, patronizing you, poor thing—look what's happened to you!"

In her active imagination dialogue between the handless maiden and her mother, Jessica wrote:

> Dear mother, please help me! Daddy promised the devil to cut off my hands. Tell him not to do it. What will I do without my hands?"
> The mother responds: "Now daughter, don't get so upset. Your father knows best. They are only your hands. It's not like he is going to kill you, or anything."
> The maiden responds: "What will I do without my hands?"
> The mother answers: "You'll manage, dear. You always do."

In Jessica's active imagination dialogue, when the maiden pleads with her father not to cut off her hands because they are her life, he responds:

> "I don't want to cut off your hands, child, but I made a promise to the devil. God knows what he'll do if I don't give him what he wants!"
> The maiden pleads: "But Daddy, what could be worse than my hands?"
> The father responds: "For heaven's sake, child, you'll still have us to care for you."

In this dialogue, we hear the pain of the daughter whose creative potential (her hands) is cut off by the father-world, with the collusion of her mother. "It's only your hands, it's not like it will kill you," to give up your heart's desire, your creative soul. However, this is precisely the temptation when we experience ourselves as handless maidens. We can be tempted to stay connected to the patriarchal world, bound by the golden handcuffs of promises of safety and financial security in our old age. We can spend our creative, generative years in jobs we hate and which suck our life energies dry—so that we will have pensions. The tragedy is, *then what?* If indeed we live long enough to come to retirement age, we may have already developed a heart condition or be battling the destructive forces of cancer. When we disregard our feminine soul, this neglect is often experienced in bodily symptoms. When we don't listen to our hearts, they will get our attention another way, perhaps by refusing to function. If we allow ourselves to be eaten up by what does not nourish our souls, our bodies will exhibit the chaos as disease, often cancer.

In her active imagination with the handless maiden (written on her father's birthday), Jessica hears the handless maiden within her respond:

> I have lost my hands, cut off by my father, who thought it would be okay because he would get all those riches and then care for me. Perhaps he thought he would be able to control me by giving in to the devil, the demon that lived in him. But losing my hands did not bind me to my father and mother. I am not helpless; I am free. My mother and father both have their hands, but they are the ones who are *prisoners*! My father can't stand up to the devil. He really believes that riches will make life easier for him. He allows the devil into his life and doesn't trust his own judgment. I was lucky to get away with my life. I knew that I had to leave, to go beyond pity and oppression, for my spirit to grow and survive.

When Claire imagined a dialogue between the miller and his handless daughter, she had the daughter say to the father: "I responded to you without fear. You could have allowed tears. You never looked at alternatives." The miller answers: "I was so afraid; I never thought to ask questions."

Where the focus of life is *fear*, a climate is fostered that eliminates love. Emancipation comes when love is able to drive out fear. Claire reported the following dream, after identifying this fairy tale as her own life story:

> A young woman, perhaps still a teenager, a gypsy girl dressed sensuously, was riding a horse bareback. She knew the horse, and she knew her own body. It was a joy to watch her ride. An older man was telling her all he could do for her. She listened and spoke not a word. He grabbed her close to him, ripping open the top of her dress slightly. She stood back and said, "Listen to me." She spoke only two words: "*I love.*" He did not really understand. Still, she kept trying to say what she'd always known (even at her young age)—that *to love is everything.*

Claire drew an image of the young gypsy girl on the horse. She noted: "This feminine image of me was stunning. I am so grateful for this dream." At the center of the dream was the gypsy girl with her ability to be one with her horse and her own body. Claire described her as dressed in a camisole and skirt, quite pretty and feminine. She wrote:

> She rode in undulating waves upon the back of the horse, legs apart, and arms aloft for balance. Here was no helpless, handless maiden. She let her instinctual energy flow through her with precision and skill. The old man was condescending toward her, telling her what he could do for her, when his intent was to possess her for himself. He grabbed her without her consent. She responded with love and compassion: "Listen to me; this is how relationship works, I *love*." She knew that to love is everything!

This powerful dream encapsulates the key ingredients in the transformation of the handless maiden into the competent, creative woman. She has strong legs on which to take her stand in life. She is riding on a horse, symbol of strength and the capacity to move freely. Her message to the negative masculine figure is, *"Listen—I love."* Love is the only antidote for the poisons of fear and anxiety. Here the girl in the dream doesn't identify what or whom she loves. It is sufficient to love, for love casts out fear.[79]

In several versions of this tale, the handless maiden in exile accidentally drops her son off her back into the water when she stops to drink at a pond. In the Russian version, she becomes frantic and runs around the pond looking for help. An old man (God) appears and tells her she can save her son herself. She plunges her mutilated arms into the water and her hands grow back. She lifts up her son with her restored hands.[80] Her love for her son (an image of her own soul) heals her wound. She is no longer powerless and maimed for life. As happened to the miller's daughter in the tale of "Rumpelstilskin," her true love for her son transforms her from a helpless young girl to a loving and nurturing mother, willing to do the seemingly impossible to save her child's life.

The Two Mothers

What are the messages about mothers in this tale? The maiden's own mother stands helplessly by as her daughter's hands (and in some versions, breasts) are cut off by the father.[81] It is remarkable how many women who are victims of incest by fathers/uncles/brothers never tell their mothers because they expect no protection from them. Some of these women believe their mothers knew and did nothing to prevent it. One woman's mother told her, "Well, the same thing happened to me as a girl, so what was I to do?"

The contrast between the two mothers in the tale is striking. While the maiden's own mother does nothing to prevent her daughter's mutilation, her mother-in-law comes up with a creative alternative. She dares to disobey the assumed order of the king and sacrifices a doe and fawn instead of her daughter-in-law and grandson. She keeps the tongue and eyes as proof that she has killed them. When she sees the true grief of the king when he hears of the deaths of his wife and son, she tells him the truth.

The tongue and eyes of the doe are a metaphor for the timidity of the woman who is a handless maiden. The doe is a passive, silent animal. The sacrifice of the doe signifies the need for transformation from the passive tongue and innocent eyes of the naïve, helpless female to a new way of being present in the world. A new voice and a new insight are needed, which cannot develop unless the handless maiden takes this next part of the journey alone. Alexis wrote:

> I am no longer the gentle doe who personified my yearning to connect with my own soul—the gentle doe, her neck stretched to drink of the water of life. I recognize in myself the elephant, balanced and grounded in discipline and the practicality of literal reality. I realize now that I have an understanding of affective reality, standing between literal and imagined reality. I am able to bring insight to the ordinary through my work as an artist.

This awareness reassured Alexis that she was leaving the path of passivity and entering the forest of transformation, balanced and grounded in her own creative energy.

The tale of "The Handless Maiden" is one of the few Grimm's tales in which the mother-in-law is a heroine. While the women in many tales are blamed for the destruction of the children, the Grimm brothers generally attribute this to stepmothers, cooks, witches, and mothers-in-law.[82] In this tale, the mother-in-law is a queen mother, symbolically indicating her capacity for consciousness of her own power. The archetypal meaning of the positive energy of a queen in fairy tales is a woman who is able to use her feminine powers with wisdom.

While both mothers are reported to be horrified about what is to happen to the daughter, one takes action while the other remains passive. Once again, the handless maiden is forced to "go out into the wide world," this time with a child, "never to return." Again the angel appears to her in the great, wild forest, a metaphor in fairy tales for the place of transformation.

Entering the Dark Forest

After wandering through the forest, the handless maiden finds a dwelling with a sign over the door that indicates that all are welcome. Gertrude Nelson translates this sign, "Here all dwell free."[83] To be welcomed means to be greeted warmly and received openly with unconditional love and acceptance. A place of welcome is one of safety, in which there is no need to be afraid.

The angel unties "the little boy from the queen's back and holds him up to her breast to suckle."[84] The handless maiden's breasts have healed from the mutilation by her father. She is now able to nourish her son, a symbolic image of her own soul.

The woman who is a handless maiden may present herself as a *puella*, a helpless little girl. Because she has not had the benefit of appropriate mothering herself, she finds it difficult to be a mother and may have ambivalent feelings toward her own child. On the one hand, her child's presence forces her to grow up and take responsibility in her relationships with others. On the other hand, the child's presence may get in the way of her ability to continue to live on the edge of life, responding to whatever comes without having to make a firm commitment. It is noteworthy in the tale that there is no mention of her choosing the king, only of the king choosing her. There are indications in the tale that he married her because he felt pity for her and was enamoured by her helplessness. If the story had ended after the wedding, with the words "they lived happily ever after," the handless maiden would never have had the opportunity to grow back her own hands. She would have died with the artificial silver hands that her husband had designed for her.

Despite having the name of Queen, the handless maiden still had not embraced her own life. The young queen is almost too good, too obedient, too complacent, and too passive. She needs a test in the opposite side of her life. She is sent into the dark forest to find her true self. One of the shadow sides of a woman who wakes up after being too passive is the potential of becoming too aggressive.[85]

In the dark forest, the handless maiden faces her own dark side. Here she does not have to serve anyone but herself and her child, an image of her soul. The young queen calls her son Sorrowful, which, translated from the German, literally means One Rich in Sorrow. She is indeed a woman whose soul is rich in sorrow. From the transforming crucible of suffering, she could potentially emerge bitter and revengeful, or she could become wise and compassionate. The woman who is a handless maiden is at risk of becoming a woman of sorrows or taking on the image of a helpless martyr. On the other hand, if she enters her suffering, as did the handless maiden in the tale, she and others can be transformed through her courage.

In the tale, the king searches for his queen-wife and his young son for seven years. He is purposeful and focused on his quest, taking "neither food nor drink." Eventually, in the fullness of time, he finds the place where "all are welcome." Taking "neither food nor drink" indicates metaphorically that he is in a state of mourning. He can neither feast nor celebrate life until he finds his wife and son.

When the king comes to the dwelling in the forest, he covers his face with a handkerchief so that he can go to sleep (that is, go unconscious). Then he hears the voices of his wife and son in his sleep. After the angel tells them that this is indeed the king, the handless maiden asks her son, Sorrowful, to remove the handkerchief from his father's face. She has taught her little boy that his father is God in heaven. The boy protests because he sees the weary king as a wild man who could not possibly be his Father in heaven!

When the king awakens and is reunited with his wife and son, he exclaims, "A heavy *stone* has fallen from my heart." The thing that has blocked his capacity to love has been removed. What is interesting to note is that his kingly persona is gone; he looks like a wild man, without any pretence. The archetypal image of a wild man in a fairy tale refers to basic instinctual masculine energy, which is not bound by collective and cultural expectations.

The king and the queen and their young son go home to the king's old mother. "There is great rejoicing throughout the whole kingdom, and the king and queen are married again and live contentedly to their happy end."[86]

Another wedding is necessary because this is a time for a new union of opposites and the emergence of new consciousness. The king initially chooses the handless maiden when she is helpless. He takes pity on her in her passivity, which earns her the promise of protection. Both the king and queen in the tale have experienced the process of radical transformation in their seven years of suffering and alienation. Neither is the same person he/she was at the time of their first wedding. Their commitment now is from a place of freedom, rather than pity or passivity.

The transformation of the handless maiden into the creative woman, who can spin and weave the fabric of her own life with her own hands, requires that she begin to trust herself and her own gifts. She needs to be united with her "wild man," the primal masculine energy within her that can live without fear. This process needs to happen not in an inflated, compulsive way, driven by anxiety and aggression, but in a freely creative way nurtured by love and acceptance of herself. The handless maiden emancipates herself from servitude when she is no longer dominated by early survival conclusions, which have their roots in self-doubt and anxiety about life and assumptions that others alone can save her.

The Emancipation

On the collective level what does the tale of "The Handless Maiden" teach us as a human community? One lesson might be that feeling sorry for ourselves as handless maidens in the industrial patriarchal world (the domain of the miller) will not gain us anything but artificial silver hands. They might look beautiful, but they have none of the billion-year memory of the development of human hands. Then, we are truly crippled with patriarchal appendages with which we can neither spin nor weave new life as women. Seeking sympathy for our mutilation resulting from acts of obedience to the father-world will not free us. However, it may soothe those of us "rich in sorrow" to know that some women and men understand our pain.

Union with the wild man, the unadorned unpretentious masculine within ourselves, will emancipate us from the world of the father-miller. We cannot escape the industrialized, corporate world in which we live. It is part of our evolutionary human history. We are here, as women, at this moment in time in that evolution. What we can contribute to the process of transformation is our own consciousness that only if we live without fear can we claim to have lived at all. We can teach our children to approach life without fear—not naively, but with their eyes open. If they see us embracing life without fear, they will mirror this in their own lives and potentially in the lives of their children and their children's children.

The tales of "Rumpelstilskin" and "The Handless Maiden" both revolve around the theme of the destruction of the daughter's creative self in order to meet the demands and expectations of the father's world. In both tales, the father is either prevented from living out his own creative life or chooses not to do so. Consequently, he tries to kill the creative life in his own daughter.

In both tales, the millers' daughters are betrayed by their fathers' inadequacies. This is a manifestation of the absence of the true masculine, which is always in the service of the feminine. The true masculine within us is our capacity to stay clear, objective, and purposeful, focused on what is essential in our lives. The true feminine is embodied in our capacity to be creative, generative, and compassionate toward others, the natural world, and ourselves.

In the tale of "Rumpelstilskin," the miller-father is proud and boastful. He lives through his daughter to satisfy his need for power and prestige. He seeks external recognition. The shadow side of the miller-father that can be taken on unconsciously by his daughter is his arrogance, ambition, and anger.

In the tale of "The Handless Maiden," the father is greedy for possessions. He is willing to sacrifice the apple tree (associated in the biblical story of Genesis with the Tree of the Knowledge of Good and Evil) for wealth and ease. This miller-father also tries to possess his daughter, and, in the process, forces her to leave. He seeks comfort and security. He is fearful of taking action and assuming responsibility for his own soul life. The shadow side of the father that can be taken on unconsciously by his handless daughter is a sense of hopelessness, melancholy, and depression.

Both miller-fathers use their daughters to satisfy their own needs. Both expect their daughters to obey with gratitude. Both millers' daughters are also inadequately mothered. In the first tale, the mother is absent, assumed dead. In the second, she is helpless and fails to defend her daughter or prevent her mutilation. Both millers' daughters have what Carl Jung refers to as a *negative mother complex*.

> Women with negative mother complex often miss the first half of life; they walk past it as if in a dream.... But if they can overcome this (complex), they have a good chance in the second half of rediscovering life with the youthful spontaneity missed in the first half. For though a part of life has been lost, its *meaning* has been saved.[87]

After living in exile for seven years (a period associated with the fullness of time), the handless maiden is no longer recognizable to those who once knew her. After the seven years of his search, when the king finds his queen-wife, he does not know her without her silver hands. She no longer needs artificial hands to cover up the mutilation she experienced at her father's hands. She has her own hands now, which she attributes to God's grace—a divine gift.

Four Years Later

Four years after our initial work with the tale of "The Handless Maiden," the women met to explore where they now were in their lives in relationship to the tale. Each of the women addressed the question: What is happening for me now in the exploration of the tale of "The Handless Maiden?"

Emily declared that she felt released from her history, and that she now experienced herself as more empowered. She reflected back on her early life experiences of having her own creative energy tied behind her back, and going out into the world maimed and begging for food for her soul. She recalled that when we first worked with the tale she had experienced her hands tingling with rage. She reported that while she still felt angry at the abuse she experienced from her father and stepmother, she is no longer full of rage. She was aware now that the God-fearing child who was obedient to her father believed in a negative God, not the God to whom Emily can relate at this time in her life.

In her reflections on the tale four years later, Emily was astounded that the queen mother believed the devil's message brought to her by the messenger who could not stay awake (that is, remain conscious). The queen mother did not trust her son, a symbol of her own masculine. Emily admitted that she too found it difficult to trust her own inner masculine and that the false negative messages she still received could still deceive her. She recognized that it demanded considerable energy for her to remain conscious and avoid getting "caught by the devil" (the negative messages that undermine her life and rob her of energy to continue her plans to develop her gifts of healing). She wrote, "I do feel different about my father now. I now see that what happened to me through his hands was my initiation into the work that I have begun to do, which is defining itself more and more to me each day."

When we revisited the tale four years later, Alexis admitted that, although she had made considerable gains in claiming her own creativity, she still, at times, experienced levels of fear that handicapped her. Her anxiety stifled her creativity and left her feeling helpless. Alexis recalled a dream she had early in her psychotherapy that she now saw as related to this tale:

> I unpacked a beautiful little clay bird that I had made and sold but had not yet delivered to the buyer. My friends admired it and had quite a reaction of delight when they saw it. As I put it on a pendant, it transformed into a beautiful silver white elephant.

Alexis recognized that she is often "in flight" from her creativity through the many distractions that make it difficult to maintain the discipline necessary for her work as an artist. In this dream, the bird (which she connected with spirit and lofty heights) is made of the clay of the earth. When she put on this aspect of herself, "it transformed it into a beautiful silver white elephant," which she associated with her own spirituality grounded in an earthly existence. A white elephant in India or China is a sign of the spiritual force returning. In contrast, we use the term *white elephant* in the West to mean something we no longer want to keep. In Alexis's dream, the elephant is made of silver, a metal she relates to the moon and to a reflection of the feminine side of herself.

Revisiting the tale of "The Handless Maiden," clarified for Alexis the importance of staying conscious and maintaining the discipline of balancing her creative energy and power in a way that kept her grounded in her body. She acknowledged her own power, and reported that she no longer felt handicapped and helpless with the timid eyes and tongue of the sacrificed doe in the tale.

Michaela felt rage when reading the tale again, four years later. The first time we worked with the story she could not relate to the handless maiden because she had never seen herself as powerless. Now, her anger was focused on the miller who had grabbed at the dark stranger's promise without asking a single question; at the daughter who succumbed to her father's abuse; and at the king who went away to war just as new life was about to be born, a time when stability (the archetypal meaning of king) was most needed at home.

In the devil's message the child was called a changeling, which in fairy-tale language means that his father was from the underworld (or even the devil himself). The consequence of all the distortions in the messages was that the handless maiden had to, once again, go out into the world, this time with her baby son tied to her back. She was forced to make new choices. Michaela acknowledged that she was now being forced to make important new choices in her own life that, while difficult, she felt that she now had the courage to make.

When we worked with the tale for the first time, the story hadn't had much meaning for Jessica. She had felt sorry for the handless maiden and thought of her as a "poor thing." Since then, Jessica had had several powerful dreams, which she realized four years later were related to the tale. She dreamed: "I was in a place I didn't know. Both of my hands were covered with bees. At first I was frightened, but then I realized they had come to give me something."

Through her reflection on this dream, Jessica realized that the bees had come as a sign of healing energy. Bees are connected archetypally to wisdom.[88] The sting of bees is used for arthritic limbs, to relieve the pain and heal the crippling paralysis that is associated with this disease. When Jessica reflected on the dream, she realized that her hands and her ability to be creative as a writer were all she needed. For this, she was deeply grateful. She acknowledged feelings of joy, which, for so many years, she had not realized she was capable of experiencing.

Estelle reported that, four years earlier, she had found it difficult to relate to the tale. She had since become more aware of her own hands. She noticed that when they were clenched in fear, she could not take in anything new. When she was able to open her hands, she could let go of her fear. This opening required faith, a belief that she had divine wisdom within herself. She now appreciated how fear and self-doubt destroyed her creativity. Estelle recognized how the miller's bargain with the devil led his daughter to conclude that she had no choice but to do what her father wanted, no matter what the cost to her personally. On revisiting the tale, Estelle identified with the miller "who didn't want to do the hard work." She was now more conscious of the cost of avoiding the hard work of putting herself out into the world as a musician. Estelle also struggled with allowing herself the tears necessary for her own healing. She acknowledged her need to keep her inner messengers awake so that she would not be deceived by the negative messages within her that robbed her of her power.

On revisiting the tale four years later, Claire recognized the sorrow-filled messages of her own heritage. She questioned: "Do I have to have sorrow in order to learn? The handless maiden called her son Rich in Sorrow—what about Rich in

Joy instead?" Claire acknowledged a self-defeating bargain she had made earlier in her life, which she now regretted. More than ten years earlier, she had severely injured her arm and hand. A few months prior to our meeting to revisit this tale, Claire had re-experienced the pain. She wrote: "If I go to take the bargain, the easy way out, I feel it now in my body and psyche. I become doubtful, fearful, and my arms and my hands give me pain." The power of the story of "The Handless Maiden" for Claire was her realization, "Once I know I'm loved, then I'm able to dwell free in my own body and soul." After we revisited the tale, Claire bought some very expensive cream for her hands to acknowledge that they are worthy of special attention.

Making the Choice to Live

Women who are handless maidens are often unsure about what is expected of them. They act as if they are powerless to respond from a place of choice. We see an example of this in a dream shared by one of the women in the group:

> Three young boys were high on the support wires of a bridge over a dam. They held live wires in their hands, but they didn't know this. On a signal from a man on the bridge, they were to put the wires together. When the first boy did it, the force of energy blew him away. The second boy saw it and still went ahead and put the wires together and was killed. The third boy just held the wires in his hands and watched his hands melt away in pain, but he lived. This was all so that destruction could take place. It was one man's way of retaliation.

The woman associated the man on the bridge in her dream, with the negative masculine force within her that tries to kill her young energy. For her, the underlying message of the dream is, "How can this potentially destructive energy be used more wisely?" The dream is about the vulnerability of her young masculine, on a bridge (a place of transition), over a dam (a wall that holds the potency of her emotional and creative life in check). The first young boy didn't know the power he held in his hands could destroy him. The second boy knew. He went ahead and put the wires together and was killed. The third held onto the live wires, lost his hands, but not his life. In the tale of "The Handless Maiden," the daughter also loses her hands, but not her life. She goes through life maimed because of her father's weakness, and her refusal to be submissive to the devil's wish to possess her.

When the woman who had shared this dream dialogued in an active imagination with the man on the bridge, she asked, "Why are you here, what do you want to say to me?"

He replied: "I want to unleash the power of the damn (dam) to see its power moving and uncontrolled, powerful, beautiful, forceful."

She responded: "Why do you need the three young boys?"

He answers: "They represent a profound statement of your power gone amuck—the first one willing to sell himself out completely to death; the second willing to sell himself in spite of knowledge; and the third still holding the wires, refusing to believe there is a power in them equal to the force of this damn (dam). He is oblivious, maimed, handless, and dumbstruck, with the unarticulated question, 'Why me?' None of the three ever asks the question, 'What choice do I have?' They act as if they have no choice but to be murdered, forced to commit suicide, or be maimed. All three, in their vulnerability, assume that they are victims of fate and that their destiny is destruction."

Women who are handless maidens often feel victimized by life and expect negative outcomes to occur. As a result, they live in a state of anxiety and fear. Unless they are able to recognize the power they hold in their own hands and allow life (often in the form of suffering and disappointment) to shock them into releasing the power held back by the dam, the wall that blocks the potency of their emotional and creative life remains standing. When the woman wrote out her dream she spelled the word "dam" as "damn." This was most appropriate, because she realized that she would be "damned to a life of despair," unless she did the necessary work to become conscious.

Four years later, as each of the women in the group took her life back into *her own hands,* the amount of creative energy that flowed from each of them was overwhelming. It was indeed as if a dam had broken open. Each woman acknowledged her own power to make choices that were healthier for both her body and soul. She no longer needed to be "full of sorrow." She "finally knew what (she) had to do and began...."[89]

Reflection Questions:

Chapter III—Emancipation from Servitude: The Tale of the Handless Maiden

1. Are there areas of my own life in which I feel handicapped, or where I experience myself as having my hands tied behind my back?

2. What are the "silver hands" in my life that substitute for my authentic creative potential?

3. What are the bargains I may have made in the past that still keep me hostage?

4. What life choices are facing me now?

5. How can I embrace my life choices consciously, recognizing that I do not have to live my life as if it is my fate?

CHAPTER IV

RISING FROM THE WELL OF GRIEF: THE TALE OF MOTHER HULDA

The looness cuts through the water with purpose.
She maneuvers freely
with my burden resting on her shoulders.
Spiraling down and around,
we arrive.
The light cast by her red eye
exposes the secret
well of grief.

(Jessica)

All of the women in the group were familiar with the *well of grief*. Finding them-selves in the pit of despair had brought them into psychotherapy, forcing them to do their inner work or die.

The tale of "Mother Hulda" is the story of the distraught daughter/heroine reclaiming the waters of life out of the well of grief. The brothers Grimm recorded it in their earliest collection of tales.[90] In ancient Teutonic myths and folk songs, Mother Hulda represents the real or original mother who we can reach only when we descend deeply into the well.[91] Associated with the cultivation of flax, Mother Hulda gives a young girl her first spindle (a metaphor for her creative feminine identity) and rewards her diligence by spinning for her at night while she sleeps. The ancient myths and songs about Mother Hulda present her in two contrasting images. In one, she is a beautiful woman in white and in the other, an old crone with a long hooked nose, big teeth, and wild hair.[92]

Mother Hulda is "the mother who holds and is able to bend,"[93] the faithful mother who can be trusted to hold us without becoming rigid or inflexible. In her essence, Mother Hulda is a manifestation of our Earth Mother, from whose womb (also imaged as a well) our bodies arise into life and to which they return in death.

In myths and tales, Mother Hulda guards the riches of the great underground river. She is the bridge between the conscious and unconscious worlds, the container for the wisdom of the ages.

Mother Hulda, the enduring mother, will hold us through the process of individuation. In her embrace, we can discover our unique identity, claim our power as women, and pursue that which gives our life meaning. As the midwife of our souls, Mother Hulda will not abandon us. She requires, however, that we be willing to descend into the well of grief, to go through the pain of being birthed anew, and to enter the crucible of transformation. If we do not descend into her mysterious dwelling place of unconscious riches, we will never find the treasure she holds for us. She will not accept shortcuts or half-hearted attempts to do the work. Those who try to deceive her live to regret it, as we shall see in the tale.

A Synopsis of the Tale of Mother Hulda

Once upon a time, in a land far away, there lives a widow with two daughters. One is beautiful and industrious, and the other ugly and lazy. Because the ugly, lazy one is her natural-born daughter, she favors her over the beautiful, industrious one.

Each day, the widow-mother sends the beautiful and industrious daughter to sit by the well and spin until her fingers bleed. One day, when the daughter tries to wash the blood off her spindle, it slips through her fingers and falls to the bottom of the well. In her distress, the daughter runs home to tell her widow-mother and to ask what she should do. The widow has no sympathy for her. She demands that her daughter retrieve the spindle from the well. The poor girl is so distraught that (in the despair of her heart) she jumps into the well.

When she recovers from her fall, she finds herself in a beautiful meadow blooming with flowers. As she walks through the meadow, she hears a voice coming from the baker's oven. It is the bread, calling out to her, "Please take us out, or we shall burn." She stops, finds a baker's peel, and takes the loaves out of the oven, one at a time. Then, as she walks on further, she hears the apples from a beautiful tree calling to her, "Please shake the tree; we are all ripe and need to come down." She shakes the tree until all of the apples fall to the ground.

Finally, she comes to a little cottage, where an old woman with very large teeth is sitting in the doorway. The girl begins to run away because the old woman looks so fierce. But the old woman calls after her: "Do not be afraid. Come and stay with me. If you take care of the house and do the chores, you will want for nothing, for I am Mother Hulda." The old woman keeps her promise, and the girl has delicious meals and a lovely place to sleep. Every day she does her chores, and she is very happy. But after she has been there for some time, the girl begins to long for home (although she is much better off with Mother Hulda than she had been at home). When she tells Mother Hulda that she wants to go home again, Mother Hulda is pleased. Before the girl leaves for home, Mother Hulda returns the spindle that the girl had lost in the well. When Mother Hulda brings her to the door, a shower of gold falls upon the girl because she has faithfully served Mother Hulda. As the door closes behind her, the girl finds herself not far from her stepmother's house. The cock on the wall announces her return: "Cock-a-doodle-do. Our golden girl has come home too!"

At first, her stepmother and sister are happy to see her, because she is covered in gold. When her stepmother hears how her stepdaughter has found such wealth, she sends her other daughter to get the same reward. But the ugly and lazy girl does not sit by the well and spin. She puts her hand into a thorn hedge to make it bleed. Then she throws her spindle into the well and jumps down after it. She finds herself in the same beautiful meadow her sister had described. But when the bread calls out to her to be taken from the oven, she refuses, because she does not want to blacken her hands. When she hears the apples call out to be released from the tree, she refuses to shake the tree, in case one of them might fall on her head.

When the lazy girl gets to Mother Hulda's cottage, she isn't frightened, because her sister had told her what to expect. She does the chores Mother Hulda asks of her for a few days. But then she becomes more and more lazy and can't even get up in the morning. Mother Hulda warns her, but she won't listen. When Mother Hulda leads her to the door to send her home, the lazy girl is pleased, because she expects that she will now be given the shower of gold that her sister received. But as she stands in the doorway, Mother Hulda pours a large kettle of pitch over her. So the lazy girl comes home covered in pitch. The cock on the wall announces her return: "Cock-a-doodle-do. Our dirty girl has come home too!" And never, for the rest of her life, can the pitch be removed.[94]

Many women sit at the edge of the well of life with their fingers bleeding from the destiny assigned to them by their widow-mother (who has no masculine focus for her own life). As long as they allow their lives' purposes to be determined by their widow-mothers, they never claim their own destinies. They live, day after day, on the edge of the source of life, in which they bathe their wounded hands but from which they never deeply drink. These women feel marginal, as if they don't quite belong in this world.

Carl Jung puts it bluntly when he writes of those who "are in the world only on parole. They have not formed a connection with this world; instead, they are suspended in the air." He admonishes:

You should leave some trace in this world, which notifies that you have been here, that something has happened. If nothing happens of this kind, you have not realized yourself, the germ of life has fallen, say into a thick layer of air that kept it suspended. It never touched the ground and so never could produce the plant ... the shoot must come out of the ground, but if the personal spark has never gotten into the ground, nothing will come out of it.[95]

The paradox of life is that to find our lives we must lose them.[96] It is more fruitful to jump into the well than to sit on the edge of life, day after day until our fingers bleed, neglecting our creative potential. When women are cut off from the nurturing feminine soul of their mothers, they are also cut off from themselves. They have no reserve of nurturance or comfort when they find themselves in a life crisis. The only choice they see (in the despair of their hearts) is to jump into the well of grief into which their feminine potential (their spindle) has been lost. They may think that their lives are now over, when, actually, a new beginning awaits them!

In this tale, the golden daughter (also know as Gold Mary) doesn't retrieve her spindle from Mother Hulda until she has completed all her tasks and is ready to go home. She initiates the transition back home, even though the world in which she finds herself seems ideal. She has all the nourishment she needs and has found acceptance and affirmation from Mother Hulda.

As we had done with the previous tales, each woman inserted herself into the fairy tale, as if it were her own dream. We worked with a series of dialogues, using the process of active imagination with the images in the tale, including: sister to sister, each sister with her widow-mother, each sister with Mother Hulda, and the widow-mother with Mother Hulda. Each woman also recorded her dreams over the time that we were working on the tale.

Unlike the two previous tales we explored ("Rumpelstilskin" and "The Handless Maiden") there are no masculine images in the tale of "Mother Hulda." Instead, there are four feminine figures: two images of mother, Mother Hulda and the widow, and two images of the daughter, Gold and Dark Mary. Each pair of images is a contrasting or shadow image of the other. Mother Hulda is the positive mother, the all-powerful keeper of the flowing source of consciousness and rebirth. The widow-mother is the negative mother, frozen in her feelings and projecting her needs onto her daughters. The two daughters also carry the shadow side of one another. One is called Gold Mary, and the other, Dark Mary.

The Negative and Positive Mothers

The two aspects of the mother in this tale are the one who rejects (the widow-mother) and the one who holds (Mother Hulda). Holding is the essential element of the mother-child relationship. "Holding includes, especially, the physical holding of the infant, which is a form of loving. According to D. W. Winnicott, it is perhaps the only way in which a mother can show the infant her love."[97] For Winnicott, holding extends beyond its concrete meaning to symbolize the totality of a positive relationship between the mother and her child. It includes the foundation for a healthy development of the ego so that the child can trust her body and build a secure sense of self worth.[98]

The girl child may experience the lack of holding as falling with nothing to hold on to. As a consequence, she may even lose her connection to her own body. If holding does not happen in infancy and childhood, sooner or later this loss will present itself in either physical or psychological symptoms. These symptoms usually occur around times of life transitions when a maternally deprived woman may experience herself falling into the well of grief. If she courageously seeks the holding for which she yearns and finds others to enact this holding of Mother Hulda, healing is possible for her.

The widow-mother in the tale offers no comfort to Gold Mary when she loses her spindle. She insists, instead, that Gold Mary jump into the well to retrieve it. The daughter could interpret this response as her mother wishing her death. Gold Mary goes back to the well and, "in the despair of her heart, she jumps down the well."[99]

In the original version of the Grimm's tale, the mother is a widow with two daughters. There is no mention of her being a stepmother to the golden daughter. The brothers Grimm introduce this change in later versions to provide an explanation for why the ugly, lazy daughter is favored over the hardworking, beautiful one.

What is clear in all versions of the tale is that the mother is a widow. There is no father in the story. Kathrin Asper clearly expresses the problem the child faces:

> The father who is absent physically or in exile emotionally, generally speaking, intensifies the problem of the non-empathic mother. When there is no father present, the child unconsciously participates in the mother's pain and anger and can be easily drowned in her sadness.[100]

The loss of her father contributes to the child feeling estranged from herself and her own emotional life. The mother, who has no support from her masculine partner, may seek her emotional energy from her child. She may project her emotional needs onto her child and expect the child to carry them.

Rita's stepmother rejected and psychologically abused her. Her father, while physically present, failed to protect her from her stepmother. There was no positive emotional connection between her father and her stepmother, and Rita found herself enmeshed in their unresolved conflicts. She was torn between a father she loved and a stepmother she feared. She felt forced, at times, to take her stepmother's side in arguments between her father and stepmother, for fear of retaliation from her if she did not do so.

After exploring the tale of Mother Hulda, Rita dreamed:

> I was on a bus with my stepmother. An old crone was sitting across from us. My stepmother fell into a well-like area in the bus. I went to rescue her. I looked over at the crone, who indicated to me that I should let her go.

Rita recognized Mother Hulda in the image of the old crone in her dream. She encouraged Rita to let go of the emotional burden that her relationship with her stepmother has placed on her life. After working with this tale, Rita composed her own fairy tale in which she is free of her stepmother. She acknowledged, after sharing her tale, "My stepmother no longer has control over me." In her active imagination work, Rita had Mother Hulda say to the widow-mother, "I will not allow you to bully her anymore." Then, Rita dreamed:

> I was in the home where I grew up. I had rearranged the furniture and moved into my office. There was going to be an important business meeting there. My stepmother came in, but I went on with my preparations for the meeting.

In this dream, Rita had returned home. The space was no longer arranged according to her stepmother's wishes. It was now arranged according to Rita's needs. In this new space, her competency and leadership skills are about to be recognized.

Images related to the negative and positive mother also appeared in Emily's dreams after we explored the tale of "Mother Hulda." She dreamed: "A friend took me home to introduce me to her parents. I was astonished to find that her mother is a giant and her father is a dwarf, like Humpty Dumpty." On awakening, Emily remembered the nursery rhyme from her childhood:

> Humpty Dumpty sat on a wall,
> Humpty Dumpty had a great fall.
> All the king's horses and
> All the king's men
> Couldn't put Humpty Dumpty
> Together again.

Emily recognized several ways that she could view the dream images of the giant mother and the dwarfed, fragile father. They could represent two aspects of the feminine and masculine energies within her. The image of the giant mother could carry the energy of what Jung referred to as her *mother complex*, an aspect of our unconscious that we all carry as human persons. Marion Woodman[101] refers to the mother complex as a layered onion of all our experiences related to our mothers. It resides in our unconscious and rises to the surface when events in our lives evoke memories of what remains unfinished in our relationship with our mothers. A similar complex occurs around our relationship with our fathers. When events trigger the layered memories, they spontaneously rise to the threshold of our awareness, even if we are trying hard to repress them.

Emily carried an enormous negative mother complex of memories and experiences related to both her birth mother and stepmother. Her mother abandoned her when she was nine months old. Then, her stepmother rejected Emily and favored her own daughter. Emily was aware that the giant mother in her dream could be all the negative mother energy she carried. Or, as she decided to interpret it, the giant mother could be the positive mother, an image of Mother Hulda herself. Emily related the fragile, dwarfed masculine image of Humpty Dumpty to her own fragile masculine energy (as she struggled to be focused in following her desire to become a healer).

In this tale, the widow-mother carries dwarfed masculine energy. She has no purpose or focus in her life. Emily saw the image of the widow-mother as an empty shell lacking the powerful energy of the egg (a source of life associated with the feminine).

The woman who experiences herself as sitting on the edge of the well of grief finds it difficult to develop her true masculine side (her capacity to focus on a goal to which she can give her energy) while, simultaneously, respecting her feminine side (her capacity for maintaining relationships, expressing her creativity, and honoring her body).

Emily's father had very little connection with his feminine side. She experienced him "as generally hating women." The only time Emily saw her father in touch with his feminine side was when he took her and her stepsister exploring in the beautiful hills surrounding their hometown. There, he came alive and was able, through his scientific background, to share the secrets of the created world with her. At home, he was explosive and cruel, punishing her for any minor infraction of the rules he had set for her. He tried to control and suppress her creative spirit. But he never succeeded because he had introduced her to her Earth Mother, Mother Hulda, the *huldemoder* of the hills. Her Earth Mother continued to share her beauty and love freely, no matter what rule Emily didn't obey, or what task she didn't perform perfectly. Emily recognized the giant mother in her dream as Mother Hulda, who she saw as her true mother, the Divine Mother, who would never abandon her.

For Emily, the tale of "Mother Hulda" powerfully reflected many aspects of her own life story. She grew up in a home with a stepmother and a stepsister who was favored by her own mother. In her dialogue between the first daughter (Gold Mary) and her mother, Emily wrote:

> As Gold Mary approaches her widow-mother, she feels that the gold is not only on her but was also inside her. Every cell in her body seems like a shining coin of gold, like a million suns shining and reflecting. She walks toward her mother without fear. The gold is like a shield of armor. She is free to act and decide. She addresses her mother: "Mother, I was so afraid to dive into the water to find the spindle. How could you have been so cruel as to demand that of me? I could have walked away and not done what you asked. But you see, Mother, along with the great despair and fear was an instinctive trust in my own abilities. When I jumped into the well, it took me on a long and dark journey. I kept going down until I suddenly found myself in the light. You might wonder, will I share this? You say I was always your child? No, mother, that is not true. You did not love me as a mother loves a child. I will share with you what I have acquired. It is up to you what you do with it. I am not going to stay with you any longer. I will go and make my own life."

In Emily's active imagination dialogue between Dark Mary and her widow-mother, Dark Mary says to her mother when she returns home covered with pitch:

In this blackness there is no life. I feel as if the image of the crippled mother marks my entire body. Mother, with your jealousy you have robbed me of my creativity, my spontaneity. You did not love me. You thought only of yourself. Mother, I have news for you: staying here pitch-black with you is going to kill me. I am resolved to go back to the well and to dive down again. I don't know how I will be received, but, Mother, that is my only way to salvation. I will do it differently this time. I will do the work. I am sorry to leave you by yourself, but I don't want to die. I want to live.

After her active imagination work, Emily dreamed:

I was swimming in a large outdoor pool with crystal clear water. My baby and my parents were with me. I was swimming around my baby in a playful manner, as a mother seal would do. I dove under her, swam away, and came back, just having fun. My parents were trying to tell me what I should and should not do, but I ignored them. Instead, I was totally concentrating on my baby.

As she reflected on her dream, Emily realized that the baby, who she saw as an image of her own soul, could swim on her own. Emily was amazed that she was able in her dream to ignore the voices of her parents without a single negative thought. Emily saw this as a reassurance from her unconscious that she was making the appropriate decision to claim her own life and follow her desire to become a healer. Her baby, a newly born image of her soul, is already capable of swimming. Emily recognized that she needed to continue to hold the tension between her conscious and unconscious world, which she associated with being above and below the water. Her dream assured Emily that she could dive under and emerge again. She would not drown in the dark side, symbolized by the presence of her parents in the dream. She could actually have fun and celebrate her own soul-life (the image of her child).

While she worked on the issues generated by her reflections on the tale of "Mother Hulda," Emily experienced pain in her breasts and ovaries. She saw these symptoms as a clear sign from her body that her longing for creativity was being blocked. Emily associated her breasts with her own motherhood and her capacity to receive and to give love and nourishment to her daughters. She saw her ovaries as a part of her capacity to create new life. Emily acknowledged that something new needed to be born and nourished within her. She was finding it very difficult to accept an offer to begin her healing work. Paradoxically, she felt overwhelmed by the *positive* support she received.

Our shadow includes all those aspects of ourselves, positive and negative, gold and dark, which we do not acknowledge as our own.

> Ignoring the gold can be as damaging as ignoring the dark side of the psyche, and some people may suffer a severe shock or illness before they learn how to let the gold out. Indeed, this kind of intense experience may be necessary to show us that an important part of us is dormant or unused.[102]

Emily finally recognized that her dream was encouraging her to accept the offer and begin to use her own creativity in ways that could give health and life to others. After making the decision to accept the offer, leaving behind the negative messages of her stepmother and father, Emily noticed that the painful symptoms in her breasts and ovaries disappeared.

Jessica also found the tale of "Mother Hulda" to be very important for her own life. It represented to her a journey of "getting to the heart of the matter," rediscovering the heart of the mothers in her life. Jessica's maternal heritage had been contaminated with toxic shame. She associated the widow in the tale with the toxic mothers in her family who were rejecting, blaming, and whose love was poisoned with pretense and the expectation that she please them. The exploration of this tale evoked a poem for Jessica that she entitled "To All my Toxic Mothers."

> What are your expectations of me?
> Don't change the rules in the middle of the game.
> When I'm afraid, help me in my fear.
> Please don't ask, "What's the matter with *you?*"
> Then I feel ashamed, blamed for intruding on your good feelings.
> When I ask for help because I am lost,
> please don't say, "You should know that."
> I wouldn't ask if I knew.
> When I ask for approval because I want to learn the proper way to set the table
> Please don't say, "You've done a great job!" then behind my back correct my mistakes.
> Perhaps I am a toxic child,

digging in my heels,
no desire to blacken my hands.
Toxic parents beget toxic children.
When I point my finger at you, am I also toxic, lazy, and
insolent?
Readily, I see the toxic shame
Paralyzed by pitch. Pleasing.
It's all your fault! Blame.
Blame who? Toxic parents?
Mother Hulda recognizes
pretense when she sees it!
I am responsible, not for my toxic parents,
but to shake the pitch off myself.
Mother Hulda has no time for pretense
when I blame and judge my toxic parents for my life,
or lack of it!
I am responsible for my life.
My children are responsible for theirs.

Jessica's grandmother had committed suicide when her mother was twelve years old. The family held this shame-filled secret for years. No one spoke of it. When Jessica was twelve years old, she learned the secret from a girlfriend. She was very angry that her mother hadn't told her. Jessica wrote:

> I resented the secret she kept from me about her own mother. I wanted her to tell me. Yet, I was afraid of her despair, her tears, and her pain. But what I was really afraid of was my own feelings of despair for her.

Jessica addressed Mother Hulda: "Mother Hulda, what was my grandmother's despair? What is my mother's despair, my own despair? Am I afraid that pretense will cover me all the days of my life? Do I have a choice? Do I *have* to pretend?"

Jessica's active imagination work evolved into a conversation between her mother and her grandmother, who had been severely depressed. Jessica realized her own mother's dilemma in feeling responsible for keeping the family together during her grandmother's rapid emotional deterioration. (Her grandfather was unconscious in his addiction to alcohol.) After her mother's suicide, Jessica's mother found herself torn between continuing to feel responsible for caring for the children and her father and claiming a life of her own in the home of her aunt, her mother's sister. Jessica now saw this aunt as an expression of Mother Hulda, a medial woman who released her mother from her perceived obligation "to save the family." She gave Jessica's mother the opportunity to claim her own life.

After her reflections on the tale, Jessica wrote:

> Looking at my mother now, I realize that I always put her down. The bit of pitch that clung to her blinded me. I never realized that she had been to the well, met Mother Hulda, and returned with the gold of courage. I feel now like the daughter all covered in pitch, resentful because I wasn't told the secret.

In her journal, Jessica wrote to her mother:

> I now marvel at your life. How you handled death and disappointment, and blackened your hands to do what needed to be done. I enjoy your sense of humor, the gold you received from Mother Hulda to be able to laugh at yourself. I got caught in feeling sorry for you so that I didn't have to acknowledge my own pain. I saw you as helpless, so I didn't have to own my own stance of helplessness. What a surprise it is to me to discover that you didn't let your mother's suicide hold you back. You didn't allow anyone to feel sorry for you or wallow in self-pity. You got on with your life. Now, it's my turn to do the same.

Jessica found an old photograph of her grandmother as a young woman and had it restored and enlarged. She sent a copy to her mother and framed a copy for herself.

In her active imagination dialogue between Mother Hulda, her mother, her grandmother, and herself, Jessica wrote:

> I reach out to my mother and tell her that I am relieved to know that she has been to the well. A burden is lifted from my heart. I move beyond my mother to my grandmother who sits beside Mother Hulda. I tell her, "I am grateful to be able to speak your name and see your face in my mother's house." Her grandmother responds, "I am so glad you have chosen to include me in your life."

Jessica concluded her conversation with Mother Hulda as the image of Sophia, Seat of Wisdom: "Your warmth and caring give me courage to believe I am not helpless. I am good enough. There is a place for me at the table." Then Jessica dreamed: "I was living in a house in which many people were interested. It was a grand house and reminded me of Aunt Elsie's. The attic was draped with sheets and very oppressive. I could hardly wait to take them down. Beyond the attic there were many more rooms."

Growing up, Jessica was one of Aunt Elsie's favorite nieces. The price of being favored, however, was high. She always had to please her aunt and give her special attention. Jessica associated an incident of shaming with the attic of Aunt Elsie's house. At age nine, she had asked for something she needed and, as a consequence, was publicly shamed. In her distress, Jessica fled to hide in the attic. She saw the dream inviting her to go beyond the place of shame (covered over with sheets), a place of remembered oppression. In her dream, Jessica was anxious to take down that which covered her shame and to move beyond the attic of disgrace to explore the many other rooms that contained treasures yet to be claimed.

Shame reduces a child to a state of wanting to disappear. This happens to Gold Mary in the tale when her mother shames her for dropping her spindle into the well. In her despair, she jumps in after it and disappears. When we experience shame early in life, we can carry it unconsciously into our adult years, where it can continue to destroy our sense of self-worth.

The night after doing her active imagination with the images in the tale, Jessica dreamed:

"I was watching some children at play. They were blowing up the monuments." This dream affirmed Jessica's decision to reclaim her own life and let go of all the "markers of significant memory" that kept her connected to the past.

A few weeks later, Jessica had this dream, which she associated with Mother Hulda:

> I went to a cottage that I supposedly rented, but no one was there. I went in anyway. I kept looking over my shoulder (into my shadow). I met this very old woman who lived with her son in a hovel (nothing more than a hole in the ground). She had spun some very crude wool with flowers still stuck in it. She was weaving a blanket. I was very impressed. It was very soft.

Jessica recognized the contrast between "the grand house" of her previous dream and the hovel or "hole in the ground" in which the old spinster weaves beauty without perfection. Jessica saw the image of the crude wool with the "flowers still stuck in it" as an affirmation of her decision to let go of having to do things perfectly. She acknowledged her acceptance of the warmth and softness of Mother Hulda's weaving within her.

The woven fabric of Jessica's maternal history was torn by her grandmother's suicide. The threads knotted around her grandmother's throat choked the voices of all the women in the family. The unspoken messages were clear: "hold your tongue," "button your lip," "grin and bear it." Jessica still found herself pressing her lips together when she was distressed. Jessica saw her dream of the old woman in the hovel as a turning point in her life. New threads were being woven together. And, the rewoven fabric contained flowers!

Then Jessica dreamed: "I found an abandoned baby girl. I cared for her, cleaned her, and changed her diaper. I wondered if I could love her as much as my own children. As I held her, I decided that I could." In this dream, Jessica recognized an image of the abandoned feminine side of herself. She removes the dirt (the toxic pitch) that clings to the child. And then Jessica decides that, indeed, she could love this newborn image of herself.

Jumping Into the Well: Plumbing the Depths

In the tale, Gold Mary goes back to the well when her mother refuses to help her retrieve her lost spindle. Not knowing what else to do, and in despair, she jumps into the well. In Claire's active imagination dialogue between the gold daughter and her mother she asks: "Have you ever despaired?" The widow-mother answers, "I have never allowed myself to imagine or dream; therefore, why should I despair? Not all are called to plumb the depths."

What a poignant response! The widow-mother has no masculine focus in her life and no feminine imagination and creativity. She lives on the edge of life itself. She is afraid to plumb the depths and to make the choice to die in order to live. She ends up trying to live through her children, instead of choosing life for herself. The dark daughter also feels forced by her mother into the plunge for which she herself is not prepared. The widow-mother lives in a state of denial and blames others for the pain and distress she will not accept as her own.

After reflecting on this tale and exploring her own willingness to plumb the depths, Alexis composed a spontaneous poem:

> Today, I feel afraid of my own depth.
> On a narrow ledge I stand
> looking at the abyss below and the leaves above
> my flesh torn apart,
> my heart exposed.

I see no exit
no other way
but to stand here and endure
as I fear my own
descent into the well.
I send signals
like rings of smoke
which only time can dissipate.
I fear, but then I love,
I love, but then I fear
my own depth.
Is there a way out of this pain?
I ask what my heart desires,
what will keep fear in check?
I look inside and see
between the two are the words,
"Be intentional with your life."

When Alexis looked up the word *intention* in the dictionary, she discovered that it meant, "a course of action one intends to follow or an aim that guides one's actions." She discovered that synonyms for "intention" included the words *import, significance,* and *purpose*. Intention is about having one's mind and will clearly focused on a specific purpose, moving toward an aspiration, a mission, and a destination. In response to this awareness, Alexis wrote:

Sophia, you have visited me in darkness in the nave of Notre Dame. You have been my companion as a child. In you I trust and put my faith. As a child of the light, I was afraid of the dark, but the dark of your womb is filled with your presence. I am in a new loop of my journey, going toward what I fear. I feel that you are calling me to explore uncharted territory. Be my light. Help me to enter into my body and to wait for a sign of your guidance. Help me wait out the darkness. I am beginning to understand that being intentional means staying focused. No matter what happens, the focus can hold the balance. I realize that my intention is not for my self-glorification but for sharing my creative gifts with others. This recognition will help me avoid falling into my shadow, my competitive side that feels threatened when someone else gets more attention and affirmation than I.

Then Alexis reflected on an image of a wolf that came to her in a dream. The wolf is usually focused and purposeful. However, Alexis associated him with an animal of Apollo, greedy, and devouring those who got in his way. She recognized these qualities in her own shadow (those aspects of herself that she would rather not acknowledge). When she did an active imagination dialogue with her image of the wolf, she asked him, "What drives you to devour?"

> He replied: "Hunger turned to greed. I wanted to remind you of the dangers of the woods as well as to guide you through them. Greed leads to competition, which leads to jealousy, which leads to manipulation to get your own way. Be careful!" Alexis responded: "So, that's how you are connected to my shadow. You represent spiritual greed, being better than others! I recognize my greed, my compulsion to be best or most favored. I thank you for this awareness. I recognize how my relationships with others have been damaged because of my spiritual greed. I have to be special, more esteemed than the others. But they are all kin to me, sharing the same struggle."

Two nights after her active imagination dialogue with the image of the wolf, Alexis had the following dream. It confirmed her newfound awareness and affirmed her resolve to be more intentional in her life. She dreamed:

> I was dancing wildly in a large room with other people. A woman commented that she realized that one doesn't recover one's creativity entirely working with only one modality. She was pleased with herself. Then, I took off and flew. I stopped by a fountain for a drink. I watched for prowlers, as I was not at ease in the dark. A young man joined me. We walked together, but he could not fly. I was frustrated, so I left him behind. I found myself in Paris and sat on a ledge of a cathedral, like a gargoyle. People looked at me, and I made a face at them. They were holding on to each other as if they were dancing a conga line. Then they all tumbled like dominoes on the ground. In the next scene, I was on the Champs Elysees. There was hardly anyone around me. The pavement was a boardwalk, a lovely smooth wooden surface. I felt the texture of the wood with my hands and slid on my stomach downhill. I went through a series of hallways, slid-

ing and flying in deserted corridors. Then, I was on a ship. I was flying, moving fast. But I wondered, "Where are the people?"

This was a very powerful dream for Alexis. It draws a very clear picture of what happens in her life when she goes into a grandiose inflation. She leaves her soul behind (the image of the young man) because it cannot fly. She turns into a gargoyle, a distorted image of a half-human, half-beast on the outside of cathedral walls intended to frighten away evil spirits. In her dream, Alexis becomes a distortion of her true self, causing others who are dancing in unison (a conga line) to fall to the ground.

In her dream, the Champs Elysees, a place generally full of people, was deserted. Alexis recognized that she loses her relationships with others as she slides and flies through empty passageways, her feet not touching the ground. In the last part of her dream, Alexis finds herself on a ship, a vessel of transfer across water. She associated the ship with a metaphor for the balance between the conscious (above the water) and the unconscious (below the water). Alexis saw this dream as a warning to wake up to the destruction that happens in her life when she loses her focus. Then, she forgets her intention to use her own creative gifts to awaken the creative gifts in others. Alexis admitted that when she "goes flying off," she has broken her intention and is at great risk of losing important relationships that nourish her own creative energy.

The Gold and Dark Sisters

The daughter who carries a mother abandonment wound may find herself moving between the two extremes of grandiosity and depression, which manifest as "fluctuating self-esteem."[103] We see this in the two images of the daughters in the tale. Gold Mary struggles with depression, while Dark Mary is caught in grandiosity.

During our weeklong retreat, Alexis made a mask of her face portraying the two sides of herself, the light, and the dark. She danced to the music of the "Ave Maria" with the light side of her mask and to songs from the opera *Carmen* with the dark side. When she finished dancing, Alexis began to sob. She realized that the dance was about healing the split between the good and bad girl within herself.

While we were working on the tale of "Mother Hulda," Alexis dreamed:

> I had an appointment with an old woman who lived on the ground floor of an apartment building like the one I lived in when I was a teenager. I had my black ebony flute with me. Somewhat embarrassed, I took it apart. But it would still be visi-

ble because I had no purse or pocket in which to hide it. The old woman opened the door, but she was busy, and I had to wait.

Alexis associated the old woman in her dream with Mother Hulda. She wrote:

> She invited me to descend to the underworld of the dark yin, to be renewed through *waiting* and *listening* to the images of the deep so that a new phase of my personal life could be gained. Moving down into the depth of my being, I awaited the dissolution of my fears to let the new me emerge. I entrusted myself to Sophia, Mother. I trembled as I began to experience the power of the feminine.

Next, Alexis had the following dream:

> A huge mansion stood in front of me. It was impenetrable. I sensed the owner was an ogre. I would have loved to explore its attics and turrets, but it was too well guarded. However, a small child ran out of the house. He was craving affection, and he rested in my arms. We loved each other. I sensed that I was being observed from the forest.

Alexis's young soul, in the image of the little boy, lived in the fear-filled house of the ogre. When she opened herself to move beyond her fears, the young child was able to escape from the mansion of the negative mother. Alexis associated the ogre's mansion with that part of herself that is critical and rejecting. She longed to explore its attics and turrets, but it was too well guarded. If she could get beyond her guardedness, Alexis would discover what she had secreted away in her attic. She recognized these secrets as her ways of thinking that kept her anxious and afraid. Alexis made a commitment to herself to explore the attic of the fears that paralyzed her. This reminded her of Gold Mary sitting by the well, weeping, with bloody hands. Then Alexis wrote:

> I am taking the bull by the horns. Today is the first day of the rest of my life. I have to put order in my life before I sink any further. I will get my spindle back and do the hard work. The two sisters in the tale are shadow images of one another: one gold, one dark; one depressed, and the other grandiose. One does the work, and the other just pretends. Dark Mary is not able to grow up and do

the work that needs to be done to claim her own life because of an overprotective, devouring mother who made her special and, thereby, crippled her. The other daughter, Gold Mary, is rejected by her mother and is forced in her despair to descend into the well where Mother Hulda rewards her with gold. However, the Gold Mary in me may feel that she has to give away the gold she received from Mother Hulda, in the hope of belonging and being valued.

After reflecting on this tale, Alexis recalled an earlier dream she had had about a young girl who gave birth to twins, one black, and one white. In her reflection on this dream, Alexis recognized that the black child was longing to be held. He was Negro. Alexis associated Negro with *negredo*, the dark substance from which gold is extracted in alchemy. Initially, she felt repulsed by the black child; then she wrote:

> How can a baby, newly born, repulse me? Who are you, so different in your mother's arms? Loved as you are, why can't I accept you? Little child, I hold you against my heart to accept, to forgive, to give back, and to acknowledge all that is dark within me: my insecurities, my envy, and my pride. Is there another repressed side of me I find difficult to acknowledge? It is my inferior function that I haven't integrated yet. I would like to be brilliant, and I am not. I would like to be sharp and assertive, and I am not. How do I accept and live with myself as I am?

Then Alexis dreamed of finding a place of nourishment for both the black and white aspects of herself:

> I was looking for my cousin in a small village; my mother was with me. We took a bus to the village, but we had not done our research. We only knew she owned a restaurant called La Grisaille. My cousin has a hooked nose. My mother sat at a table in a café under the trees and ordered a pancake, which she shared with a little girl. They had fun pretending they were angels. Meanwhile, I continued my search. On my way to find a telephone book to look up the address, I stumbled upon the place. When I looked down, I saw *La Grisaille* written on the doormat. I woke up.

Alexis associated *La Grisaille* with the French word for gray, a color that is neither black nor white, but a combination of both. It was important for Alexis to find the threshold where the extremes of black and white meet. She left her mother, who was playing with a little girl. They were pretending to be angels. Angels are not of this world and, therefore, not grounded in the reality of everyday life. Alexis went on searching and "stumbled upon the place." This frequently happens when a woman is searching for nourishment for her soul but hasn't done her "research." In other words, she hasn't exercised the discipline necessary to have a clear focus or map of where she is going. Things happen to her, she stumbles upon the answer. In the dream, Alexis stumbled upon the place for which she was searching. The name is on the doormat at her feet. If she hadn't looked down (that is, reconnected to her ability to stand on her own), she would have missed that for which she was searching. Alexis noted an interesting detail in the dream in the reference to the cousin's hooked nose. She recognized her as Mother Hulda!

In response to the tale, Alexis wrote: "The big issue in my life is that I retreat in fear each time I take a step forward. My early survival conclusion was to only trust others and not myself. Yet, I feel guided. I feel that someone within me knows." This awareness inspired Alexis to write the following poem:

> In the well she appeared as reflection of truth.
> Why look for her outside when she dwells within,
> in the depths of my own well?

Alexis continued:

> So familiar was this face that I knew it was my own *self*—not the doubting self with its hesitation, or the wounded one who decided so early on to put her trust in others but the one who knows the way, the one who gives life, the Divine Presence that has been coaxing me to go forward. I worked to hold on to your image, but it was as if my own doubts, whenever they surfaced, obliterated your face.

Alexis realized that the tale of "Mother Hulda" was inviting her to develop a deeper relationship with the Divine Feminine within herself, who Alexis knew as Sophia, the Mother of Wisdom.

In My Sister's Shadow

Other ancient tales also carry the theme of the gold and dark sisters. Perrault published a story entitled "Diamonds and Toads," in 1695.[104] In a version of this tale, the trial of the two daughters also takes place at a well. The first daughter graciously gives the fairy (disguised as an old woman) a drink from the well. As a reward, she receives the promise, "Every word you speak shall come out of your mouth either a flower or a jewel." The mother sends her second daughter to the well for the same reward. However, the second daughter goes grumbling, annoyed at her mother's insistence. When she meets the fairy (this time disguised as a princess), she is very rude and does not give the disguised fairy a drink. For her rudeness, the fairy gives her the promise, "With every word you speak there shall come out of your mouth a snake or a toad." If we disrespect Mother Hulda, in the variety of forms in which she manifests herself, we will pay the price!

Unfortunately, in the tale of "Diamonds and Toads," the first daughter is blamed for her sister's dilemma. "O mercy," cried the Mother, "What is this I see? It is your sister that has been the cause of all of this, but she shall pay for it." Immediately, the mother ran after her daughter to beat her. The poor girl fled and went into hiding in the nearby forest.[105] The forest in fairy tales and myths is the place of trial and transformation.

Several of the women experienced deep pain and rage when they did their active imagination dialogues between the two sisters in the tale of "Mother Hulda." In Emily's dialogue, the dark sister returned to blame Gold Mary for her fate: "You lied to me! I hate you!" The experience of being blamed for something that had happened to their sisters was one that many of the women shared. Some also carried the pain of rivalry with their sisters for their mothers' attention and affection.

As a group, we explored the stress we experience as women when we are constantly compared to our sisters or other female relatives. Rita did an active imagination dialogue with a cousin with whom she was always negatively compared. She woke up in a rage. Many of the women in the group had unfinished business with sisters who had "blackmailed" and negated them. What was alarming was how often this negative situation went on for years until one of the women decided to change the relationship.

After her active imagination dialogue between the dark and the gold sisters, Estelle dreamed: "I was in the Caribbean visiting my sister. She told me to get my own voice!"

In an actual conversation with her sister, Estelle had encouraged her to find help to deal with her depression. Her sister, who was in an abusive marital relationship, replied: "I'm not ready to dabble in the unconscious. Besides, it's a lot of nonsense. The next thing you'll be telling me is that our father sexually abused you."

Many of the women in the group had experienced pain in their relationships with other women, including being hurt by their lies and spite. Claire reflected on her experience of women mentors stealing her creative work, diminishing her value, and discrediting her competency.

In the tale of "Mother Hulda," Gold Mary wants to be reconciled with Dark Mary and her widow-mother. Of her own choice, she decides to return home. Her deepest hope, as Emily expressed it, was to discover: "Now I belong. They finally will accept me!" In this hope we hear the plaintive cry of the abandoned child: "Please accept me. Now that I bring you gold, am I not, finally, good enough?"

The abandoned child, now woman, needs to discover her own gold, the precious qualities of her own unique life, her right to be alive, and to simply exist.

Healing the Split

Kathrin Asper writes about the "fluctuating self esteem" of women who have experienced early maternal deprivation.[106] Gold Mary and Dark Mary are the two sides of this woman. She may go from feeling excited and positive about her life to feeling depressed and despairing. Some women with a maternal wound find it easier to focus on the dark or shadow side of their personality. It is essential that these women also acknowledge the side of themselves that is Gold Mary, or they will remain split within themselves.

In Michaela's dialogue between the two sisters, the radiant Gold Mary says to her dark sister when she returns home, "I would like my good fortune to be yours." If the maternally deprived woman can focus on the radiance of her own essence, then she can welcome home the dark side of herself as well. This requires integrating her own shadow, those aspects of herself she does not know or acknowledge, into a new understanding of herself.

> The term *shadow* refers to that part of the personality that has been repressed for the sake of the ego ideal.... Practically speaking, the shadow more often than not appears as an inferior personality. However, there can also be a positive shadow, which appears when we tend to identify with our negative qualities and repress the positive ones.[107]

The maternally wounded woman doesn't need reminders of her dark side. Her task is to find her way to the light through the well of grief. Her grief is deep. Her loss vibrates in her body, in the very matrix of her soul. She needs to find Mother Hulda and to rise from the well to be born into a new way of knowing herself.

The ancient alchemists always began the process of bringing forth gold with the negredo, the ingredients of darkness. The most precious aspects of ourselves are often found when we reintegrate the shadow side of our personality, that is, those parts of ourselves that have been lost to our awareness. It is essential that the maternally wounded woman distinguish her *own* shadow from the projection of the shadows of others that she may have assimilated as her own.

Jessica wrote in her response to this tale:

> It is only when I am in the *light* that I am able to *see* my own shadow! The shadow lives behind my mask. It lives in the darkness because I am ashamed to bring it out. I am afraid if I take off the mask there may be no one there. Or, do I not take off the mask because what is underneath is too precious, and I don't want to defile it? I feel as if I am my shadow, and I am watching myself go about my life.

After Alexis danced with her mask (which was white on one side and dark on the other), Jessica had the following dream: "I was hit in the chest by a white light from Alexis's mask." Jessica woke up, startled out of her sleep. She realized that she continued to carry the shadow of her maternal heritage in her body and psyche. The silent sins of the mothers weighed her down with sadness. She recognized that *joy* was in her shadow. She acknowledged that she could not allow herself to feel or express joy. It was as if the daughters in the family had been assigned the task of continuing to mourn the loss of their grandmother. A great weight was lifted from Jessica's body when the white light in her dream touched her heart.

Each of the women carried negative messages about herself, often expressed through the voice of negative images in her dreams. When the light of her new understanding of herself erased the false shadows projected on her by others, each woman was able to discover her own shadow. In the process of our work, we did not focus on probing negative experiences. The woman who is maternally deprived needs to learn to accept the positive gifts of Gold Mary within herself first. Then she is in a healthier position to integrate her Dark Mary shadow side.

Our experience as a group confirmed this. When each woman claimed her positive shadow, then the darker shadow side of her personality manifested itself in healthy and constructive ways.

Facing the Dark Mary side of herself was more difficult for some of the women in the group than for others. If her early survival conclusions were in the direction of only trusting herself and not others, the woman had more difficulty in claiming her dark shadow side. Her shadow had to be cloaked with a coverlet of gold for this girl child to survive. For her to pull the cover off too quickly would risk precipitating a headfirst plunge into the well of grief and despair (against which she had developed successful strategies over many years). The danger of potential exposure left her in terror.

On the other hand, the woman who developed early survival conclusions that she could only trust others and not herself is more amenable to exploring her dark shadow. Sometimes, she may be *too* eager to disclose her dark side. She assumes that when she reveals her darkness others will be ready and willing to give her the help she desires. The danger for this woman is that she can then be reconfirmed in her inability to trust herself. However, if she has integrated the positive aspects of her shadow (those parts of herself that encourage her ability to claim her own personal power) then a significant shift can occur in her relationship with herself and others.

After reflecting on the tale of "Mother Hulda," Estelle had the following dream:

> Alice and I were at Edith's house (not her actual home). She was preparing a meal in the kitchen, and we were helping her. She was being very bossy and controlling and making put-downs and negative comments about herself and us in a joking kind of way. Eventually, I couldn't stand it any longer, and I told her that I didn't have to put up with her criticism and abuse, and that I was leaving. I told Alice to meet me at a certain gas station, and I left. I was surprised at my courage and ability to get out of that situation. I met up with Alice, and we went for a drive along a road beside a beautiful beach. I think we were in the Caribbean. We loved the scenery. We had a really good time and felt comfortable with each other.

When Estelle worked with the images in this dream, she identified Edith as dark, bossy, and critical and Alice as light, bright, funny, witty, and warm. She recognized the two feminine figures in the dream as shadow sides of her inner self. Interestingly, Estelle's own sister, with whom she had a strained relationship, lived in the Caribbean.

Many sisters struggle in their relationships with one another. One sister can carry one side of the parental shadow, and the second sister the other side. Or, one becomes the good daughter, and the other the bad daughter. One may align with

one parent and the second with the other parent. Estelle was more closely identified with her mother and tried to be a good daughter to her. Her sister, who had
moved far away from her parents, was aloof toward their mother. Neither daughter had a close relationship with their father. Estelle's sister acted toward their
mother in the same way that she had observed her father relating to their mother.
Her sister had also entered into a marital relationship similar to that of their parents. However, she assumed her father's role in the relationship. When Estelle
suggested to her sister that she develop her gift for singing because she had such a
beautiful voice, her sister ignored her. Estelle was trying to share the gold from her
own experience of developing her own voice, but her sister wasn't open to receiving it. When competition between sisters develops early in life, usually around the
perception of a scarcity of love and attention from mother, their relational pattern
is difficult to change, even when one of the sisters desires to do so.

A week later, Estelle dreamed:

> I was in a strange place; I didn't recognize my house. It was in
> a run-down part of town. A black family lived across the street.
> There were always lots of people in that house, for some reason.
> The children, two little black girls, were always hanging around
> outside. They knew my name. I wasn't sure why or how they
> knew my name, but they called to me whenever they saw me. I
> just ignored them. I didn't have anything to do with them. I had
> to go to the store because my fridge was empty. When I went
> outside to leave, I couldn't find my car. It had been stolen! I was
> really upset. How could someone steal my car in broad daylight
> right outside my house? To make things worse, my purse had
> been in the car, along with a library book on creativity that I
> wanted to share with my friends.

This dream occurred after an incident in which her mother had not been
encouraging and supportive of Estelle's musical performance. In her analysis of
this dream, Estelle recognized the ways she became trapped in seeking her mother's approval. She felt that her mother only half-heartedly supported her creativity.
She experienced herself being "damned with faint praise." Estelle allowed herself
to feel the pain of not receiving the support she desired from her mother. The
impact of the message of the dream hit Estelle hard. In her attachment to her
mother's approval, she was left with no nourishment (the fridge was empty), no
way of moving out into the world (her car was stolen in broad daylight), and no
purse (her identity and money were lost). She had also lost a library book about

creativity. In other words, her knowledge about creativity was only on loan! In the dream, she ignored the two black girls who lived across the street and who called out her name. For Estelle, they represented the young feminine shadow energy trying to make itself known to her, but she didn't pay any attention. Her house, an image of her sense of herself, was run-down and neglected.

While the widow-mother in the tale of "Mother Hulda" favors one daughter over the other, Mother Hulda treats both equally. There is no scarcity of her love and attention. All she asks is commitment to the task, the work of life. Gold Mary in the tale is never able to fully get her widow-mother's love and approval, even when she returns showered with gold. In order to be free, she needs to separate from the expectation that she must have her mother's love in order to survive.

After working with this tale, Estelle had the following dream:

> I was back at my mother's house. I had been eating some kind of yellow, sticky toffee, which was sticking in my throat. I was trying to pull it out. As I pulled, more and more became stuck at the back of my throat. Finally, I managed to pull it all out and stuffed it into a garbage bag. I didn't want anyone to see the mess.

In her dream, Estelle struggled to get the sweet stuff, the "sticky niceness" out of her throat. Until she did this, she could not speak in her own voice.

A few weeks later, Estelle had lunch with her mother. She discovered that her mother had not felt loved by her own parents and believed that they preferred her sister (Estelle's aunt). Her mother experienced her own mother (Estelle's grandmother) as distant and aloof and her father as verbally abusive. Once more, the cycle continued—except, now Estelle was conscious and could make another choice for her own life and for her relationship with her spouse and children. Estelle made the decision to break the pattern experienced by her grandmother, her mother, and herself. She committed herself to not passing on this toxic legacy to her own daughter.

After reflecting on this tale, Jessica also explored the issue of "toxic niceness." She wrote in her journal:

> A crow came three times, insisting that I pay attention. Crows are harpy and associated with witches. Mother Hulda demands that we look at pitch; everything isn't nice, either black or white. Life isn't always "nice!"

Then Jessica remembered a nursery rhyme she had heard as a child, "Sugar and spice and everything nice, that's what little girls are made of." This is the dilemma of the child who survives by accommodating to the desires of others. The message she receives is, "You must choose between being 'nice' (always responsive to others' expectations) and being 'harpy' (resentful, rebellious, controlling, and judgmental)." Jessica recognized that she had a third choice. She could claim her own soul and live freely without having to judge, blame, *or* save others.

After we worked on the tale of "Mother Hulda," Jessica dreamed:

> I was standing on the top rung of a ladder to get a striped water pitcher off a high shelf. The ladder was very shaky and weaving back and forth. I got the pitcher down safely. Then I looked down and saw below me a pit filled with coins at my feet. There were pennies on top. Then, as I looked further down, I saw silver coins underneath. Also, I discovered that there was an old printing press stored in another room. I wondered if there were any printer's trays.

Jessica associated the water pitcher in her dream with her mother-in-law, a woman caught up in pleasing others. In the dream, Jessica tried to claim her feminine container (the water pitcher), which she connected with her emotional life. This part of herself has been stored away almost out of her reach. The ladder is shaky and "weaving" back and forth." Weaving is generally related to the feminine activity of making a new pattern, pulling threads together, and generating new life. Once she safely retrieves her emotional container from the place where it had been "shelved," Jessica sees the rich source of her energy (associated with money) that lies in a pit at her feet. The riches are hers! She just has to sort the coins and claim this energy for her own creative life. The dream also suggests that what is needed for the expression of her creativity is available in another room. This dream encouraged Jessica to continue her writing and to let the emotional impact of her mother and grandmother's story be expressed. Then she dreamed:

> I was sorting through my mother's stuff deep in the basement. There were linens there which are very old, dusty, and dirty. There was also a large, bread-making table. People were coming and taking what they needed and wanted. I was happy to have the clutter removed. I would keep the bread-making table.

Months later, at our weeklong retreat, Jessica made bread for the group as part of her ritual of celebrating her own life and the rising of her creative energy out of the well of Mother Hulda.

The Dilemma of Dark Mary

In the original version of the tale, when the dark sister returns home, the cock on the well announces her return: "Cock-a-doodle-do! Our dirty *slut* has come home too." The dark sister prostitutes herself for what she expects will be gold. There is no heart in the tasks she performs; it is all a pretense in the hope of an easy gain.

In Jessica's dialogue with the dark sister, Dark Mary expressed her rage at being crippled by her mother's message that "all you have to do is go through the motions." After she avoided blackening her hands with work (her refusal to take the bread out of the oven), she ended up covered in pitch that could *never* be removed.

In the tale, Dark Mary does not choose to jump into the well of grief. She is pushed by her widow-mother and by a greedy desire to obtain the riches that her sister has received. She does not feel the despair that, when acknowledged, finally frees. She is just going through the motions. Gold Mary jumps into the well because of the "despair of her heart." Dark Mary doesn't feel with her heart. She calculates with her head. She pretends to be about the process of self-discovery in order to achieve a secondary gain. But Mother Hulda has no time for pretenders. She cannot be deceived. She sees the intentions of our hearts and responds accordingly, although she always gives us the chance to learn, if we are open to doing so. She is never partial and always fair and just.

Dark Mary is given the same opportunities as her golden sister. She finds herself, like her sister, in the beautiful meadow and follows the same path. But Mother Hulda knows that the blood on the spindle is not from Dark Mary's attempts at spinning (that is, at claiming her true feminine potential). Her wound is self-inflicted. To make her spindle bloody, she put her hand into the thorn hedge. Even her wound is one of deceit!

Here we find an interesting contrast between the fate of Gold Mary and that of her dark sister. While Gold Mary claims her feminine (in the image of the spindle) and is willing to shed her blood (that is, do the work of becoming a woman), Dark Mary only pretends to grow up. She refuses to get her hands dirty (blackened) by honoring what is risen in her and ready to be taken from the oven. (In the Italian culture, to have a "bun in the oven" means to be pregnant with a child.) Dark Mary also chooses to avoid the ripened apples (her own ripe feminine nature), claiming that they might injure her by falling on her head. This avoidance is a metaphor for having to change her way of thinking.

Dark Mary is a puella, an eternal little girl, a woman fearful of growing up. She passes by the ripe opportunities she is given to claim her own unique life. She chooses instead to live *as if* she is a woman, while protecting herself (through mainly unconscious deceit) from the consequences of moving from childhood to womanhood. Although seemingly favored by her widow-mother, Dark Mary is also maternally deprived. The chosen, and often overprotected, child is also contaminated by her mother's ambitions for her. This child may actually be more severely psychologically damaged by her mother's toxicity than the neglected child who does not identify with her mother and who, therefore, remains separate.

Gold Mary, in her grief at losing her spindle down the well, goes to her widow-mother in tears. Her mother shows no sympathy for her and, instead, reacts with rage. In contrast, Dark Mary even deceives her own mother. She doesn't spin as she was sent to do. Instead, she inflicts a false wound on herself with the thorn hedge.

Women who are caught in their Dark Mary side often feel isolated. They find it difficult to connect in mature relationships with others, because this would demand that they grow up and take responsibility for their own lives. They find it difficult to stay with the process of doing their inner work on the path of individuation, although they may appear enthusiastic at first. Their motives are often related to secondary gains: the gold they expect is the disappearance of painful symptoms, the restoration of life as it once was, or the regaining of control in their lives and the lives of others. But Mother Hulda is not deceived. She gives Dark Mary a fair warning, which she doesn't heed. Instead, Dark Mary continues to believe that she will receive the reward of gold (consciousness), even though she doesn't do the work necessary to obtain the insight she needs. Her condemnation is severe. She comes home covered in pitch, announced as a "dirty slut." She has prostituted her soul for the promise of gold. She returns, not with the radiance of her sister, but with the black pitch "sticking to her fast and, never as long as she lived, could it be removed."[108]

Redeeming Our Shadows

Our conscious commitment to no longer prostitute our unique and creative souls *releases* the Dark Mary in us from the name of *slut*. We may make this decision when we find ourselves pregnant with a child and facing the responsibilities of motherhood. Or, we may make it when we discover our hidden creative gifts and choose to manifest them to others: in poetry, painting, preparing a beautiful meal, composing a song, or leading an organization.

Our shadow sides may continue to distress us. They are, by their very nature, designed to afflict our comfort. But our shadows do not have to overwhelm us.

Their presence is important for us to live honestly, grounded in our connection to Mother Hulda.

If we refuse to acknowledge our shadows, we will, like Dark Mary, blame others for the losses and disappointments in our life. We may also blame our sisters (and other women) for what we have actually brought on ourselves. We may even find ourselves seeking to wound them in revenge.

Our shadows are always with us. When we acknowledge and claim our dark sides, new energy is available for our lives. This does not mean that our shadows have disappeared. It simply means that, in the new light of consciousness, other shadows have formed. Each of us can be deceived by the ambitious widow-mother in us who believes that going through the required steps, taking the right courses, getting the degree, and completing the therapy will relieve us of our shadow sides. Then we would, indeed, be as naïve as Dark Mary!

The good-enough mother must reflect both the light and dark sides of her child, or the child can become stuck in a cycle of narcissistic need. Remaining in the idealized state of the little girl (a puella), the child/woman sees gold as her right and goes into a depression when she doesn't receive from life that to which she feels entitled.

Several women in the group recognized the toxic Dark Mary within themselves. When we acknowledge both the shadow and the light within, we are free to be who we truly are. We are delivered from the pretense that Mother Hulda will not tolerate.

As we began our work on the tale of "Mother Hulda," Claire had the following dream:

> A woman had inherited the job as queen or chieftain of a tribe
> of people. Through false pretenses, she lured young women to
> the village and ended up using them as prostitutes. One man
> was able to help three women escape by tying them around his
> waist with their feet off the ground, putting huge clothes on over
> them, and walking out with them. He brought them to where
> I was staying. We went back for more. I helped some of them
> escape by taking them by boat over the water, but I was pursued.
> I hid behind an outcrop of rocks, but they still followed me. So
> I speared one of them and got away. When I left the mission, I
> walked along a hallway with many pictures of similar pursuits.
> Then I went down a set of stairs to the ground.

Claire noted that the woman wounded in her own feminine might wound the feminine in other women. We see this clearly in the tale of "Mother Hulda." The widow-mother is wounded in her feminine nature and refuses to be in a relationship with Gold Mary. She treats her like a prostitute, using her for her own needs, continually reminding her of her inferior status in the family.

When Claire, in her dream, attempted to rescue the prostituted women ensnared by the deceptive queen, she had to confront the negative force with her spear, a symbol of her own incisive masculine power. She knew there had been many similar encounters in the past because they were recorded in the pictures in the hallway. Claire recognized that she needed to explore how the dream image of the tribal queen mirrored her own encounters with her inner feminine persecutor who holds her soul captive.

For Claire, the tale of "Mother Hulda" points to the return of her own masculine, that part of herself that is focused and purposeful and claims her own power. She reported that she felt "fired up" after working with the tale. She saw Mother Hulda as having a "penis for a tongue. What she spoke happened; power spewed from her mouth."

Claire envisioned herself claiming her own power from Mother Hulda. Then she shared the following from her active imagination work:

> A woman walked out of the forest to a cliff trail that overlooked the beach and the water, a huge panorama. It was rugged country. She was older than I, but very agile and free in her movements—light, energetic, lilting movements. She walked among the rocks where the rattlesnakes lived. She gave them enough warning of her coming, and neither was disturbed by the other. I called out to her. I wanted to talk with her before she got too far ahead. She waited for me and said there is nothing to fear. The path is clear and unobstructed, and I realized that she is basically me without the fear. I realized that this meant that I could live my life with less effort and experience more energy.

This reflection was a marvelous, freeing experience for Claire. She was the heroine of her own soul. She was neither her own persecutor, the negative feminine chieftain queen (who she associated with her internalized negative mother), nor is she the abducted feminine prostitute (a victim in despair). Claire consciously chose a third path, one without fear, which offers her the promise of creative energy for her own life.

Welcoming Gold Mary

As she reflected on the tale of "Mother Hulda," Michaela noticed resistance within herself to entering the story and allowing its meaning to penetrate her consciousness. To move through her resistance, she chose to do an active imagination dialogue between Gold Mary and her widow-mother. Michaela wrote in the voice of the beautiful daughter who returned radiant and covered in gold:

> Oh Mother, I wish you could see where I've been. I met an old woman who took me in. I was so happy with her, but something drew me back here to you. It seems to me that your life is not very happy, and I want to tell you what I've learned. I would like to see you as happy as Mother Hulda.

Michaela realized that this was a moment of choice for the widow-mother. She could remain frozen in her old way of thinking—or, she could open herself to hear Gold Mary's invitation. Michaela recognized that she was, of course, talking about her relationship with her own mother. The part of her who is Gold Mary yearns to reconcile with her mother and to share with her all that she has learned. Michaela's mother, now deceased, was actually a widow-mother who struggled to support her family after her husband's early death. With tears, Michaela acknowledged the many ways her mother had responded to her needs when she was growing up, something she had not previously been able to do.

Then, as we continued exploring the tale of "Mother Hulda," Michaela dreamed:

> I came out of the subway right onto a GO train and discovered that I was going in the wrong direction. I got off, but a woman was trying to hold me back. I had to go through a maze of derelict buildings to get out. I was feeling very tired. Then I met two women. They told me that where I was standing was a bus stop. Another woman, who was Chinese, joined us. We were chatting about our mothers.

Another dream in which Michaela's sister appeared followed a few days later:

> My sister Sarah was driving very fast, passing a bus on the right-hand side. The visibility was very poor, and she was really speeding. I was frightened and concerned for our survival.

In the first dream, Michaela associated having to take the GO train with not having her own way of moving in the world. When she emerged from the subway (the well of her unconscious underground) she went in the wrong direction. A woman, who she associated with an image of Mother Hulda, held her back and forced her to go through a maze of derelict buildings. Michaela saw this part of the dream as a reminder that she needed to stay with her vulnerability (the derelict, shadow side of herself), which she would prefer to ignore.

Michaela associated the bus stop with a place where people boarded the vehicle whose route was determined by the collective patriarchal world in which she found herself. There were two other women waiting for the bus. A third woman appeared who was Chinese. Michaela associated this image with a foreign side of her feminine that she did not know. They were chatting about their mothers. Her sister Sarah is a soul mate and heart-friend to Michaela. She was a surrogate mother to Michaela when she was growing up. Michaela connected Sarah with a part of herself that disregards the rules of safety and potentially threatens her survival. In the dream, Sarah was determined to get past the bus even though it was dangerous and there was the possibility of a crash. Michaela wrote, "I was afraid of a collision with the bus," an image for her of the collective patriarchal world. "I needed to trust, even though I could not see the road clearly." Michaela awakened from her dream with the message, "Trust that what you are doing is right."

Michaela lives in the corporate world of academia. The images in her first dream caution her to pay attention to the direction in which she is going. She knows she must not be too quick to run from her vulnerability. She also appreciated that the conversation at the bus stop in her dream was about mothers. Michaela realized that, in rejecting her mother, she joined the patriarchal world of her father, where she felt she would have more power than her widow-mother.

Choosing to Go Home Again

In the tale, when Gold Mary expresses her "great longing to go home," Mother Hulda replies, "It pleases me that you should wish to go home."[109]

Michaela was drawn to dialogue with her deceased mother through the process of active imagination. She expressed her gratitude to her mother and her regret at her emotional estrangement from her mother when she was alive:

> I can feel your loving presence with me now. My wounds are deep, Mom, but they are healing, and I'm beginning to see myself as a beautiful woman. I have finished Mother Hulda's work, and I am coming home.

Before the Gold Mary leaves, Mother Hulda gives her back the spindle she has dropped into the well. Her own feminine identity, the symbol of her creativity, is returned to her. Mother Hulda expresses her pleasure that Gold Mary wants to return home. She can now take what she learned from her plunge into the well of grief and bring it into her conscious life so that her experience can inform her new life choices. She no longer has to live as if her role as the rejected daughter, weeping and bleeding at the side of the well, is her fate. Mother Hulda has generously showered her with the gold of enlightenment. She is rewarded because she is willing to do the work.

Michaela noted that Mother Hulda does not force Gold Mary to leave, and she does not give her a time limit. She waits until we are ready to allow the new consciousness and awareness of our choices to come to the surface. Gold Mary does not ask Mother Hulda's permission to leave. And, she did not ask her what she *should* do, as she had asked her widow-mother when she lost her spindle in the well. Then, she followed her widow-mother's instructions. Now, she makes her own decision. In receiving her own spindle, the golden daughter has reclaimed her power to spin her own life threads and weave a new life pattern that allows her feminine creativity to be acknowledged and valued.

Estelle wrote in her active imagination dialogue between Gold Mary and her widow-mother: "Mother Hulda taught me how to do the work that needed to be done. I am glad, not just for the gold (new consciousness), but for the release the work has brought me to claim my own life and to honor my own creative gifts."

Being the Good-enough Mother

Exploring the images of Mother Hulda as a positive mother and the widow as a negative mother led to a discussion among the women about being good enough mothers to their children. While recognizing that no one can take on the role of the all-faithful Mother Hulda, each of the women expressed her concern that she would not pass on the toxic mothering she had experienced to her own children. The questions raised by the mothers in the group included:

- Where is my grounding as a mother?
- How do I live my life in the real world, even when it is difficult to do everyday chores that never seem to end?
- What happens to my creative life when I am bound to the everyday demands of my family?
- How do I know if I am a good enough mother?

Becoming a mother is at once immensely creative and profoundly grounding. To maintain the balance requires maturity and consciousness in the daily struggle to be present to the child in a healthy way.

The woman who is carrying Dark Mary into her role as mother has the potential to either grow up through motherhood or to continue to be a child with her child. To leave her childhood state, the little girl in Dark Mary must discipline herself first and then, her child. This is necessary so that the child can learn the importance of being grounded in his/her human existence.

In the story of Peter Pan,[110] Wendy Darling, a child herself, is asked by Peter and the other "lost boys" to be the mother they each had lost in infancy. Peter reports that he fell out of his pram and his mother never found him. He flies from place to place, refusing to grow up. In fact, he wants Wendy to mother him so that he doesn't have to grow up. When Wendy returns to her own mother, Peter extracts a promise from her that she will come each year to do his "spring cleaning." Wendy longs to keep flying with Peter, but she recognizes that she needs to make another choice. She becomes a mother, and the cycle continues with her own daughter and her daughter's daughter. Women (like Wendy), who have come back down to earth in order to be more than a pretend mother, are at risk of partnering with *puers*, that is, little boy/men who don't want to grow up. Such men often withdraw from their responsibility as fathers, leaving the women living like widow-mothers.

The tale of "Mother Hulda" accentuates the importance of women who are mothers acknowledging their own true masculine side (not a Peter Pan substitute), so that their children don't find themselves being raised by widow-mothers with no inner masculine power.

Some women in the group found themselves in the position of being daughter-mothers, that is, mothers to their own mothers. Alexis, Estelle, and Claire were able, through much struggle, to feel compassion for their mothers' pain and, at the same time, disentangle themselves from their roles as their mothers' rescuers.

Four Years Later

We revisited the tale of "Mother Hulda" four years after our original work on the tale. Alexis shared with the group how she had come to recognize Dark Mary within herself. She realized that she frequently yearned for what was missing in her life, instead of celebrating the gold she had been given by Mother Hulda. She wrote:

> The first time we reflected on the tale I saw Mother Hulda calling me to more discipline, inviting me to take the middle path

of balance that is narrow and requires awareness and diligence. Now, I am more aware of my return from the well of initiation in the darkness. I now ask myself, "What do I have to bring back?"

Then, Alexis dreamed:

> I was going down and down into the earth. First I passed down cement steps, which then turned to earth. I continued down until I came to an underground river. Then I realized I could see the sky above me. I could not stay there, even though it was quite beautiful. I needed to go back up. I met a young man and I hitched on to him. We came back up together.

Alexis acknowledged that she was now ready to claim her own masculine energy and focus on her creative work with renewed discipline.

Estelle associated our first exploration of the tale of "Mother Hulda" with her struggle to let her children follow their own hearts' desires. She found herself, four years later, continuing to discern how to share her music in ways that inspired other women to also share their creative gifts. Revisiting the tale reopened the old wound of her unresolved estranged relationship with her sister. Estelle reported being more conscious now of what it meant to be a sister to other women. She recognized that, even though there hadn't been healing in her relationship with her own sister, she was committed to her relationships with the women in the group who had become her sisters.

When we revisited the tale four years later, Claire was reminded of how, over a period of more than twenty years, she had met a series of toxic women from whom she had had to reclaim her power. She recognized how these devouring women drew her into relationships of trust and then robbed her of her creative work. She vowed: "*Never again!* Now I can come home knowing what ails me. I know there is no other way; I can't skip the journey, and I need to do my own work and move out from the past. I long for the time when I could hug my mother, and she wouldn't suck."

Four years later, Emily was able to honor all the healing that had taken place within her as she used her gifts in healing others. She wrote, "Frau Hulda is beckoning to me. How will I respond? When I see snowflakes, I am reminded of her."

Emily remembered that when we originally worked on the tale she had imagined Mother Hulda having a picnic with her stepmother in the meadow at the bottom of the well. Emily offered prayers of compassion for her stepmother. A short time later, her stepmother called unexpectedly to ask Emily for her for-giveness. Emily recognized that she no longer had overwhelming negative feel-ings toward her stepmother and stepsister. She acknowledged that her stepmother would never be able to be a mother to her. "I no longer need to go into the details of the story of my life. It's not about blame anymore, but choice."

When Michaela revisited the tale four years later, what continued to be power-ful for her was "being able to go back home," which, she recognized, "involved compassion for myself and my mother." She expressed gratitude that through her initial work on the tale she had been able to reconcile with her mother. Michaela had emotionally abandoned her mother more than forty years earlier because she believed her mother had abandoned her when her brother was born.

Four years later, when we revisited the tale of "Mother Hulda," Jessica wrote:

> I feel I owe Mother Hulda a great deal. I feel released from toxic shame. All I ever knew was a toxic mother, but Mother Hulda taught me that there was another way. I've finished writing my mother's story. So much of what I learned from Mother Hulda is in the story. I have also claimed my own role in the story. I feel relief from pretense and release from my maternal family curse. My growing edge has been not to get caught back in toxic shame, to stay vigilant, to be positive, to be creative, to be open to possibilities, and to celebrate each day.

The tale of "Mother Hulda" taught Jessica to recognize her feelings of fear of abandonment and to reclaim her own feminine soul. She wrote:

> Mother Hulda taught me to accept my limits and do what needs to be done, to realize that to love with compassion is what makes my spirit come alive. She taught me to give without expecting anything in return, freeing myself to accept the gold of conscious freedom. I now understand that discipline doesn't restrict me, only expectations do!

We began our exploration of the tale of "Mother Hulda" with the recognition of the two sides of the mother: the positive side, which holds, and the negative side, which rejects. We examined how this split in the feminine within the mother resonates in the split between the positive and negative aspects of the daughter. In the tale of "Mother Hulda," the daughter is split into Gold Mary (who fights depression because of her connection to a rejecting, powerless mother) and Dark

Mary (who is caught in grandiosity because of her bond with a devouring, doting mother).

There is no magical healing for the daughter who carries a mother abandonment wound. She must make the descent into the unknown place of the unconscious where "the mother who holds dwells" and do the work necessary to claim the gold of enlightenment.

Many of the women in the group associated Mother Hulda with Sophia, a biblical feminine image of Divine Wisdom. As our spiritual mother, Mother Hulda is a faithful midwife of the unfolding process of discovering our true selves and claiming our power to live creative, meaningful lives. She longs to bring us home. But the only way home is through the descent into the well, the passageway of our own rebirth. There are no shortcuts, and she will not be deceived. If we enter the process to get gold for our own personal gain, we will be left with pitch sticking to our egos.

If we jump into the well of grief and have the courage to plumb the depths with a heart open to transformation, ready to make whatever changes we need to make in our lives, then Mother Hulda will offer us the gold of enlightenment. In recognition of this gift, Michaela wrote, "The gold with which she showers us is lightness of heart."

Mother Hulda is an image of the true mother and the midwife of the restoration of our creative souls. Awareness of her presence within each woman in the group brought energy for holding one another in a faithful, loving way through times of pain and loss. Filled with her promise of life, we found the courage to be soul midwives to one another through the birthing canal of the well of grief.

Reflection questions:

Chapter IV—Rising From the Well of Grief: The Tale of Mother Hulda

1. How do you experience Mother Hulda's presence in your own life?
   - How is she manifested in your unconscious, in your dreams?
   - What do you need in order to move your own healing process forward?
   - Who needs to be included in that healing process?

2. Are there unresolved issues in your relationships with your sisters or other women who are a part of your life? What next steps can you take to move to a place of reconciliation, either with them or within yourself?

3. Who is the Dark Mary within you? How do you recognize her presence in your life?

4. Who is the Gold Mary in you? How is she manifested?

CHAPTER V

WAKING FROM THE SLEEP OF AGES: THE TALE OF BRIAR ROSE

> I was bred and conditioned to passivity like a milk cow.
> Waking is the sharpest pain I have ever known.
> —Marge Piercey, "The Judgment"

The tale of "Briar Rose," popularly known as "Sleeping Beauty," has been dramatized in movies and ballet performances across the Western world. All of the women in the group had been exposed to the story when they were young. Many remembered the song they had sung as young girls, "Some Day My Prince Will Come." While this song is part of a Disney movie entitled "The Tale of Snow White," in actuality the movie is an attempt at combining the tales of "Sleeping Beauty," "Cinderella," and "Snow White" into one. Beneath the romanticized version of the tale lies another story, which the women identified when we explored the tale as a group. It contains a profound message about the fate of the girl child with a silent mother who grows up under the benevolent protection of the patriarchal world of her father.

When I began editing the notes for this chapter, I had just attended the forty-ninth session of the Commission on the Status of Women held at the United Nations in New York. In 1995, at the conclusion of the fourth World Conference on the Status of Women, held in Beijing, China, the majority of the participating nations had agreed to work toward achieving gender equality. Ten years later, six thousand women, from all over the world, gathered to measure how and if those promises had been kept.

As I reflected on my experience at the conference and recalled the reactions of the seven women in the group to the tale of "Briar Rose," what struck me were the parallels between the two experiences. Both were about the reality of living in a patriarchal world in which the fathers make the rules and hold the power.

While I was sorting through my notes trying to decide how to begin this chapter, I noticed a book on my shelf wedged between a copy of *The Maiden King*, by

Woodman and Bly,[111] and *Sophia, Goddess of Wisdom,* by Matthews.[112] The title wasn't visible, as the binding was black and the letters were worn off. It had long since lost its paper jacket. It pricked my curiosity (which was what led Briar Rose to find the spindle) and I got up from my chair to see what it was. When I picked up the book, I began to laugh! It was entitled, *Kiss Sleeping Beauty Goodbye,* by Madonna Kolbenschlog.[113] Published in 1979, it was among the first of my collection of books on the psychology of women. Since the "library angel" had led me to the book, I took the time to review it. As I read, I discovered that, twenty-five years later, while some things have changed for women, much has remained the same.

The tale of "Briar Rose" can be found in a variety of forms since Charles Perrault first published it in *Histories of Times Past* in 1697. The first version was entitled, *"La Belle Au Bois Dormant"* or "The Sleeping Beauty in the Wood." Variations of the tale are evident across Europe from the fourteenth century on. Some early tales report the rape of the sleeping princess, who awakens to find herself pregnant.[114] The version of the tale we used for our work was Grimm's "Briar Rose."[115] We also explored the original ending of the tale as translated from the French version by Perrault in 1729.[116] While the Grimm's tale ends with the awakened princess and prince living happily ever after, the earlier tale goes further to explore the fate of Sleeping Beauty. The following is a synopsis of the Grimm brothers' version of the story.

A Synopsis of the Tale of Briar Rose

Once upon a time, in a land not far away, a king and queen long to have a child. One morning, while the queen is in her bath, a frog jumps out of the water and announces that she will have a child before the year is out. The little frog's prediction comes true, and the queen gives birth to a beautiful baby girl. The king is so filled with joy that he decrees that a great celebration will be held in the castle and that the wise women of the kingdom will be invited to come and shower his daughter with the finest virtues and gifts. As he only has twelve gold plates, only twelve wise women can be invited, and the thirteenth one has to stay home.

At the banquet, after eleven of the wise women have bestowed gifts of beauty, grace, wealth, and kindness on the little princess, the thirteenth wise woman appears. She declares in a loud voice, "When the princess is fifteen she will prick her finger on a spindle and fall dead." The king and queen are horrified! The twelfth wise woman then steps forward; as she cannot reverse the curse, but only modify it, she says, "The princess will not die, but only fall asleep for one hundred years."

To protect his daughter and prevent the curse from coming to pass, the king confiscates all the spindles in the kingdom and has them destroyed. The princess grows up, as the wise women had predicted, to be beautiful and kind. All those who know her, love her. On the day that the curse is to take place (her fifteenth birthday), the king and queen are away. Curious to explore the parts of the castle she hasn't seen, Briar Rose climbs the steps to an old tower, where she finds a rusty key in the door. When she turns the key the door opens, and Briar Rose sees an old woman with a strange object in her hand. "What are you doing?" she asks. The old woman replies, "I am spinning." "May I try?" Briar Rose asks, and the old woman hands her the spindle. As soon as she grasps it in her hand, Briar Rose pricks her finger and immediately falls into a deep sleep. In that moment, the wind dies. Just then, the king and queen return to the castle, and they and the entire kingdom fall asleep, including the flies on the wall. As the years pass, a great briar hedge grows up around the castle, until finally it completely covers the roof—not even the flag was visible.

Stories of the beautiful sleeping princess are told from one generation to the next. Many young princes attempt to get through the briars, only to get caught and die a painful death. One day, just before the hundred years are up, a young prince comes into the neighboring village inquiring about the castle with its beautiful sleeping princess. All those he meets discourage him, as they had witnessed the terrible deaths of those who had tried to get through the briars. But the young prince is determined to see the sleeping princess. Much to his amazement, as he approaches the briars they blossom and part to let him through. Then, they close behind him. When he enters the castle, the prince finds the king and queen and every creature in the kingdom asleep, even the flies on the wall. He searches the castle until he finds the sleeping princess in the tower. She is more beautiful than he had imagined! When he bends down and kisses her, she opens her eyes and smiles. In that moment, the wind blows, and the entire kingdom awakes. The prince and princess come down from the tower together and are greeted by the king and queen and the entire kingdom. A great feast is prepared and Briar Rose and the prince are married and live happily together ever after.[117]

Following the process we used with the previous fairy tales, we explored the tale of "Briar Rose" by inserting ourselves into the story, primarily taking on the role of the daughter. I invited each of the women to engage in a series of active imagination dialogues with the characters in the tale, as if they were images in her own dreams. We set up dialogues between the princess and the following images: the king and queen, the thirteenth wise woman, the old woman with the spindle, and the prince. Although we explored the tale together, each woman approached the story in her own way. Each one shared with the group whatever part of her reflections she chose. She also recorded any dreams that occurred during her active imagination work and after our exploration of the tale in the group.

The Overprotective Father

Although the king in the tale is presented as loving his daughter, his need to control her life and to protect her from her own destiny is the very thing that brings about her one-hundred-year sleep-death. Perhaps he thinks he can outsmart the thirteenth wise woman. However, the consequences of his attempt to protect his daughter for "her own good" bring about her long, deep sleep (an unconscious state) and that of the entire kingdom. He also falls asleep and cannot be awakened until she regains consciousness.

In the tale, the king attempts to save his daughter by destroying all the spindles in the kingdom. Spinning and weaving are connected with the feminine capacity to conceive and give birth to a child. As noted in earlier chapters, the spindle in many European cultures was associated with the mother's family, who were referred to as the *distaff* side of the family. The spindle is also a symbol of the wise old woman. The father who breaks all the spindles, the instruments of preparing the threads of life, renders the feminine world of the girl child powerless. She is then dependent on his world for protection. The father who idealizes his daughter and attempts to protect her from life's struggles, and the mother who has no spindle of her own, create a state of extended paralysis throughout the kingdom.

In the original version of the tale, the description of the sleeping castle was brief. The Grimm brothers, however, evidently couldn't resist embellishing the scene with details of the entire court asleep, including all the animals, and even the flies on the wall. This graphic image paints a picture of the paralyzing effect of the suppression of the feminine in the girl child herself, and in the entire natural world. Briar Rose tries to claim her feminine identity when she takes hold of the spindle and attempts to spin. But she has never been taught what becoming a woman is all about. As soon as she touches the spindle, a symbol of her creative feminine potential, she pricks her finger and immediately falls into a deep sleep. In tribute to her lost spirit, the wind dies and all life becomes paralyzed, frozen in that moment.

Taking hold of the spindle and drawing blood on her fifteenth birthday is also associated with the first menstrual cycle of the young princess.[118] The awakening of puberty for girls who have not been prepared for their passage into womanhood can have the effect of putting their sexuality to sleep.

In her active imagination as Briar Rose, Estelle pleaded with the king and queen: "If only you had taught me to spin! You wanted to protect me, but I felt and took on your fear. I had to hide my sexuality."

When Estelle dialogued with the old woman in the tower, she asked her: "Where did you get your spindle? I thought all of them were destroyed." The old woman replied: "I hid mine, so that they couldn't find it and destroy it."

When that which is of value to her feminine nature is hidden, the adolescent daughter feels frightened and confused by her awakening sexuality. "Depending upon a girl's relationship to her own sexual nature, the pubescent girl will bloom or suddenly fade."[119]

Many women learned about menstruation as *the curse*. The word *bleeding*, however, comes from the Old English word *bloedsen,* which means blessing.[120] For the women in the group, becoming a woman and being fertile for spinning and weaving new life was not a time of celebration. It was whispered about, if discussed at all, with the caution not to mention it to fathers and brothers. It was interpreted to them as a secret curse only incurred by girls and women, from which men and boys were exempt.

The curse comes to Briar Rose because one of the wise women is excluded and ignored. Her mother and father are out of the castle the day she becomes fifteen, the day the curse was to take effect. She finds herself alone in her pubescent world. Her curiosity to explore that from which she has been sheltered naturally emerges.

The king thinks he has destroyed all the spindles (a metaphor for having thoroughly repressed the feminine energy in the kingdom), so he does not feel he needs to worry about the prediction of the thirteenth wise woman. But the rejected wise woman refuses to be ignored or repressed. She hides the feminine spindle, a symbol of the capacity for creativity and life, in a tower, a phallic image of the patriarchy.

Patriarchy is based on fear of the mother, the feminine, and the body. Because her creative feminine energy has been repressed by her father all of her life, when Briar Rose goes to the tower (a phallic symbol of power) she is unprepared to handle the spindle. She draws blood and goes into a state of unconscious withdrawal from her creative feminine potential. This same state happens to many women who enter the tower of the corporate world without a sufficiently developed feminine identity to survive the test. Consequently, they are unable to live balanced lives as women and to access their true inner masculine that is in the service of their feminine nature. Instead, they take on the competitive, compulsive nature of the corporate lifestyle, often suffering the consequences in their bodies and psyches. Both Rita and Michaela attested to this from their own life experiences.

When Briar Rose pricks her finger, after grasping what she does not yet know how to hold, her entire world goes to sleep. The kingdom becomes paralyzed when the feminine is not allowed to develop and mature in a conscious, healthy way

Jessica realized how closely she identified her own life story with this tale. In an active imagination dialogue with Briar Rose, Jessica wrote:

> What is your longing, Briar Rose?
> Lying on your pallet, what does your heart seek?
> Are you waiting for a man to come and rescue you?
> What is your secret?

Briar Rose responds:

> Pity the man who comes to wake me up. If he thinks we'll live happily ever after, I've got news for him. I feel like a caged tiger. I'm so mad. He's more likely to get a kick in the crotch than a kiss on the lips. I'll no longer pretend that life is a bowl of cherries. I'm beginning to see into the pitch, the darkness, and it isn't pretty. How many times have I spoken up and then done battle with myself because I wasn't a nice girl? Well, no more pretending. I've had my back pinned against the wall long enough. I'm no longer waiting to be admired like a pinup girl, sweet, waiting for his desire, with no voice, no standpoint, and no choice of my own. What happens when he doesn't come, and no one tells me I'm pretty? Am I then unworthy?

We clearly hear the pain of Briar Rose's dilemma as reflected through Jessica. She no longer wants to pretend to be what she is not in order to gain the attention and protection of men. She doesn't want to be pinned up against the wall as an idealized image of what the men in her life want her to be. Following her reflections on the tale, Jessica wrote a poem. She shared the following concluding lines with the group:

> Don't pin me up like a pinup girl at the end of your spear.
> I want to get down and go through the door.

The image of the spear is an ancient metaphor for the paternal side of one's family, just as the distaff or spindle is the image of one's maternal family. Jessica experienced herself in a rage at all the patriarchal expectations that she had assumed, as a young girl, she had to meet in order to be worthy of the affection of men. She was expected, above all, to be "pretty and a nice girl" if she was to receive the praise and admiration of men. To be "unworthy" meant she had no value. After this reflection, Jessica dreamed: "My therapist's friend, Sharon, had committed suicide. I was aware that the wind was blowing outside."

When Jessica explored the images in her dream, she associated Sharon with a part of herself that tries to be cute and is always taking care of others. Sharon, in the dream, is her therapist's friend and, therefore, connected to her own healing process. It was significant to Jessica that the part of her who is cute and caring killed herself. Jessica recognized that when she got into the place of feeling compelled to be cute and caring, it did kill her soul. The last detail in the dream, "the wind was blowing," Jessica found to be an encouraging sign. She associated the wind with spirit and the breath of life. She acknowledged that she held her breath when she felt obliged to be cute and caring for others and unable to voice what is true for her own soul. Jessica remembered that the wind came up when Briar Rose awakened from her state of paralysis.

The Thirteenth Wise Woman: The Curse Turned to Blessing

Paradoxically, most of the women in the group saw the good king as the negative force in Briar Rose's life. They identified the evil thirteenth wise woman as the one who redeemed her from the deadly existence of remaining a dependent little girl all her life and not claiming her potential as a mature woman.

When Jessica did an active imagination dialogue with the thirteenth wise woman she related her to one of her great-aunts who always said what was on her mind. Jessica recognized that the thirteenth wise woman gives what is needed. Through Jessica's active imagination, the thirteenth fairy speaks to Briar Rose:

> I will not play your silly fairy tale games and pretend that everything is just peachy and harmonious. I can see that you are not happy. I can see that life is tough. I'm not upset about not being invited to the party, which is trivial. It is easier for you to believe that I am upset about rejection. Life is not about wishes. You have all the virtue you need already. You may as well be dead if you hide the truth about life. Life is tough. Life is unfair. Life is painful. Life has both dark and light sides. If you pretend that life is always pleasant, then you will wonder if there is something wrong with you when life gets tough. It is an illusion to think that if you are good, that life will be good to you. How will you

cope with the pain when you discover life is tough? You need to be able to stand on your own two feet, or you will just be another pretty face, waiting to be rescued, another wasted life, holding back, holding up, waiting.

Continuing her active imagination process, Jessica had the thirteenth wise woman then address the king:

Is she a toy, a plaything to perform and bring you joy, to be discarded when she turns fifteen because she is no longer cute and sweet to bounce on your knee? All she knows is how to perform for you. When others look at her pretty face she smiles and responds. You can't take it, you are jealous of her beauty. Rose is paralyzed, stuck, and confused. Your protection stifled her and caused her pain, grief, and sorrow. Lying in her bed, turned in on herself, what she is thinking?

Then, the thirteenth wise woman continued to admonish the king:

Who cares about the stupid party anyway? That is frivolous. Open your eyes and look. Can't you feel the toxic niceness—the little girl dressed in her party dress waiting to have everyone dote on her and tell her how pretty she is? She is the center of attention, pretending she is a princess. She has all that she wished for. Where are her virtues? They are withered and dead from lack of use. How will she cope with reality? Don't you care? Will she remain beautiful and sweet forever? What about old age? What about injustice? Is beauty enough?

The Benevolent Sexist King

The denouncement of the king's behavior in Jessica's active imagination dialogue resounds in the recent research by social psychologists, in which they make the distinction between benevolent and hostile sexism. They define benevolent sexism as solicitude for women who are seen to be weak and needing protection and hostile sexism as antagonism toward women for usurping the power of men.[121] None of the women in the group were familiar with this research. Their responses to the tale were based on their own life experiences.

The father/king in the tale of "Briar Rose" fits the description of the man who has embraced a benevolent sexist attitude toward women. Benevolent sexism is a "subjectively favorable, chivalrous ideology that offers protection and affection to women who embrace conventional roles," that is, those deemed appropriate for them by men.[122] Such a man may feel that he is cherishing, rather than restricting, the women to whom he promises protection. Many women may also experience his behavior as desirable. The cross-cultural research indicates that, while women generally reject hostile sexism, they are as much or more ready than men to choose benevolent sexism.[123] These women are prepared to hand over their spindles (their creative feminine energy) in exchange for protection, which would inevitably put their true feminine potential to sleep. The promises of the father/king are, of course, offered, "for her own good."

After we worked on the tale of "Briar Rose," Claire had the following dream:

> We were on a long passage of rock, which opened up into a very rugged, rocky shoreline overlooking the ocean. We had to find a path for our vehicle. It was treacherous and beautiful at the same time. Then, a group of us were in a dining room at an inn. Eileen was telling me about a physical therapy treatment she found helpful. She said she would get the man to demonstrate it. I watched, horrified, as the man, who had her standing, pulled, and yanked at her, put his foot on her, and mauled her so that her clothes started to fall off. While this was going on another woman was being done beside her. Two men were the practitioners. The other woman fell to the floor, trying to grab at her clothes and keep them on while the man was doing therapy on her.

Claire reported after her reflection on the dream, "I thought it was very invasive." Then she recalled: "The man working on Eileen stopped and rested his forehead on the wall. I saw that his left hand was like a hoof of a pig, a split hoof." This reminded Claire of an image of the devil, disguised as a healer. She commented that women, including herself, did not need to be abused in the process of what others, particularly the men in their life, saw as "for their own good."

Sometimes, what appears to be benevolent sexism is actually hostile sexism, "an antipathy toward women who are viewed as usurping men's power."[124] According to extensive social psychological research with over fifteen thousand men and women in sixteen countries across five continents, hostile and benevolent sexism are "complementary, cross-culturally prevalent ideologies, *both* of which are predictions of gender inequality."[125] In other words, where men hold the view that women are pure creatures who need to be protected (and whose love they need in order to feel complete), they often also hold the opposite view of women who step out of their expected roles or who are seen as threatening the power of men. This split view of women, as either pure and good (a Madonna/virgin) or tainted and evil (a whore/bitch) is called ambivalent sexism.[126] Many women have swallowed these projections and internalized the split. As a result, they experience conflicts within themselves around their feminine sexuality and power. Working on the tale evoked these internalized conflicts for several women in the group.

After working on the tale of "Briar Rose," Alexis had the following dream:

> I was going to a baptism. I had a large book of fairy tales, which I have had for a long time that is now tattered and torn. I was bringing it as a gift for the child. However, I was hiding it under my arm so that no one would see it. My mother was not there. Apparently, her house had been broken into and she had been threatened with being killed or violated. She invoked all her virgins and Madonnas and their miraculous powers. Then, I woke up.

In her dream, Alexis was bringing a book of fairy tales as a gift for a child who was going to be baptized. It was a book she had had for some time and it appeared to have been well read, as it was tattered and torn. Alexis knew the fairy tales in the book that she wanted to share with the child. But she was hiding the book, as she didn't want anyone to see her gift. There is evidently some secret she wanted to tell the child through the tales. In working with the images in her dream, Alexis realized that the secret is about her sexuality. In her dream, she saw her mother as frightened of being violated or robbed of her virtue and calling on her virgins and Madonnas and their miraculous powers to save her. Alexis clearly recognized the source of the repression of her sexuality as a young girl. Now, she wants to bring a new message to the child in her dream. After this reflection, Alexis wrote:

> In my family, children were puppets, well dressed and well behaved. In fact, the quieter they were the better. They were to be docile, obedient, respectful, and a credit to their parents. What mattered, above all, was what others would think of their upbringing. The tension was unbearable between my mother and myself during my adolescence. Bound in her own repressed sexuality, she was unable to talk to me about it. My virginity was protected at all costs, and I was kept in ignorance. The ideal set for me was purity, and I did a very good job of it. I wouldn't let

myself come close to anyone and kept others at bay. Sexuality outside of marriage was the gravest sin.

When Alexis addressed the king and queen in her active imagination as their daughter, they told her clearly: "We shall mold you into our image. You shall marry a rich prince and take care of us in our old age." That night, Alexis dreamed:

> I was in an old mansion. In the attic I found a crippled son who had been kept in the dark. He was so happy to see me!

When she reflected on the dream image of the crippled son, Alexis recognized this aspect of her young masculine as a part of her that had the potential to determine and follow a direction for her life consistent with her own destiny. But he was crippled and hidden away in the attic (a place where things are stored that are not in daily use). Alexis acknowledged that she needed to claim her own vital masculine energy, stand on her own two feet, and clearly choose a path for her own life. Then, she had another dream:

> I received a wedding announcement from England. My cousin Frances was getting married. The announcement was very original. It was illustrated with symbols made with ink in an oriental style. At the church, the bride came in by herself. She had a blue tulle veil over her shoulders. It hung loose and was not attached. I helped her with it. I was aware of how beautiful I looked. Several members of the family, including Lily (who is now dead) remarked how much I looked like my father. During the reception, an album was passed around with photographs of the groom's family. My sister and I were disgusted by the vulgarity of all of them. Not only were they obese, ordinary, and vulgar, they were also patriarchal. I turned to my sister and said: "Here is a good candidate for therapy. She needs to leave her father's house."

In her reflections on this dream, Alexis noted that the bride was not wearing a white veil, the sign of purity and virginity. Instead, she had a blue veil around her shoulders, which was a break with the tradition in her family. In Alexis's family, the sign of a virgin bride would be a white veil worn over her face and head. At the altar, her father would remove the veil from her face when he presented her to her husband-to-be. In this dream, not only was the veil blue, it was not over her face and head but around her shoulders. Also, there was no father present to "give her away" or hand her over to the protection of her husband. Alexis associated the color blue with the energy of her throat and her ability to speak what she knew to be true.

The dream reminded Alexis of how much she looks like her father. Amused by the ending of the dream, Alexis recognized that she still had aspects of herself that needed to leave "her father's house." She acknowledged that she had more conscious work to do to finally leave the protective realm of her father's, and now, her husband's house.

The Captivity of the Idealized Daughter

At her christening, at the father/king's invitation, twelve wise women come to bestow gifts on Briar Rose. Some give her beauty, others virtue and wealth—all of which would have made her a desirable wife for any prince approved by her father. The tale indicates, "She grew to be so beautiful, so modest, so sweet tempered and wise that no one who saw her could help loving her."[127] Young Briar Rose lives out all the socially desirable traits that are still prescribed for the idealized woman today. And, at the same time, we know (because everyone loves her) that she is successful at avoiding all the traits that are not determined as socially desirable in women: rebelliousness, arrogance, or being controlling and cynical.[128]

The daughter who believes that she must meet the expectations of her father at all costs may unconsciously go numb to any feelings that she herself may have, for fear that they may threaten her privileged status under his protection.

Briar Rose thinks she is free because she can roam the castle. She has no appreciation that she is imprisoned within its walls and within her role as her father's idealized daughter.

One evening, after we worked as a group on this tale, Estelle had the following dream:

> After a trip to hear a lecture about an ancient archeological site, we were all exhausted. My psychotherapist went to lie down on some paving stones next to a large old building that was an institution of learning. I thought it was amazing that she could do that. She didn't have any blanket to lie on, just the bare stones that were warm from the sun. I decided I also wanted to do this. I wasn't going to care what anyone thought.

What gets the king into trouble with the thirteenth wise woman is his concern about appearances. He only has twelve gold plates, so he only invites twelve wise women. His invitation to the celebration of the birth of his daughter is restricted by what he perceived as his limitations (the twelve plates).

Estelle associated the archeological site in her dream with the traditional rules and customs of her own cultural upbringing. She realized, in her reflection on the dream, that she needed to find her own way beyond the rules established by her father's world. Estelle associated the image of her psychotherapist in the dream with her own inner wise woman, who lies down on the "bare stones that were warm from the sun." Estelle saw this dream as an invitation to become more conscious of her own grounding in wisdom. In order to accept this invitation, she must let go of others' expectations of how she must behave. She wrote, "I no longer have to live up to the family name or to remain captive to my father's high expectations of me."

Then Estelle dreamed:

> I was with a group of people. We were trapped in a high-rise building and were trying to escape, to find a way out. Someone managed to open a door that led outside. We saw that we were extremely high up and would have to climb down a rope ladder. I was really scared. I had the new music I had composed with me in a portfolio. There was no way I could carry it and climb down the ladder. I don't like heights at the best of times and my balance isn't very good. It would mean that I would have to leave my work behind. I didn't want to do that, but I would be forced to do so if I wanted to escape. Then I was sitting, huddled in a room with a group of people. A storm was raging outside. We are close to the ocean and could hear the waves pounding and the wind howling. We were talking about the positive and the negative forces and the coming together of both of these. I asked them to explain the story to me.

This dream occurred as Estelle was preparing for her first solo concert. She wrote in response to her dream: "In reality, it is hard to 'follow one's bliss'; one has to cope with all the negative forces that arise. The negative voices within me tell me I am not competent, that I will be a failure, that I won't be ready on time." Estelle felt the fear of failure in her body as back pain between her shoulder blades.

Estelle recognized that her dream of being in a high-rise building (a tower) was about the high expectations she had of herself that keep her trapped. She recognized that she needed to find a third way out of the dilemma, beyond the alternatives of either taking her portfolio with her and potentially losing her balance on the ladder of success or leaving her creative work behind.

Briar Rose is trapped in the tower of her father's expectations with his promise that she will always be protected from the negative side of life. Instead, he propels her into it. It is in the tower (a metaphor for a phallic, patriarchal way of thinking where everything is under presumed control) that she met her fate.

When a girl is raised in a world where she feels forced to be an idealized woman, she continually lives with the fear that she cannot measure up to the high expectations that are placed on her. Indeed, her perception is accurate. She cannot live up to expectations that she will always be perfect. The dilemma Estelle faced in her dream put her in a state of terror (the storm raging), causing her to feel pain across her back. Estelle carried the burden of perfection in the area of her heart between her shoulder blades. She felt weighed down by the burden of carrying the inflated expectations of the "good daughter." Estelle acknowledged that she needed to let go of the yoke of perfection. Then she dreamed:

> I was going to leave home and go out on my own. My mother was advising me that I should take certain courses that would help me. I was trying to tell her that I was quite competent and self-sufficient and that I didn't need any courses.

This dream revealed to Estelle that she had internalized the message from her mother that she didn't know enough to go out on her own. Now, however, Estelle was clear. She was ready to trust her own wisdom and to claim her own destiny.

As Estelle continued to claim her own life beyond her mother and father's expectations, she had the following dream:

> I chased my son home through an underground tunnel. When I got home (it was not a house I know) he was trying to move a cupboard away from the wall. A strange woman was helping him. He eventually moved the cupboard. Behind it we found a whole secret compartment filled with keys. Before the strange woman left, she advised us to renovate the house before we sold it. She said we should change the room where we were (the bedroom) into the dining room and change the dining room on the other side of the kitchen into a bedroom. Then she left. I thought this would be a good idea because the dining room would lead onto the patio and be closer to the swimming pool.

Estelle recalled that, in the tale of "Briar Rose," there was a rusty (unused) key to the tower room where the thirteenth wise woman hid the last spindle. Estelle interpreted the dream image of the "secret compartment filled with keys" as a sign of her own hidden power to claim her own spindle and weave a new pattern for her life. The wise woman in her dream encouraged Estelle to reorganize her life after helping her find the missing keys. Then, according to the dream, she needed to sell the house and move to a new home, a new way of being.

Waiting for the Prince

But, you might wonder, what about the prince? Isn't he the hero of the tale? The prince is the personification of the idealized father, the romantic rescuer, and gallant knight for whom many women are waiting, often holding their breaths (a sleep-death state) for the moment of his arrival.

The prince carries the image of what Hollis calls the Magical Other.[129] Women living with the hope of meeting the prince (who someday will come) often appear in a somnolent state, not quite awake to life passing them by, day after day. Some, as adolescents, never crossed the bridge from childhood into womanhood. Others, caught in the illusion that they must remain thin to attract the prince, are imprisoned in eating disorders. One of the symptoms of anorexia nervosa, a disorder prevalent in adolescent girls, is the suppression of menstruation. This state effectively prevents them from growing up and claiming their potency as women.

These women (and they are numerous among us) are waiting to "have a life," and for the right "other" to bestow it upon them. They haven't yet recognized that, within themselves, they already have everything they need to claim their own lives.

> One of the great ideas that drives humankind is the fantasy of the "magical other," the notion that there is one person out there who is right for us, who will make our lives work, a soul-mate who will repair the ravages of our personal history, know what we want and meet those deepest needs; a good parent who will protect us from suffering and spare us the perilous journey of individuation.[130]

Claire's dialogue with the king in the fairy tale disclosed that he was afraid and therefore unable to let his daughter live her own life. While we were working on this tale, she found a photograph of herself as a young child riding on her father's shoulders. In the picture, her father's head covers her mouth. She responded vehemently to the image, "No way will I be piggybacked on my father's reality." Then

Claire had the following dream: "Students appeared for the class I was about to teach. They all waited in line in the basement."

Claire saw the dream image of the students in the basement as the part of herself that was waiting to awaken from the unconscious place, the part of her that was eager to learn. She then expressed her resolve, "I'm tired of being a lady-in-waiting."

The reality is that there is no prince out there, beyond ourselves, who can save us from the transformational suffering of life. The prince is an image of the true masculine within. He is that aspect of our inner selves that has been graced with the capacity to determine a direction for our lives and to stay focused on our intention in a purposeful, thoughtful way. He is neither capricious nor impulsive, but rather courageous and grounded in reality. He may be a part of ourselves that we've forgotten or lost, like the crippled little boy left in the dark attic who appeared in Alexis's dream.

Estelle had an interesting dream about a prince, the night after we worked on the tale:

> I was staying with Jane, who is married to Elvis Presley. We were all sleeping in one bed. When Elvis came home, he woke Jane, as he wanted to make love. She was annoyed with him for waking her. She felt he was taking advantage of her. She gave him a book to read (one I had given her) on hostility and allowing oneself to be taken advantage of by others. I couldn't believe it! How could she refuse Elvis in this way? I wouldn't have minded making love with him, but I couldn't suggest this, as Jane was my friend. Then they were driving me home. We all had to go to a wedding later on. I asked them to come in, but they had their little boy with them and wanted to take him home to sleep before the wedding. Later, we were at the wedding. I can recall sitting at a round table and noticing that one of the little coffee cups was cracked. The broken piece broke into three smaller pieces (it was like a triangular chip out of the cup which then broke into three smaller triangular pieces). Then, I was with Dorothy who was doing a critique of my creative work. We were talking about the location and pattern of the shadow and how the shadow could affect the work in an adverse way.

In this dream, Estelle associated Jane with a controlling and manipulative side of herself. Elvis, for her, carried the image of the handsome idealized masculine, indeed a symbol of Prince Charming for many women. But the Jane image in her dream didn't want to wake up for the prince to make love to her. Then, the cup at the wedding was chipped in the shape of a triangle, which then broke into three more pieces.

Estelle explored what the triangles in her dream might mean. For her "to be in a triangle" meant to be caught in the role of the persecutor, the victim, or the rescuer. All three are roles in which she isn't free to be herself. The last part of her dream indicated that she needed to be aware of the shadow patterns in her life that could affect her in an adverse way. Estelle connected this image with her relationships to the men in her life. She recognized that she needed to stay conscious of the ways in which she becomes ensnared in the shadow side of those relationships (by getting caught in the "triangle" as their rescuer or savior) and then feels victimized.

Estelle acknowledged how easy it was for her to accommodate to the needs of Prince Charming. In the dream, she gave her friend a copy of the book on hostility and allowing oneself to be taken advantage of by others. Estelle realized that she needed to read the book herself!

If we have to sacrifice ourselves to meet the needs of the prince, then he's probably a projection of our fantasy lives (a role Elvis played for many women). The true masculine of our internal prince is always in the service of our feminine nature, which includes: our generative and creative gifts, our openness to meaningful relationships, and our awareness of our bodies and the natural world.

When the one hundred years are over and the time of Briar Rose's awakening is at hand, the true prince is able to get through the briars. They bloom, open, and then close behind him. The prince stays focused on what he came to find. He goes through the courtyard and the court itself. He isn't distracted from continuing to search until he finds the princess. The prince within us as women is that internal force that keeps us searching until we find our own beauty and power (hidden away in towers with rusty keys).

When he finds Briar Rose, the prince is so struck by her beauty that he bends down to kiss her. "No sooner have his lips touched hers than she opens her eyes, wakes up, and smiles sweetly."[131] Together, they go downstairs and out of the tower to the place of grounding. It is only then that the king, queen, and the rest of the court wake up.

When Claire did an active imagination dialogue between the princess and the prince, she imagined the princess saying to him, "We have to bow into coming awake." Claire interpreted this to mean, "We have to surrender to becoming conscious."

Claire's inner prince replies: "We cannot live in a tower. We must come down into the kingdom gone awry." The message in this for Claire was:

> I cannot stay in an idealized state of fantasy in my life, with the expectation of a prince who will come and rescue me. I have to come down to the ground and do my own work in the kingdom gone awry.

We then explored, as a group, our own resistance to waking up and becoming conscious of the mature choices we need to make as adult women. The prince within us recognizes our unique beauty and power. He invites us to remain awake (stay conscious) in a world that is not perfect and that may, indeed, carry pain that we would rather not have to endure.

In Claire's active imagination, when the prince asked the princess what she wanted, she replied: "The truth and no lies. I will not be piggybacked any longer."

What comes across clearly is Claire's determination to neither depend on the fear-filled father/kings in her life to protect and defend her, nor wait for an external gallant prince to rescue her. She is clearly choosing to claim her own true masculine, her inner prince. She knows that she can't live in an ivory tower of fantasy but must descend onto the ground of her everyday life.

When our true inner masculine and the power of our feminine nature awaken and come together within us, the briars open and bloom and our consciousness shifts. Jung referred to this as the process of individuation. In the tale of "Briar Rose," individuation is the experience of the entire kingdom and natural world waking from its dormant state. The Grimm brothers' version of the tale indicates that when Briar Rose woke up, she smiled sweetly. However, the reality for most women may be closer to the words of Marge Piercy's poem, "Waking is the sharpest pain I have ever known."[132] Consciousness (waking up) challenges us, as women, to claim our own lives, let go of our idealized, protected state as daughters of the benevolent sexist king, and abandon our roles as ladies-in-waiting for the kiss of the rescuing prince.

The Protected Occupation of Womanhood

Once we become conscious of our womanhood as a "protected occupation,"[133] and not an expression of our equality as human persons with men, it forces us to choose between the comfort of protection (that is, living with the assumption that we cannot survive without the emotional and economic support of men) and the challenge of coming down to the ground of our human existence as women. We cannot be both carried and equal. We have to make a choice.

Jessica wrote about this choice in a poem she composed in response to the tale.

> A good girl turned bad by rejection.
> The penis sticks out like a sore thumb.
> Daddy's gone; it's over.
> I'm no longer under your power, thumb, penis.
> I remember the wise woman who sees clearly.
> Where does she live?
> Where is she when I need her?
> I feel her call. Longing to be free,
> I cry HELP.
> I feel the pitch, heavy, thick, pulling down.
> No use! Why bother?
> Not good enough! I rise. I fall.
> It's cold in the shadows.
> The pitch squeezes, hardens, paralyses.
> Alone! Will I survive? I turn inside myself.
> The wise woman beckons.
> She did not abandon me.
> She speaks, "You have all you need."
> The sun travels across the sky.
> The pitch softens, melts, drips on the earth.
> I stretch, yawn, breathe.
> Blood rushes through my veins.
> Awake, oh sleeper.
> I extend my hand,
> The fearless prince helps me to my feet.
> Standing on firm ground
> We dance.

Throughout the time of our work on the tale of "Briar Rose," we recognized the sharp contrasts of light and dark within the tale. On the one hand, what initially appeared dark, in the image of the thirteenth wise woman, was later revealed to be light. She provided Briar Rose with the opportunity to step out of the naivety of her girlhood and into the fullness of her womanhood. If the thirteenth wise woman had not hidden the spindle so that the king could not confiscate it, Briar Rose would not have had the opportunity to claim her true feminine identity.

On the other hand, what initially appeared as light, in the image of the loving, protective father/king, was later revealed to be dark. In attempting to shield his daughter from the painful side of life, the father/king actually ended up imprisoning her in a cage of pseudo-protection.

After she reflected on the tale of "Briar Rose," Michaela had the following dream:

> I was at the Center, when a young, dark, Latino man carrying something that looked like a musical instrument came in. I started to say to him, "You don't belong here," but I stopped myself. I realized that he was the opposite of Peter. Instead, he was a positive young masculine figure. I felt embarrassed at what I had started to say, at my first reaction that he did not belong.

Then Michaela wrote: "When I woke up, I knew his name was Miguel, Spanish for Michael, the messenger from God who brings light (the masculine counterpart of my own name)!" This dream came to Michaela on the anniversary of her father's death, a loss she experienced just as she was entering puberty (about Briar Rose's age when she fell asleep). Michaela's father had been her light and protector. He left her just when she felt she needed him the most.

When Michaela did an active imagination dialogue with the object that Miguel was carrying in her dream, she discovered that it was a long tube woven out of grass and reeds that is used to purify the roots of a South American plant before it is ground into flour. She recognized that grass and reeds are fragile but that when they are woven together they can be quite strong. Michaela also associated reeds with musical instruments played with the breath. Indeed, in the dream, Michaela thought that the object Miguel was carrying was a musical instrument.

In Michaela's dream, we see the contrast between images of dark and light. Miguel is dark-skinned, yet he is the "messenger of God who brings the light."

During this same week, Michelle dreamed of the Ku Klux Klan. In this dream, she was trying to prevent them from killing. The members of the Klan wear white as they seek to kill or suppress those who are black, or who they determine to be inferior. This was an image for Michaela of energy within her that is split into shadow and light.

When a young girl falls into an idealized state, particularly in relation to her father, she cannot exist in her own right. She may feel split off from her shadow side. She may believe that her very existence depends on always being good, and pleasing her father. But secretly she may never be sure that she could actually succeed.

"Please, Daddy," Jessica wrote in her response to the tale, "please tell me you care for me not because I am cute or sweet or make you feel good but because of who I really am." She then wrote:

> I am aware of my father and how he was never there.
> How I stood by his side, how I propped him up.
> But it didn't matter.
> I thought he was perfect.
> I couldn't see his faults
> I wonder if he loved me?
> He never told me
> Can I let it be?
> He didn't want to know my pain
> He came and went like a shadow
> My fear separated us.
> Whenever I heard his big shoe thumping on the stair
> I shivered.
> I wonder if he loved me?
> He never told me
> Can I let it be?

Getting Through the Briars

Our egos, the sentinels of our survival conclusions, stand guard at the door ajar to the light of consciousness. The door is covered with layers of defenses against knowing what our egos have decided might be too threatening for us to know. The door freely swings open, however, in the images in our dreams, in myths, and in fairy tales (which are collective dreams). The defensive briars of the ego have no power over the unconscious world. But the thorns of our ego defenses cling together like hands to prevent us from breaking through to an understanding of the images the unconscious presents to us.

Michaela put it very clearly in her reflection on the plight of the many princes who came too early, got trapped in the hands of the briars, and subsequently died painful deaths. She wrote: "I tried and tried, and then one day I finally surrendered. In that moment, the briars parted and began to bloom."

Michaela realized that her attempts to get through the briars were about her ego trying to maintain control and letting only little glimpses of consciousness in at a time before closing off again. She had a physical experience of the briars closing in on her, which she described as an "I-don't-want-to-know-this headache." She recognized that her surrender was not to an external prince or authority but to the recognition within herself of a gift of divine grace from Sophia, Mother of Wisdom. Michaela acknowledged that, indeed, she had everything she needed for her life journey. She was neither deficient nor deprived because she had no external prince to rescue and protect her. She had found her prince within. This awareness led Michaela to a deeper appreciation of the beauty of her own feminine nature, which she had denied for so many years while she was in the pursuit of external achievement and recognition by men.

The hundred years are over when we finally surrender to being who we are, not who we wish we were, or who we perceive others want us to be. When the briars have grown up around us (as a defense against becoming conscious) it can take a hundred years (or the equivalent of the fullness of time) for the individuation process to reach the time of blossoming.

But why does the entire kingdom and natural world go to sleep? What does this say about the repression of the feminine in the name of protection? Why do the briars cover the entire kingdom, even up to the flag on the top of the castle, so that it is completely covered and, therefore, impenetrable?

The briars represent the collective defenses of the patriarchal world of the father/king. They block any knowing from entering the kingdom that would disturb the established order. They prevent any reinterpreting of the father/king's solicitude for the safety of his daughter as a form of enslavement that robs her of her power as a woman.

While we were working with this tale, Jessica heard a blackbird in her back yard squawking outside the birdhouse that contained a sparrow's nest. At first, she was afraid that the blackbird might try to destroy the nest and take the eggs, but the sparrows stood their ground and chased the blackbird away. Jessica wrote:

> Who are you that you barge into my life demanding that I listen? Robber bird, trying to rob me of my power and choke off my creative source, don't tell me I have to do more, be more. Don't block my way. Let me through the briars—I am ready to wake up!

The Negligent Mother

Where is her mother while Briar Rose is growing into womanhood? The only mention we have of her mother is prior to her birth and when she is absent on the day of her daughter's fifteenth birthday (when the curse of the thirteenth wise woman is to take effect). Because the tale clearly states that the king confiscated *all* the spindles, we can assume that her mother also turned hers over to be destroyed. There is no mention of her protesting the destruction of all of the spindles in the kingdom. She, as well, under the guise of protecting her daughter, colludes with the king in nullifying her own feminine potential. She, too, falls into a somnolent state from which, according to the tale, only her daughter's awakening can redeem her.

After working with the images in the tale of "Briar Rose," Emily recalled a dream: "A blonde woman came down an avenue of linden trees on a horse. She was a doctor who prescribed herbs. I ask her for some." On awakening, Emily was shocked to recognize the woman-doctor in her dream as the mother who had abandoned her when she was only nine months old. Emily was stunned! How can the healer also be the one who inflicts the pain?

As previously noted, according to Jung, a woman with a negative attitude toward her mother (that is, a negative mother complex) has the best chance of achieving higher consciousness. This is because her intrinsic psychological situation forces her to fundamentally reappraise her feminine nature. She is unable to be a woman, unless she becomes conscious.[134]

This was the first dream that Emily recalled in which the image of her birth mother appeared. It was a clear sign to her that her relationship to her mother (now deceased) was shifting. In the dream, her mother was coming to heal Emily of the shame and blame she had carried for her own abandonment. Emily remembered that, in the tale, the king and queen left Briar Rose on the very day she needed them most, the day that was predicted as the time when the spell would begin.

According to an older version of the tale, on the fateful day predicted by the thirteenth wise woman, Briar Rose's mother and father go out to a "house of pleasure."[135] While we are not entirely clear what this means, what is clear is that their pleasure takes precedence over their concern for their daughter. Besides, they think they have everything under control. They imagine that they have outsmarted the neglected wise woman. This is a big mistake. Never underestimate the power of a woman spurned, particularly the inner feminine! You will pay her what is her due at a point in time you least expect, although she will generally give you fair warning.

Emily realized that it was for her mother's pleasure, out of her own narcissistic wound, that her mother had abandoned her, and inflicted her with the same wound.[136] Even in her vulnerability, Emily accepted the gift of healing that she was being offered through her dream. On the most important day in her life, when she turns fifteen, Briar Rose is left alone. This reminded Emily of all the days that she was left alone. She wrote:

We cannot protect our children from their destinies. They each have to climb the narrow winding staircase of their lives. When we are asleep, those around us are asleep as well. The work of our awakening will also affect others.

Emily remembered with deep pain what her birth mother had told her sister when her sister had questioned her years later about why she had abandoned them. Her mother had replied, "Your father was having such a good time while he was away, I decided I needed some fun, too." Her mother had sought her own "house of pleasure" when her children needed her most. Emily was only nine months old, and her sister about age three, when their mother left one day and never returned.

After reflecting on this tale in the group, Emily had the following dream:

> I was with an aboriginal group of people. Their skin tone was the brown of Australian aborigines. I knew I was a stranger amongst them and felt fear. It was the same kind of fear I always felt as a child. In this place, men were the rulers, women subservient. We were all standing around talking. We then proceeded to the next room, which was cave-like, but with high ceilings. As is the custom in the Western world, the men went first. Then I saw a very confident young, blonde, blue-eyed woman coming toward me. She identified herself as a doctor and totally calmed my fears. I learned, in fact, that men and women were equal here. My fear was a misconception.

Emily associated the Australian aborigines in her dream with people who "acknowledge the sacredness of dream time." Healing is beginning to take place in Emily. The blue-eyed woman is the doctor who can calm her fears. In her dream, Emily discovered that it is not true that men are more important than women. They are equal in the dream. Her fears are a "misconception." Ironically, Emily's mother was also blonde and blue-eyed. Emily connected this dream image with the earlier dream she had had of the woman herbal healer on horseback, who she had recognized to be the mother who had abandoned her. Emily was angry. She addressed the image in the dream: "How dare you come back as a healer, a doctor! What right do you have to bring healing?" On the other hand, Emily recognized that it is precisely that which wounds us that carries the key to our healing.

Emily shared Estelle's pain over not having any guidance about sexuality from her mother. Emily wrote: "I didn't have guidance in anything. All the comments from my father and stepmother were negating." Ironically, Emily remembered her father calling her a *spinner* when she talked about loving classical music. For him, a spinner meant someone who was crazy.

After the group reflection on the tale of "Briar Rose," Emily had the following dream:

> I was with my two daughters in my husband's boat (although it looked different than his actual boat). This one was a wide-bellied wooden rowboat. My youngest daughter was in the boat and called for help, because the boat was drifting away from the dock. I hesitated, and my oldest daughter encouraged me to jump. I did, and we were all three in the boat. I was very concerned about my little bird, which was still on board. I picked it up. It was so very tiny and all wet. I was terribly concerned about it. Now we were all three climbing out of the boat, and I again voiced my concern for the little bird. My oldest daughter assured me that it would be all right.

In Emily's active imagination with the image of the tiny bird from her dream, she discovered that the bird desired her to "blow life into it again." Emily interpreted this message as an invitation to begin breathing deeply. She understood the little bird to be an image of her injured young spirit. After recording her reflections on her dream, Emily heard a robin singing in the garden outside her window. After her active imagination with the image of the little bird, Emily dreamed:

> Before my eyes, someone was working at a potter's wheel, making a cup. The wheel was turning and turning as unseen hands made the clay rise up, lovingly shaping a cup. The clay was of the same muted pastel colors as the bird in the previous dream. When it was finished, I had to bring the cup to a young man I knew, to be fired.

In this dream, Emily associated the image of the young man with a creative, healthy side of herself. For her, the clay from Mother Earth is providing a receptacle from which to drink the water of life (an image for Emily of the grail cup). This cup needed to be taken to a friend to be fired. He placed it in a huge oven. The fire was needed to transform the raw, soft material into a strong, useful container. In her active imagination, Emily waits to see what colors will emerge in the firing of the cup. When it is removed from the fire, the cup is all the colors of the rainbow. It will only need a clear glaze. The rainbow contains the full spectrum of natural energy. This new cup represented for Emily her redeemed beautiful feminine side, which held all the creative energy she needed for the transformation of her life.

Then, Emily had a dream inviting her to let go of the garbage from the past:

> I was standing in front of my house, taking out the garbage. I had three large garbage bags full. A large black Labrador retriever had snatched a baby plastic diaper panty and was dancing around with it. The panty looked like a cap. I was laughing out loud, watching him.

Emily gradually began to reconcile herself to her mother's abandonment. She wrote: "I am now able to see myself as Moses in the cradle. I realize, with deep emotion, that my mother leaving me actually saved my life." Like Briar Rose, all the years of being asleep, unable to recognize the depth of her own beauty as a woman, had now come to an end. The briars had opened and bloomed for Emily.

When Rita did an active imagination between Briar Rose and her father, she asked him: "Why didn't you stay with me on that day? Didn't you realize I was in danger?" Rita had deeply felt the loss of her father when he left her to go to war after her mother's death. She never felt safe with her stepmother. After working with this tale, Rita dreamed:

> I was on a road looking for a large high-rise department store. When I got there I realized that the elevator wasn't safe, so I got off. A young man showed me how I could get on a new road. Then I was in a house where there was menstrual blood on the bedspread.

Rita recognized the image of the elevator in the department store as a way to get to the tower, the top of a place of material consumption, which she associated with money and achievement. She decided to get off, as it wasn't safe. She saw the young man in her dream as an image of her inner prince, who could show her a new road to take in her life. Rita connected the menstrual blood on the bedspread with the tale of "Briar Rose." Rita's stepmother did nothing to prepare her for the transition from girlhood to womanhood and treated any fears and concerns Rita raised with disregard and disdain.

> Without a mother who can instinctively give her a deep rever-
> ence for the mystery [of menstruation], reverence for the child-
> birth associated with it and reverence for her own body as the
> instrument through which life incarnates, the daughter reacts
> with terror.[137]

Rita felt doubly abandoned by her mother's early death and her father's decision to go to war and leave her in the care of a woman who was cold and rejecting.
She lost her spindle (her ability to recognize and claim her own feminine potential) when she was very young.

After her reflection on this tale, Rita recognized that her father had left her and
gone to war because he felt unworthy as a father. She was concerned that he had
carried feelings of guilt for her mother's early death. Rita then dreamed:

> I was visiting my father. He was driving down the main road.
> He was dying, but there wasn't much change in his condition.
> He said, "I'm doing okay." I felt that I hadn't spent enough time
> with him the last two times I'd been home.

When she reported this dream, Rita acknowledged that it wasn't safe for her
father to be driving, but she loved him so much that she let him drive. When he
announced that he was going for a ride, she responded, "I'm going with you (even
if it means death for both of us)."

Rita realized that her father lived through her. She acknowledged that her relationship with him could be described as psychological incest. She saw her father
as deeply wounded by her mother's death. Rita was a reflection of her mother to
him, an image of the woman he had loved and suddenly lost.

The daughter who is tied at a young age to meeting the psychological needs of
her father is at high risk of not being able to claim the worth of her own life. Like
Briar Rose, she may fade from life and from relationships with other men, remaining the little girl her father needs.

The mother who feels slighted or ignored by the father's extra attention to the
daughter may take her anger out on the daughter, rather than confront the father
and ask for what she herself needs. The daughter may be seen as stealing affection
and attention from her mother and, through displaced anger, the mother may
turn to wounding her own daughter.[138] This is especially true when a stepmother
feels "second" to the daughter in her relationship to the father, which was the case
in Rita's life.

While the Grimm brothers end the tale of "Briar Rose" when one hundred years have elapsed and the prince has arrived, the original tale continued beyond this point. In the 1729 English translation of Perrault's story, "La Belle Au Bois Dormant," the prince has an ogress for a mother. For this reason, he does not tell her of his marriage to Briar Rose until after his father, the king, dies, and he inherits the kingdom. In the meantime, he and Briar Rose have two children, a girl called Morning, and a son called Day. When the young king is called off to war he leaves Briar Rose, now queen, with their two children, in the castle. The ogress queen mother sends them to a cottage and plans to devour them, one by one. However, the cook and the clerk of the kitchen trick the queen mother. They hide the young queen and her children and substitute other animals for the food. When the ogress queen mother discovers that she has been tricked, she plots to have all three thrown into a tub filled with toads, vipers, snakes, and all kinds of serpents. Luckily, the young king arrives home in time and the ogress, enraged, throws herself into the tub and is devoured in an instant. Perrault's version of the tale ends, "The young king could not but be very sorry, for she was his mother, but he soon comforted himself with his beautiful wife and his pretty children."[139]

When we explored this ending to the tale of "Briar Rose," Rita talked about her experiences of feeling invisible and having to stay hidden from her stepmother, who was very cold and rejecting. Her father had hoped that his new wife would be a mother to young Rita. Instead, her stepmother told Rita she didn't want her and subjected her to psychological abuse against which Rita's father appeared helpless to protect her.

Gertrude Nelson talks about the girl child who grows up with "the lack of maternal feeling, the warmth and tender attention and affirmation that were her due as a child." She states that this loss may continue to cause the girl child to be so emotionally hungry and needy that she will perceive hurt, become suspicious, and anticipate neglect at every turn. Her sense of her worth as a woman may be "so eroded that anger and hurt may contaminate many of her relationships."[140]

What saved Rita from this fate was the kindness she received from her birth mother's sisters and brother who truly loved her. Even though she spent only brief periods of time with them, she knew the taste of love.

Each of the women in the group affirmed the personal significance of participating in the process of exploring this tale together. What keeps the Briar Rose within us in a semiconscious state is the belief that we are all alone with our ambivalence and anger at being smothered with benevolent protection. We believe that nice girls are supposed to be grateful. And so, we retreat further into our somnolent state rather than claim consciousness and give expression to the truth of what we experience. We fear becoming, as Jessica expressed it in her poem to Briar Rose, "good girls gone bad."

Four Years Later

We revisited the tale of "Briar Rose" four years later to discover what it had to tell us since we had first explored the story.

Michaela shared her insight that overcoming our resistance to awakening occurs only if "we give up trying and finally surrender to letting it happen. Our desire is sufficient. We need faith, courage, and determination to allow the briars to blossom."

Estelle recognized how she had grown in her appreciation of the destructive potential of overprotection. As she did her own inner work and claimed her own life, she was amazed at the ways in which those around her changed and grew. Estelle had an active imagination dialogue with a native woman who appeared in a dream and encouraged Estelle to trust her own inner wisdom. This reassured Estelle that she was making the right decisions for her life.

Four years later, Alexis acknowledged that she had received the curse of the hundred-year sleep from the patriarchal culture in which she was raised. She wrote:

> When we began our work on the tale of "Briar Rose," I was bemoaning my "wound." Now I feel gratitude for it and see the trauma that I experienced as a profound opportunity for growth. I am still waking up to what is dormant, the potential within me, and finding keys to new doorways. Being awake, for me, is like being amazed. I have needed to be disobedient to the members of my "tribe." I have been amazed that I survived, and so have they. Things have shifted!

When Jessica reflected on the tale four years later, she realized, once more, how powerful the story was for her. She reread the poem she had written about being a pin-up girl and related it to an image one of the other women had painted of an African woman. Behind the black image in the painting, Jessica could see a second white image that reminded her of Marilyn Monroe. Jessica felt that she was now able to move on with her own creative work and openly share it with others. She felt the briars fall away.

Four years later, Claire reflected on her questioning during her adolescent years, "When would I know what I needed to know?" Now she asked herself, "What have I locked up in a tower for one hundred years?" Claire realized that celebrating her sexuality was an important place for her to be at this time in her life.

Reflecting on the tale of "Briar Rose" four years later, Emily realized how much healing had taken place in her relationship with her mother, stepmother, and father. She didn't feel as vulnerable as she once had. She no longer saw herself as "the odd woman out," the thirteenth wise woman, single, and uninvited. She was amazed at how much energy she experienced as she began to claim what *she* wanted to do in life. Emily reported finding a little hummingbird trapped in a pipe in her garden. She had been able to release it gradually with much patience and prayer. She recognized the fragility of her own young spirit in the trapped bird. Emily then celebrated her capacity to free herself from past patterns of emotional isolation and fear.

The invitation of the tale of "Briar Rose" is to awaken to the importance of becoming conscious, so that we don't live out our lives as if they are our fate. All of the women in the group recognized that their personal awakenings were not just for themselves. When we do our own soul work, reclaiming our true selves, we also change the world around us. In the tale, when Briar Rose awakened, the entire kingdom awakened, even the flies on the wall and the wind in the trees. This may be difficult for us to imagine, because we often see ourselves as separate entities in a global fog.

What happened to the women in the group was profound, as each of them supported one another through the process of celebrating her womanhood. Many of the women experienced shifts in their relationships with their own mothers. Feelings of compassion for them began to emerge. Some felt less caught in old ways of behaving with their fathers, freer to speak the truth with kindness. Others felt significant shifts within their own bodies. Their awakenings brought relief from old pains and burdens. All the women felt a renewed commitment to finding their prince within, instead of searching for him outside of themselves. A renewed energy emerged to let go of ego defenses and allow the briars to open and blossom.

The hundred years are over. We no longer have to continue our roles as ladies-in-waiting. As women we have the choice of claiming our womanhood, no longer as "a protected occupation,"[141] but as a power to be celebrated and a commitment to be lived with integrity.

Reflection Questions:

Chapter V—Waking From the Sleep of Ages: The Tale of Briar Rose

1. What are the briars (ego defenses) that have kept me (or continue to keep me) in an extended sleep or unconscious state, in which I am unable to claim my own life and destiny?

2. What do I need to surrender or let go of, now that the hundred years are over?

3. What will it cost me if I wake up and become conscious of my life choices?

4. In what ways have I sought the protection of the benevolent father/king in my life?

5. How can I remain truly awake to who I am, not who I wish I were, or who others wish me to be? What does this mean in my life now?

CHAPTER VI

LIFE UNDER GLASS: THE TALE OF THE RAVEN

Transparent glass is something like solidified water or air,
both of which are synonyms for spirit.

—C. G. Jung, *Collected Works*

The woman who has been wounded by maternal deprivation often feels like her spirit has been frozen or solidified. She may find herself unable to breathe or take in the spirit of life. Early in our work, Claire had a dream that illustrated this:

> I was a little evergreen tree in a large forest. All the trees around me were grown tall. But I couldn't grow or breathe because I was under a glass bell jar.

Whenever Claire was under stress, she would get a respiratory infection. If the stress were severe, it would turn into pneumonia, from which it would take her up to six months to recover. Her beautiful evergreen soul was being smothered by the solidification of her spirit. She had been raped as a young child coming home from school. Her memory was of her mother being annoyed that she had to leave work to come to the hospital where her child was being examined. No one ever spoke again of this profound insult to her budding feminine spirit. She was never given the opportunity to grieve the loss of what had been stolen from her. Years later, in psychotherapy, she discovered that it was an oral rape. Her capacity to breathe was cut off in this cruel violation of her young body. After the incident, her brothers were assigned to walk with her on her way to and from school. By the time she was five years old, a glass bell jar had descended over her young soul.

The Grimm's tale of "The Raven" is a story of what was necessary for her release. It is the story of many women whose young spirits were solidified by early trauma and who are yearning to breathe freely once more.

A Synopsis of the Tale of the Raven

Once upon a time, in a land far away, there lives a queen with a baby daughter. Night after night the child cries and is restless. One night, as the queen is trying to quiet her daughter, a flock of ravens flies by the castle window. The queen cries out, "I wish you were a raven and could fly away; then maybe I could get some rest." No sooner are the words out of her mouth then the child turns into a raven and flies out of her arms. The queen weeps and weeps for she didn't mean what she said. But it is too late; her daughter does not return.

Years later, a young man who is wandering through the forest hears a voice cry, "I am a king's daughter. I am bewitched, but you can set me free." The young man looks up, and all he sees overhead is a raven. He asks, "What shall I do?" The raven answers: "Go further into the forest until you find the house of an old, old woman dressed in feathers. She will offer you food and drink, but you must refuse it. Behind her house is a large stone; stand on it at noon and wait for me. On the first day, I will come in a chariot drawn by gazelles, on the second day in a chariot drawn by leopards, and on the third day in a chariot drawn by lions. If you are sleeping when I come, you will not be able to set me free."

The young man promises to do as the raven requests. But he is so hungry and thirsty that he forgets her warning and eats and drinks what the old, old woman offers him. So when the raven comes at noon on the first day, in the chariot drawn by gazelles, he is fast asleep. When he awakes and the raven is gone, he promises himself that on the second day he will refuse the food offered to him by the old, old woman. But the next day, as he stands on the stone waiting for the raven, the temptation becomes too great, and he tastes the food and drink the old, old woman brings him. Once again, when the raven comes in the chariot drawn by leopards, he is fast asleep, and she cannot rouse him. On the third day, the young man again decides not to taste the food and drink the old woman brings. But alas, once again, the temptation is so great that he succumbs. When the raven comes on the third day, in the chariot drawn by lions, the young man is again fast asleep. The raven leaves him a loaf of bread, a haunch of meat, and a flask of wine. She takes a gold ring from her claw and places it on his finger. Sadly, she bids him farewell with the words, "You could have broken the spell, but now it is too late."

When the young man awakes he is very distressed and ashamed that he has fallen asleep for the third time. Now he is determined to rescue the enchanted raven. He gathers up the bread, meat, and wine she has left for him and sets out to find her. He wanders through a wasteland for days and days. Then, one night, he sees a light coming from a large cave in a cliff. Suddenly, the light disappears. Then the young man sees the shadow of a giant coming out of the cave. The giant greets him warmly: "You have come just in time. I have been looking forward to a good meal." The young man is startled, but remembering the bread, meat, and flask of wine that the raven has left him, he offers to share them with the giant (as they would be more delicious than he). The giant agrees to taste them, and they sit down together for a meal. Because what the raven has left is magic food, no matter how much they eat and drink, more appears. The giant is quite satisfied by the feast, and he and the young man become friends.

The young man tells the giant of his search for the enchanted raven and his commitment to finding and releasing her from her spell. The giant has never heard of the raven, but he has a magnificent map of all the wonders of the world. He and the young man pore over the map for seven days. At last, on the seventh evening, the giant discovers a glass mountain a thousand miles away. According to the map, every day at noon a raven flies out and circles the top of the mountain three times, crying, "Alas, I am a king's daughter, but I have been bewitched." The young man is overjoyed, because he knows this must be the enchanted raven. He leaves the giant early the next morning and travels the thousand miles to the foot of the glass mountain. There is no way he can climb the mountain, as the glass is smooth and the mountain steep. So he builds a small hut at the foot of the mountain and waits for the raven to appear. He is rewarded the next day when he sees her emerge at noon and hears her cry. But he has to be content to stay at the foot of the mountain until he finds a way up.

Then, one morning very early, he hears men quarreling outside his hut. When he looks out, he sees three robbers arguing over three things they have stolen. These include a stick that can open any door, a cloak that makes its wearer invisible, and a horse that can overcome any obstacle. The robbers cannot agree on how to divide their stolen treasures. The young man offers to inspect all three and give the robbers his opinion. They agree. The young man grabs the stick, jumps on the horse, throws the magic cloak around him, and flies up the glass mountain. When he reaches the door at the top, he strikes it with the magic stick, and it immediately opens. The raven can't see the young man because the cloak makes him invisible, but she knows someone has entered. She cries out from the golden cage in which she is trapped, "Beware, whoever enters, an evil sorcerer lives here, and he will ensnare you if he returns." Just then, the evil sorcerer enters the door. The young man throws off his magic cloak and strikes the evil sorcerer such a strong blow with the stick that he falls dead. Suddenly, the door of the golden cage opens, and the raven flies to the young man. He catches her and slips the gold ring onto her claw. Immediately the raven turns into a beautiful princess, and the glass mountain becomes a magnificent crystal palace. The young man falls to his knees, overwhelmed by her beauty. She reaches out, brings him to his feet, and says, "If you wish, I will be your wife." He immediately consents. The princess and the young man are married and, now that the sorcerer's spell is broken, they live happily ever after.[142]

In ancient Teutonic myths, the realm of the dead was often referred to as the *glass mountain.* A Prussian myth declared that the dead would have to climb this mountain. For this reason, the claws of bears and lynxes were cremated with the bodies of the dead to help in the ascent up the slippery slope.[143] If a girl child were transported to the glass mountain, she would be residing in the realm of the dead.

The Rejecting Mother

The daughter in the tale became a raven because of her mother's impatience. The queen, as Alexis expressed it, didn't ask for what she needed or seek the resources that would have helped her resolve her frustration with the child. Instead, she made a wish. In her active imagination dialogue between the queen and her daughter, Alexis questioned:

> Why didn't you know to *ask?* Wishing is different than asking. Wishing is not directly addressing what you need. It's a passive-aggressive response, a denial of one's responsibility to take the necessary action to resolve one's dilemma. Wishing can be dangerous, because you might get what you wish for and live with regret that you didn't take responsibility for your life.

Claire's response to the queen from her role as the restless daughter was: "I will not be quieted, so that you can have peace. Being alone doesn't necessarily bring you peace, although it is sometimes painful to have to be with something new."

The mother in the tale is not able to be in tune with the life of her newborn feminine child. Because she is not attentive to what was distressing her daughter and does not want to do the work necessary to listen to the child's need, she loses her forever.

Jessica phrased the child's departure from her mother, "Sleep now, Oh Queen, we will not meet again." It was Jessica's perception that the child would have died if she had remained in that kingdom.

The mother in this tale is represented by the metaphor of "the dark birds circling around her house."[144] The shadow side of the mother contaminates her daughter and sends her into a dark exile. The mother herself was, very likely, maternally deprived and out of touch with her own feminine nature.

In her active imagination dialogue between the queen and her raven-daughter, after she had been released from her spell, Emily greeted the mother she had not seen since she was an infant: "Mother, it is so good to see you! I have been living with a mountain on my shoulders, dark, and full of the echoes of ages."

In the tale, the child (cursed by her mother for not being able to meet her mother's needs) becomes a raven. The image of a bird is generally symbolic of the energy of spirit. The raven in ancient folklore was considered a messenger of the great spiritual realm.[145] It was associated with the process of transformation and the potential for a change in consciousness. In the children's book, *The Secret Garden*,[146] a raven shows motherless little Mary how to find the key to the abandoned garden. The raven is also associated with the archetype of the trickster (a negative image that brings about a positive outcome). Of the many species in the crow family, the raven is the largest. The sharp persistent cry of the raven reminds us to pay attention to those aspects of ourselves that we might wish to ignore or deny.

As we were working on the tale of "The Raven," Jessica encountered a flock of crows in her orchard. The following poem was her reflection on her reaction to their appearance:

> Distracted by crows harping on and on.
> Unable to focus, I feel pulled off-center.
> The crows swoop and dive, screaming at one another.
> Are they trying to get my attention?
> Harping on and on. My ears alive
> straining to resist their complaining
> discord.
> Gentle voices whisper, "Spring."
> Mourning doves cooing, sparrows twittering.
> Robins singing, Cardinals whistling
> And yet, crows swoop and squawk.
> I demand a life of pleasant sounds.
> Harmony.
> If only I could eliminate the crows.
> My crows.
> The crowing voices deep inside of me
> that pierce the stillness of my soul.

Through her poem, Jessica creatively expressed the distress that the call of the bewitched raven-girl evoked in her. The plea of the rejected feminine is insistent.

Once we hear her call, we cannot drown it out. Even though we may try to distract ourselves with more pleasant, harmonious sounds, she will keep pleading with us: "Please hear me. I am bewitched, but you can set me free." She begs us to make the choice for freedom.

In this tale, the rejected daughter's spirit is assigned to the glass mountain, the realm of the dead from which she must be rescued. Our deliverance from a life under glass, a state in which our feminine spirit is stifled, depends on our ability to access our true masculine spirit—that part of us that is able to be focused, purposeful, and clear about what needs to be done to claim our own lives.

Who Is the True Masculine? Where Is He Found?

When I use the terms *feminine* and *masculine*, I am referring to characteristics present in both women and men that are primarily distinguished as inner/outer, yin and yang, two aspects of one reality. While masculine attributes may appear to be more readily espoused by men and feminine qualities more espoused by women, both men and women have the capacities for developing both aspects of their lives. In our dreams, whether we are men or women, the masculine energy usually comes in the image of a boy or a man, while the feminine energy generally comes in the image of a girl or a woman. Since fairy tales are like collective dreams, the same relationship applies to the images in the tales.

The true masculine, our yang energy, is always in the service of the feminine, while the true feminine, our yin energy, comes to fruition and flowering in the embrace of the masculine. Our masculine energy includes our ability to clearly identify the direction needed in our lives and to develop the discipline needed to move decisively in that direction. Our feminine energy, on the other hand, includes our ability to form meaningful relationships with others, the natural world, and our own bodies, and to develop our capacity to be creative and generative. It is the balance of masculine and feminine energies that creates a healthy life in men and women. Both sources of energy are out of balance in the woman with a mother-wound of rejection and neglect. Her feminine spirit is stifled and her masculine energy is unfocused and wandering, as is evident in the tale of "The Raven." In the story, the young man promises to release her. But he keeps falling asleep. Women who have not claimed personal agency for their own lives have a sleepy (unconscious) masculine. The rejected feminine needs the conscious masculine in order to be set free from the curse of the abandoning mother.

Marion Woodman has identified three basic capacities of the conscious masculine: definition, differentiation, and distinction.[147] These three capacities are needed to cut through the chaos and confusion in our lives, so that we can come to a place of clarity. To these capacities I would add: discipline, determination, and direction toward courageous action.

Women can either claim these capacities within themselves or seek them outside of themselves in their relationships with men who are father/kings (or in powerful institutions run by father/kings). Or, they may project their own masculine side onto prince/lovers, who they hope someday will come to save them.

In "Rumpelstilskin," the first tale we explored, the beautiful daughter is the pride of her father, a valued piece of his property. He turns her over to the greedy king and endangers her life, rather than tell the king the truth. She is expected to spin straw into gold to satisfy the king's greed and to save her father's pride. Both the father and the king use her for their gains. She can trust neither. Her immature masculine, the dwarf, gets her through the crisis but can't sustain her. Only her mature messenger (androgynous in the tale) can name what must be named before it destroys her.

In the tale of "The Handless Maiden," the obedient daughter, who is mutilated by her father, turns to the security of the king's palace. She soon discovers that she is still not safe! She must go out on her own to claim her own life and destiny.

In the tale of "Mother Hulda," there are no masculine images. Mother Hulda herself carries the balance of both the masculine and feminine energies needed for the transformation of Gold and Black Mary, the shadow sisters.

In the tale of "Briar Rose," the daughter is dependent on her father/king for his protection from the curse of the thirteenth wise woman. When he is unable to save her, she goes into an unconscious state for a hundred years. As she awakens after the one hundred years are over, the prince welcomes her into her newly conscious state with a kiss.

Women who carry a mother abandonment wound need to *define* their life issues, *differentiate* themselves from their mothers, and make the *distinctions* necessary to cut through the chaos and confusion in their lives. Then they can move forward with *determination* and *discipline* in the *direction* of courageous action. Then, and only then, will they be able to claim their own destinies, having been released form the curse of their mothers' rejection.

In the tale of "The Raven," this task is assigned to a young man wandering through the forest. He doesn't seem to have any purposeful direction or focused determination (unlike the prince in the tale of "Briar Rose"). He is just wandering through the forest (a metaphor for the place of transformation) when he hears the voice of the raven. This seemingly inept masculine is very descriptive of the woman who has been estranged from her mother. She generally does not feel powerful in the patriarchal world of the father/king and longs for the day the prince will come. She may find herself wandering through life, barely hearing her stifled spirit calling to her.

Awakening the Masculine

Jung refers to the spirit as the *subtle body* or *breath soul*, which is nonmaterial and finer than mere air. Since the soul's essential characteristic is to animate and be animated, it represents the life principle.[148]

In this tale, the feminine spirit, in the image of a raven, is assigned to the realm of the dead. She is under glass and cannot breathe. The young man, who has the capacity to animate her and to bring her back to life, carries an image of her soul. The estranged spirit longs to be reclaimed by the soul. He holds her hope for deliverance from the spell of the negative mother.

He hears the raven's cry, "I was born a king's daughter (in other words she was a princess) and have been bewitched, but you can set me free." Since he does not appear to be on any purposeful journey, he stops, looks up, and asks the voice, "What shall I do?" Then, he sees that it is the raven that spoke to him. He has no evidence that she is *really* a princess but asks no further questions. He goes deeper into the forest, closer to the place of potential transformation. He doesn't protest, "I have somewhere else to go," or, "I haven't got time." He just goes. While this is a sign of readiness for action, he hasn't yet made the clear differentiation and distinction necessary for the next step. Then he meets the old woman dressed in feathers, which signals that she has something significant in common with the raven-girl who is also clothed in feathers. Both are of the world of the spirit.

The raven prepares the young man for the triple spiritual tests he will have to face. This is the time for conscious action. The bewitched raven warns him not to eat or drink what the old woman offers him. "She will offer you meat and drink, but you must touch nothing." If we explore the tale as if it were our own dream, we hear the instructions for our redemption: "*Stand* on the big stone and *wait*." The stone is a metaphor for the ancient philosopher's stone, a place of grounding and wisdom. Our release will come if we *stand and wait* when the sun (a symbol of consciousness) is at its highest peak of light (that is, noon). This is the time of our appointed liberation from the dark curse of our negative mother complex, which includes all the layers of painful experiences we associate with our experience of being mothered.

But although we promise ourselves that we will stay conscious and awake, when the "old, old woman" offers us food and drink, we forget our promise to ourselves. When we have a wound of maternal deprivation, we are deeply psychologically hungry and thirsty for mother-food and comfort. It is so easy to unconsciously revert to old patterns. We get back into the addictive cycles that keep draining us of the energy we need to live out our commitment to claim our own freedom.

Sibylle Birkhauser-Oeri puts it bluntly:

> People caught in a mother complex often spend years on end in a state of insufficient consciousness about themselves and what they do. Sometimes they do not wake up until they have daydreamed half their life away. To choose another image, they could be said to while away the time in the jail of their own complex.[149]

All we need for our escape is waiting for us, if we remain conscious and stay awake. The boundless swift energy of the gazelle, the cunning of the leopard, and the courage of the lion are all harnessed and ready to free us from the spell of the dark mother. However, the temptation to revert to old patterns is too great, and we fall asleep again.

The Taste of Temptation

The word *temptation* refers to that which lures, fascinates, charms, entices, and/or seduces us into making a choice we would otherwise not make. A temptation may lead us to take a path of action that we had previously decided *not* to take.

When we are lured back into addictive patterns in our lives, we are not able to define the issues, and to differentiate and discriminate between the paths of action to be taken. Instead, we become caught in our own chaos and confusion. We lose our ability to think clearly, and fall into an unconscious state.

The instructions from the raven are simple: *stand and wait!* This is the courageous action that will bring about the redemption of the captive feminine spirit from her spell: *stand, and wait!* We well might ask, "What kind of action is that?" Probably one of the most difficult actions is that which appears to be inaction. The raven is clear. Our release will happen in the right spiritual moment, and not when we orchestrate it to happen. This message is very difficult to hear in the midst of our hunger for resolution and our need for control.

The raven comes the first time in a chariot drawn by gazelles, which are associated with speed, adaptability of mind and the ability to see at a distance to avoid danger.[150] These are precious instinctual energies she is ready to make available to the young man. Instead, he forgets the raven's warning not to eat and drink what the old woman offers him and falls asleep. The young man in the tale is that part of us that commits to the journey of individuation with good intentions but then promptly forgets what we have promised ourselves. We have let ourselves grow hungry for what appears to satisfy. Consequently, we are easily persuaded to take what we perceive we need. Then we fall asleep again.

On the second day, the raven comes in a chariot drawn by leopards, which are associated with overcoming distractions and claiming a renewal of vision and vitality. Leopards have strong intuitive abilities and heightened sensibilities. They carry, metaphorically, the energy to trust our inner instincts and to possess the agility to leap over what appear to be obstacles on our path.[151] These are the gifts the young raven-girl brings to the young man. But, once again, even though he promises that he will not taste the meat and drink the wine that the old woman offers him, the temptation was too great.

This time, the young man is aware of his commitment to free the raven but succumbs to temptation. We can assume that the food looked so good that he had to taste it. He forfeits the energy of the leopard, the ability to trust his own inner instincts, and is distracted from his purpose. He has the opportunity to claim a renewal of vision and vitality in his life. He passes it by for the taste of temptation and falls asleep again.

As a group, we explored what it meant to make a clear intention to liberate our own inner spirit, only to be caught again in our addictions. When we are trapped in an addictive cycle, we experience a hunger that cannot be satisfied. We cannot stay awake! We examined the temptations of our lives that cause us to become unconscious when an opportunity for our release from the prison of hopelessness presents itself. Several of the women in the group struggled with chemical dependencies. Others acknowledged their addictions to perfection and pleasing (that is, always having to do the right thing). Each woman understood, all too well, the shame and grief of the young man in the tale when he realized that he had allowed himself to be caught again.

On the third day, the raven comes in a chariot drawn by lions, whose energies are associated with the power of the sun and the emergence of intuition, imagination, and creativity.[152] But, once again, the young man falls asleep and misses his third golden opportunity to free the feminine spirit of the bewitched raven-girl.

But who is the temptress, the old, old woman dressed in feathers, living deep in the forest? She is the Baba Yaga of many ancient tales, the hag who puts us to the test. Feathers are associated with the wind and relate to the human spirit and its connection to the Divine. Metaphorically, they are connected "to changes and leaps of consciousness about to be revealed and a call to unfold the wings of enchantment within one's life."[153] In the alchemical process, feathers were used in the process of purifying and condensing a substance in order to extract its true essence. The old, old woman lives deep in the forest, the place of transformation in fairy tales. She dresses in the feathered robes of a shaman.

Claire saw the old, feathered woman as presenting the outer image of spirit but really wanting to maintain the status quo by seducing the hero into an unconscious state. This reminded Claire of the tale of the "Maiden King" in which the Baba Yaga tries to keep the young man, Ivan, from connecting with the lost feminine.[154] In the tale of "The Raven," the old feathered woman continues to test the young man's willingness to take the steps necessary to move out of old life patterns.

Alexis saw the old, old woman as the hag of transformation who invites us to consume things to fill our hunger and, at the same time, challenges us to resist the temptation. After her reflection on the tale, Alexis wrote: "When we succumb, we fall asleep to the possibilities that are right before us. Our shame and grief for what we have lost can then move us out of our idyllic innocence."

Too Late

The raven, the abandoned feminine spirit, has all the food the young man needs in the chariot, if only he would wait for her. She leaves him a loaf of bread, a haunch of meat, a flask of wine, and a ring of gold. The way of redemption was opened, but now it is too late. For some women, the patterns of enslavement repeat themselves over and over until they get to the point where it is too late. Suddenly, they wake up and recognize all the opportunities for freeing their solidified spirits that have passed them by while they were asleep. Our inner feminine spirit leaves a gold ring with the message that it is now "too late." She makes a commitment to our forgotten, creative self with the pledge of a ring.

What happens after the "too late" message is that we *finally* understand. Now we have to find our release the hard way! We discover ourselves in the "wasteland" of depression, in which we may come close to being devoured by our own inflated shadow (the giant in the cave). All the negative images and feelings about ourselves become exaggerated and take on enormous proportions. But, if we are able to stay focused with even a small amount of masculine energy, we can still call on the resources our unredeemed feminine spirit provided for us. These gifts of our inner feminine, which are constantly replenished no matter how often we use them, include: our capacity for commitment in relationships, our acknowledgment of our creativity, and our compassion for our bodies and the entire natural world.

When we befriend our giant shadows, rather than allowing them to consume us, this transformed energy is available to aid us in the pursuit of our own freedom. However, our release from our captivity in the glass mountain is not immediate. Our shadow side has the map and can show us the way. However, it takes seven full days to examine the map, in other words, a long time! On the seventh day, the place of captivity is discovered: a mountain of glass a thousand miles away. Every day at noon (metaphorically the time of heightened consciousness) a door in the peak opens. The raven flies out and then reenters the mountain.

At the Foot of the Mountain

There comes a time in the process of our individuation, which is our journey to reclaim our true selves, when we receive fleeting glimpses of who we really are. Once we have this knowledge, even though it may be transitory, we can no longer forget that we are living an exiled existence. Now we will do anything necessary to set the abandoned part of ourselves free.

This was the situation for each of the women in the group. Each had come to the point of no return and had made a commitment to do whatever was necessary to free her captive spirit. Each one had built "a hut at the foot of the mountain" from which she could glimpse the part of herself that was calling to be free.

> The process of discovering who you are as a unique person often begins with confronting an unsolvable problem: when there is no way out, no visible alternative, no apparent freedom to move. Finding yourself without a place of warmth or welcome, when all your work seems to come to nothing in the face of ingratitude and non-recognition, a trap door opens.[155]

Under this trap door are inner reserves of creativity and strength that we never imagined. Suddenly, ways up the insurmountable mountain appear in the most unlikely places. We need to be awake to spot the opportunities that, in the past, we would have ignored or thought impossible to pursue.

In this tale, three robbers appear who have exactly what is needed. This is our chance to look into our lives to see what is robbing us of our opportunity to claim our unique creative feminine spirit. Once we identify the robbers, we need to reclaim what was stolen from us:

- the *stick of discrimination* that opens any door so that we are aware of the possibilities open before us to choose a path to follow;
- the *cloak of clarity* and self-knowledge that allows us to acknowledge our true essence, erase the false images we use to defend ourselves, and remove the masks behind which we hide;
- the *horse of strength* to overcome any obstacles in our way so that we can exercise the discipline and determination needed to release those aspects of ourselves imprisoned in the realm of the dead.

In the tale of "The Raven," the young masculine claims what was stolen and ascends the mountain on the magic horse. But entering the glass mountain is not the end of his ordeal. He must still release the raven from her golden cage, confront and kill the sorcerer who keeps her captive, and give her back her gold ring. When he accomplishes these three tasks, the raven becomes a smiling princess. Then the glass mountain shifts, melts, and re-forms itself into a beautiful palace of crystal that reflects the sunlight. The princess tells the young man that, if he wishes, she will be his wife. The masculine and feminine join, the evil sorcerer's spell is broken, and the power of the negative mother complex collapses.

Wished Away

As we had done in our exploration of the previous tales, each of the women set up active imagination dialogues between the bewitched raven princess and the other images in the tale. One of the first questions raised for active imagination by the women in the group was, "What would the redeemed raven-princess say to her mother when she returned?"

In her active imagination, Emily addressed the stepmother who raised her and who resented her presence:

> Well, Mother (and you might picture me in a strong womanly stance with my hands on my hips), it is good to see you. I call you Mother (evil witch would be more fitting, but this I don't say out loud. I don't want to hurt you). *Mother,* what a strange, misused word this is! It has so many connotations. I can now call you mother (and I notice this time I wrote it with a small 'm') with love in my heart. I wish to hold you in a way I was never held as a child—in the way I expected the men in my life to hold me. Mother, I have been on a long journey, trapped in a mountain of dark glass through which very little light shone. That mountain sat on my shoulders and was filled with trapped echoes. The echoes were so strong they drowned out everything else. Those echoes were ancient; I could tell by the way they sounded. I began to understand the echoing words, to capture them and hold them and then release them. Then, light began to enter. I could see. I could hear. I could feel. Dear Mother, may I take your hand so that you might walk with me on my journey? Maybe, somewhere down the way, we might meet in love.

Emily was astonished at what came out of her active imagination dialogue. She wondered if her feelings about her relationship with her stepmother were *really* changing, or if she was just avoiding the pain in wishful thinking. Emily acknowledged that the echoes of the curses thrown at her as a child were losing their impact on her life. After her active imagination work, Emily had the following dream:

> I was in a forest, and it was springtime. The buds had not yet broken open. There were at least two dogs with me. One dog, on a long rope, had climbed a tree and was now swinging down but was quite safe. The rope prevented him from falling. There was a big bear there, as well as another dog beside me. I was not in a panic but did not feel quite safe, either. The trees were very tall. Because there were no leaves, the light was falling through.

In her reflection on the images in her dream, Emily associated the dogs with loyalty and unconditional love. She realized that a part of her is still afraid and climbs a tree to avoid the bear. Another part of her is not afraid and stands beside her. In this split, Emily recognized how, like the raven in the tale, she longs to be free of the curse and, at the same time, doubts that she will ever be. A part of her ambivalence is "up a tree." In the image of the bear, Emily saw the ruler of the woods—powerful, ancient—inviting her to acknowledge the power of this aspect of herself. It was springtime, a time of awakening, and the time of celebrating her birthday. Emily noted that the bear had come out of hibernation. She wrote, "The time of introspection is over; it is time to act."

The bear is an archetypal image associated with the fierce Divine Mother, who never abandons her young. At the time of her dream, Emily was unaware that the claws of bears were placed in ancient Prussian graves to assist the dead in climbing the glass mountain.[156] When she discovered this, Emily recognized the special gift of her dream. She wrote, "With the knowledge of bear medicine within and the assurance of my dogs walking freely beside me, I have nothing to fear."

As she worked with the images in the tale of "The Raven," Emily recognized how closely the tale reflected her own life story. With her birth mother's abandonment, she had become a raven, a discarded child, who was also a nuisance to her stepmother. While working with the images in the tale, Emily experienced layers of skin being peeled away, layers of negative messages from her father and stepmother which she had absorbed as if they were true of her. Now, in her dream, "the light is falling through" the forest, the place of transformation. The mother bear, a symbol of divine unconditional love, is now her companion.

Emily's reflection was followed by another dream:

> I was standing with others on a dance floor. It was made of beautiful hardwood. I didn't have dancing shoes. Edward went to the closet and took out a pair of black ones. At first sight, they looked like they might not fit, but then I saw that they had a slit in the back of the heel. Edward bent down to help me put them on, and they fit perfectly.

Emily had found the true masculine side of herself that was in the service of her feminine. She now had the shoes, the grounding she needs, to join in the dance of life with others. The ground on which she stood was made of the hardwood trees of the forest of transformation.

The daughter who feels discarded as a nuisance to her mother finds it difficult to be grounded in her own feminine nature. To experience the ground of her own reality as an embodied spirit, she must claim the discriminating, determined, and action-focused part of herself. This awareness will then free her from her state of paralysis. She needs to experience herself as a participant in her own destiny and not just an observer of her fate. Once the light came through in Emily's dream, and she recognized the powerful divine energy of the mother bear within her, she was ready to engage in the dance of life. But she had no dancing shoes. Edward, whom Emily associated with a masculine friend who was consistent in his affirmation and support for her work, found the shoes she needed in her own closet. This was a significant detail in her dream. What she needed, she already had. She just had to claim this aspect of herself as her own. What she required to claim her own life was already in her possession! When Emily didn't believe the shoes would fit, we saw her ambivalence surfacing. She longed to begin the dance of life from which she had felt excluded for so many years, but she didn't believe she would have what was needed to make that choice. The shoes were black, the color of the raven's wings. Shoes are the opposite of wings. Shoes ground us in the present (here and now) and in our bodily existence, whereas wings distance us from the ground of our being. Edward, an image of her focused masculine within, knew immediately where to find the shoes needed for her to begin the dance of life. And they fit her perfectly! Emily remembered the tale of "Cinderella," in which the discarded daughter found the dancing slippers of her own destiny that fit her and no one else.

In the tale of "The Raven," the young man frees the raven-daughter from her cage, slips the ring on her *foot,* and brings her back to the grounding of her human feminine existence.

The woman who has felt discarded or set aside by her mother may be so distanced from her own feminine nature that she may attempt to move in the world as if she were someone else (perhaps as a man who can command attention). This is particularly true if the daughter has felt discarded in favor of a son.

Just after we explored the tale of "The Raven," Michaela had a curious dream:

> I was walking to the bank with the automated bank machine to get some money. I was barefoot and had a coat on over my nightgown. However, when I looked down, I realized I did have something on my feet, *someone else's shoes*, and they hurt. I decided not to go to the bank machine as it hurt to walk. Returning home, I realized that I had on men's shoes. They were brown and more like a low boot. The left one in particular didn't suit my foot. In fact, it looked like a right shoe. Then I discovered that I am wearing two right shoes!

In her dream, Michaela had put on men's shoes that didn't fit. When she reflected on the dream, Michaela realized: "I have no left shoe so my energy is off balance. I'm continually trying to put my right foot forward." She recognized that the tale was reawakening memories of feeling set aside by her mother in favor of her brother. She acknowledged the ways she continually pressed herself to "try harder," or "be more," in order to be accepted and valued.

After recording this dream, Michaela recalled an earlier dream. In the dream, one of the cushions on the living room couch of her childhood home was stained. While it was out to be cleaned, another small cushion, which didn't quite fit, was put in its place. Writing this in her journal awakened feelings of anxiety in Michaela. She developed a headache, which was usually a signal to her that some important aspect of herself that she did not want to know was about to be revealed. As she wrote out this dream in her journal, the words to an old song came to her, "It's now, or never; my heart can't wait." This convinced Michaela to explore the dream image further. She did an active imagination dialogue with the cushion lying on the floor. When she asked the image of the cushion, "Why are you on the floor?" the cushion replied, "I'm waiting to go to the cleaners." Then Michaela wrote:

> I look at the little cushion on the couch that has replaced me and say with disdain, "Look at that little thing; it's small and does not fill the space. It certainly can't replace me, and it better not think

it can. I'm coming back, and I'm getting my space back on that couch."

As she recorded the active imagination dialogue, Michaela realized why she was feeling so much anxiety. The soiled cushion was an image of herself as a young child, being sent away when her brother was born because she had a contagious disease. She was determined not be replaced by her baby brother and blamed her mother for "wishing her away." Then, Michaela wrote, "I decided, at age five, to come back home and survive and to push my vulnerability out of my consciousness."

Michaela realized how the addictive patterns in her life were forcing her to acknowledge her vulnerability. The old woman in the tale continued to tempt her to go back to sleep and to not stay awake long enough to redeem her estranged feminine spirit.

Michaela reflected, in her active imagination, on the process of putting the now-cleaned cushion back on the couch. She asked herself the question, "Where does the little cushion go now?" The answer that came was, "It becomes a decorative piece," which is how her little brother had been treated. He became special; something for her mother to show off, while Michaela felt abandoned and set aside. The depth of her anger and rage at the memories of her abandonment frightened Michaela. When she was able to acknowledge her vulnerability and her feelings of powerlessness in the face of the choices her mother had made, she could let go of her fear. She wrote: "I am not a child any longer, nor am I a cushion for others to sit on. I have choices to make. Sophia, Seat of Wisdom, help me to stay awake to the potency I carry in my life now."

Longing for the Lost Mother

The daughter who is wished away because she is too much trouble continues to live with a deep hunger for a loving relationship with her mother. Estelle was able to identify with this longing deep within herself. Even though her mother was alive and involved in her life, Estelle still carried deep emotional pain, which she could not allow herself to feel. She wrote: "When I think of this pain, I feel a tightness in my chest. But I hold on. I cannot let it out." She longed to feel totally accepted and warmly loved and held.

The night after we worked on this tale in the group, Estelle dreamed:

> Agnes had invited us for dinner at her house. My partner and I went. I had a pot of flowers for her that had wilted in the car. I decided to take them in anyway. We rang the doorbell. She

opened the door, but she seemed agitated and not pleased to see us. Her husband and children were in the hallway with a photographer. She said her husband was in the middle of working on a deal that could be worth millions, and his prospective partners were with him now. So, our arrival for dinner was not really good. We felt out of place. I asked her if she wanted us to leave. She said yes.

Estelle associated Agnes with a mentor she had looked up to as a mother figure, but who no longer supported her musical career. In the dream, she was invited to dinner but then rejected because something more important was going on. Agnes invited Estelle to come for the nourishing affirmation of the mother for whom she longed. But the "mother" is busy with things that are more important to her. Even the flowers wilt in the house of rejection! Estelle recognized how sensitive she is to rejection by women. She felt like the raven-daughter who was too much trouble for the mother to nourish and comfort.

The next night, Estelle dreamed:

> I was driving down a dirt road. Two old women were hitching a ride in the other direction. At first, I didn't want to stop for them. I told them I was going into the city, to Eglinton Avenue, and asked if I could help them. They said they would come with me. We drove into the city, and the traffic was very busy. Somehow, I had to stop the car, and we all got out and began walking. I had a young boy with me. We lost the old women and kept on walking.

When Estelle reflected on the images in this dream, she associated the two old women with her own inner wise woman, two images of the Baba Yaga from the tale. However, she didn't change her direction because they wanted to go the other way. Instead, they come with her. Her young masculine also continued on the journey with her. Estelle recognized from the dream how easy it was for her to be drawn off her own life course, the path of her own destiny, when she gave in to satisfying her hunger for "mother love and approval." Estelle saw herself in the image of the young man in the tale who tasted the food of the old woman. It satisfied his hunger, but then put him to sleep. As a consequence, he missed his opportunity to redeem the bewitched raven. Estelle acknowledged that her temptation was to accommodate herself to the needs of others in order to find the mother-love she sought. She committed herself to staying awake and to avoiding the temptation to be lured in directions that would take her away from the course of her own life.

Several of the women in the group had mothers who projected their own unlived lives onto their daughters. These women were forced to fly beyond their own mothers' insecurities to avoid being caged in anxiety. Their mothers had internalized the message that life was too hard and that their daughters simply didn't have what was necessary to face life's difficulties. The unconscious message of their mothers was, "You might as well give up, take whatever Baba Yaga offers, and go back to sleep."

After working with the tale, Alexis felt that this unspoken message from her mother was what moved her into beginning psychotherapy. She wrote:

> I was terrified of opening my mouth in front of a group. I wanted to share my gifts, but I felt frozen. I had images of birds in a cage yearning for freedom and for connection with my soul, which fueled my distress. The recognition of the power of creativity and the autonomy of the unconscious frightened me. In my family, I couldn't stand up to my father. He was too powerful. My mother was helpless and ineffective in imposing her will on the children, so she responded with irritability at her own ineffectiveness. Something in her touch did not convey a sense of security. I felt bounced around. She cuddled her babies but was not able to appease them. I later watched her with her grandchildren. They tended to run away from her for fear that they would be swallowed up. She lacked a quieting presence. When brushing my long hair, I remember the quick movement of her irritability. She was herself frozen with great aspirations to improve her knowledge through education, but feeling helpless. She gave me the message that everything I attempted or aspired to for myself was too difficult for me. I felt that she hung on to me and would not let me try my own wings because those opportunities had been denied to her. I have begun to value her more in recent years, understanding her struggle, her feeling of powerlessness, and her paralysis when voicing her opinions. We are so alike. We share the same interests. I now see her passion for life, her strong spirituality under all the devotion and cultural expectations. She outwardly manifests a complete lack of self-confidence and, yet, has an inner strength that radiates, even a mystical quality.

Alexis continued her reflections:

> I cannot recognize my own voice until I shake off the bewitch-
> ment, the insecurity tied in with my mother's bewitchment. I
> need to let go of my fear so that both of us can be released. I
> need to stop seeing myself through others' eyes and to learn to
> perceive the world from my own original standpoint. I need to
> find my own ground and live out my own destiny.

Acknowledging the Trauma: Grieving the Loss

Several women in the group had lost their mothers due to death or physical abandonment when they were very young. They felt a deep kinship with the raven-
daughter who had no way to reach her mother because as a raven she was now
under the spell of a sorcerer. For some, the sorcerer came in the guise of a stepmother. For others, the sorcerer was manifested in the painful experience of a
mother who was physically present but emotionally absent.

The girl child who is cursed by her mother's wish for separation feels traumatized and forsaken. She perceives herself as powerless in her state of isolation.
However (as happens in the tale of "The Raven"), she remains a king's daughter.
This, metaphorically, means that she carries the birthright of sovereignty, that is,
power over her own destiny. The image of the king in fairy tales is a metaphor for
the one designated to hold the consciousness of the kingdom and to rule wisely
so that the kingdom will flourish. But where is the king in this tale? There is no
mention of his presence in her life and no plan to rescue her from the curse of the
sorcerer, the dark side of the negative mother complex in which she is ensnared.

When a child feels the loss of her mother's love either through death, abandonment, or emotional withholding, she experiences a profound personal trauma. To
be traumatized means to be wounded by forces so powerful that they overwhelm
our capacity to respond.[157]

In the tale of "The Raven," the loss of the mother occurs suddenly, while the
daughter is still young and vulnerable. It is a traumatic, life-altering moment with
profound consequences. The daughter becomes a raven, a disembodied spirit,
wandering in the forest of transformation. The trauma of the loss of her mother's
love left each of the women in the group with a deep psychic wound that she had
not previously had the opportunity to fully grieve.

Grief is the process through which we allow ourselves to acknowledge and
deeply experience our psychological and physical reactions to a loss. To be bereaved
literally means "to be robbed," to be deprived of what we value as precious. When
we don't have the opportunity to grieve what was taken from us, the effects of the

loss remain in our psyches. These effects may be manifested psychologically, in signs of depression, anxiety, vigilance, and hypersensitivity, and/or physiologically, in cardiac dysfunction, hypertension, and even hair loss.[158] The women in the group experienced many of these symptoms in a variety of ways.

When we experience a trauma in our lives, a personal disaster over which we have no control, the consequences are feelings of victimization and powerlessness. If not addressed, these feelings ultimately lead to despair. For the wound (trauma) to heal, an acknowledgement of the traumatic experience and telling the story in a contained safe environment (until it loses its potency) is required. The fairy tales selected for the group were all traumatic stories of daughters without mothers. Repeatedly working with the stories as a group enabled the women to identify their own losses with the collective trauma of the abandoned daughter. Some of the women had already identified the powerful emotions associated with their loss. Others had found their feelings too difficult and too frightening to address until they were able to feel safe enough to do so within the group. Even then, it was important that they worked with their losses in small doses to avoid becoming overwhelmed.

When a young girl suffers an early loss, particularly of her mother, the person with whom she establishes her primary bond, the resulting separation anxiety can cause her to doubt the very worth of her existence. To restore a sense of her personal value and to create meaning out of the trauma she has endured, she must establish trusting relationships with others so that she can feel worthy of life again. Only when she is able to process her trauma and mourn her loss can she embrace a new set of beliefs about life that were not previously possible. Her healing process also needs to include reclaiming the gift of embodiment that she received from her mother. For this reason, movement and conscious care of her body are essential in the healing process.

Over the course of the past thirty years, the long-term consequences of early trauma, particularly trauma associated with the loss of the mother, are being recognized and addressed in the psychological literature.[159] We have come to recognize how a child's young spirit can become frozen in time, solidified in her fear that if mother and her love can vanish, what else could disappear? Is it safe to be alive? This child-woman may live on the edge of life in anxious anticipation of another loss. Or, she may feel that she, herself, is not worthy of life.

Rita's mother died suddenly when Rita was two years old. Her mother went to the hospital to have a baby and never came home. While we were working on the tale of "The Raven," Rita dreamed:

> I looked at the top of an evergreen tree. There was a black bird,
> a raven, on top.
> There was also a cat in the nest below.

Rita did not know about Claire's dream of the bell jar over the evergreen tree of her life (which was referred to at the beginning of this chapter). Rita felt stunted in her own life because of the early loss of her mother. Her dream contained the promise that her spirit could live in a tree that was always green and therefore, alive. But it also warned her of a cat *in the nest*—a potential devourer of her spirit if she returned there. Rita recognized the image of the devouring cat as her stepmother, who she experienced as using every opportunity to crush her young spirit.

Following this dream, Rita had a nightmare:

> I was with my partner at our home. I went out and I couldn't
> find my way back. I kept losing my voice. I tried to tell a man
> that I would call information to get the phone number. But then
> I realized that the phone hadn't been hooked up yet. I felt like I
> might have Alzheimer's disease. I kept looking in my wallet, but
> because of my profession, my name didn't carry any weight. A
> woman came to me and said: "You can't move the car." Then I
> went out on my own. It was stormy. I saw a car backing up, and I
> was afraid the driver would run over me. I jumped into the bushes
> and fell on my face in the gully. I awoke feeling paralyzed.

In this nightmare, we hear the residual symptoms of Rita's early trauma: anxiety, feeling lost, disoriented, confused, and helpless in the face of the power of others. She was not able to drive her own car, that is, move in the direction she chose for her own life. She was in danger of being run over by someone who didn't see her. While growing up, Rita had felt invisible in her home, neither seen nor acknowledged by her stepmother.

One of the major clinical signs of a traumatic reaction is, "A state of helplessness ranging from total apathy and withdrawal to an emotional storm, accompanied by disorganized behavior bordering on panic."[160]

For the child-woman who has experienced the trauma of losing her mother's love, the voice of the sorcerer within her (the dark side of the layers of her negative mother complex that ensnare her) says:

> Who do you think you are?

You won't go anywhere or accomplish anything.
You will never amount to anything.
You are not even worthy of a mother's love.

    Rita struggled to move out from under the spell of the sorcerer. She wrote after her reflection on the nightmare: "I'm feeling fed up with how I am. I'm feeding on the negative feeling of being no good." Then Rita had another dream: "I knew that there were murders being covered up at work. The furniture was a royal blue and white fabric. I knew it had to be recovered." Royal blue was Rita's stepmother's favorite color. Rita recognized the sorcerer in the tale as her stepmother who kept her spirit caged in the glass mountain realm of death, from which, as a child, Rita believed she could never escape. The next night, Rita dreamed:

> I was at a New Year's Party, but I had to go home and change out
> of my leotards and red tunic. I couldn't tell where I was going,
> and I realized that I was deaf. My cousin was there vacuuming up
> old mud. She assured me with the words, "Not to worry!" As I
> left, I wondered, "Will any food be left for me when I return?"

    Rita recognized that her dream invited her to a new year, a new beginning, for which she didn't feel prepared. She needed a new persona (that is, more fashionable clothing) for the celebration of the new beginning. Rita realized that she needed to shed her dark standpoint (the black leotards) and her red tunic (her repressed anger and rage), which have left her confused and unable to hear her cousin's reassuring words, "Not to worry."

    Rita had a positive relationship with her cousin who was vacuuming up the mud. She associated the mud with old dirt that needed to be removed from her life. She also connected muddiness with lack of clarity and feelings of confusion, which she frequently experienced. When she compared herself with her cousin in terms of her professional success, Rita wrote, "I'm nothing more than a stick of wood by the fireplace, of no value except to be thrown into the fire and burned."

    When she reflected on the images in her dream, Rita's throat went dry, and she lost her voice. She then realized: "I feel like I repress the good within myself. I couldn't touch royal blue. It was my stepmother's favorite color. It is also the color of the furniture in my boss's office." Rita associated royal blue with danger. She exclaimed: "I'm afraid they will get me. I'm always fearful of being trapped."

    In Rita's dream, she lost her voice and her capacity to hear, both of which are essential for human communication. Her ability to claim her own goodness was overshadowed by her fear of being confirmed as having no worth except to be "thrown into the fire." She was also unsure that there would be any nourishment left for her when she came to the New Year's Eve party (a time of celebrating new beginnings).

Rita wrestled throughout her life with a strong internal voice that continued to ask the questions: "Should I stay, or should I go? Should I live, or should I die?" Through her work in psychotherapy, Rita made the decision to stay alive. However, the residual symptoms of her early trauma continued to haunt her whenever she found herself in situations where she felt her value was being questioned.

During a serious epidemic in her hometown, when Rita was ten years old, her stepmother sent her out to sell greeting cards door-to-door. When one of the women in the neighborhood asked her if her mother knew what she was doing, Rita replied that her mother had sent her to do it. The woman told her to tell her mother that it was too dangerous and that she wasn't to continue. Looking back on the experience, Rita realized that her stepmother wanted her out of her life. She didn't want her alive! Rita recognized that this was the murder in her dream that was being covered up, a murder, which was repeated through the "soul-murders" she experienced at work and other places where she felt worthless, like "a little stick to be thrown into the fire."

After working with the image of the sorcerer from the tale and recognizing herself as the raven-daughter, Rita dreamed:

> I was walking along a road and I had to go through a tunnel.
> There were some cars coming through. It was very dangerous,
> but I got through to the other side. Then, I was with a little boy-
> child, about a year old. He had welts on him, as if he had been
> beaten. I was to take care of him.

While working on the images from this dream, Rita recognized the significance of the tunnel as a rebirthing passage. Although it was dangerous, she had survived and come through to the other side. Her young masculine soul had been beaten, but he, too, had survived. She had now been assigned to nurture and care for this part of herself that had been so abused and neglected. Rita perceived this image as a sign that she was being released from the glass mountain. For many years, she had felt as if she were living in the realm of the dead, with her father's grief over her mother's sudden death and her own grief, which she dared not express lest she increase his pain.

Rita was struggling, at the time we were working on this tale, with a decision about whether or not she could be released from another glass mountain that felt like the realm of the dead for her. This glass mountain was a stressful job in which she didn't feel valued for what she had to offer. She dreamed:

> My partner and I were walking outside the city in the wetlands. There were mother ducks and their chicks everywhere. I saw two blue wild pigs, and then a blue heron. I realize that I needed to untangle myself. Then, I was waiting for tickets to go into a museum or zoo. I was leaning over some plants to get my tickets. Then the question occurred to me, "Why buy tickets to a place where I can't stay?"

The dream gave Rita the answer. She needed to go where there was new life. She no longer needed to fear the color blue. Rita also recognized that she could no longer invest her life energy in a job she did not want. She made plans to "untangle" herself.

Several weeks later, Rita decided to sell her house and buy a cottage, which she could finally identify as her own home. Then she dreamed: "I see a plucky three-year-old lugging a suitcase through a meadow to her new home." Rita knew that she had been released from the glass mountain. Her abandoned and abused little child was going home again.

Trauma and Addictions

In the tale of "The Raven," the young man promises to release the beautiful raven-daughter. He recognizes her distress and expresses a commitment to work toward her release. But as soon as he is tempted by the food the old woman brings, he tastes it and falls asleep.

The experience of trauma and addictive behavior often accompany one another. Sometimes, they even appear to reinforce each other. Addictions to food, chemicals, sex, work, or pleasing others may help us temporarily forget the trauma. However, addictions are basically a repeated pattern of behaviors that ultimately never fully satisfy. Instead, they keep us feeling defeated and powerless while they occupy our attention and distract us from the pain of the trauma. Then the wound never heals, and the raven-daughter remains unredeemed from the curse of the sorcerer, her own dark negative mother complex.

Our addictions are like the giant in the tale, the inflated shadow side of ourselves that will eat us alive if we do not befriend him. The giant doesn't know where the raven, our abandoned feminine spirit, lives. But he does have the map. The shadow energy of our addictions holds the power to show us the way, if we only ask. It can hold up a mirror to the illusions that keep us deceived about who we are and what we need to release ourselves from our glass mountains.

The inflation of the negative devouring shadow (the giant) is often a response to a traumatic experience in which we felt helpless and overwhelmed. If we swallow the shadow (blame ourselves for the trauma), concluding that it must have been our fault that we lost our mother's love and were banished to the glass mountain, then the inflated shadow will surely consume us.

After her reflection on the tale of "The Raven," Jessica worked with the image of the swallowed shadow. Jessica recalled that her Aunt Margaret's behavior was always the opposite of the family ideals. She was the scapegoat of the family, the one assigned to carry the sins or shadow side of the tribe. Jessica recalled that Margaret appeared to believe that she could "*never* get it right," while Jessica felt compelled to "*always* get it right." Jessica realized that while she acted out of the illusion of perfection, Margaret acted out of the illusion of imperfection. Jessica recognized that *both* are responses to the perfectionist ideals of her maternal heritage, "the tyranny of the shoulds"[161] that ruled the women in her family.

Jessica acknowledged that her addiction to perfection, "to *always* having to get it right," was a response to an early trauma of rejection by her godmother, who was a substitute mother for her. It felt to Jessica like her need "to always get it right" was like the hungry devouring giant in the tale. Jessica recognized, however, that to take on her Aunt Margaret's illusion of imperfection was equally destructive. Jessica realized that she did not have to carry the sins of her family *or* defend herself against them. She had a choice.

Then, the day after we worked in the group on the tale of "The Raven," Jessica dreamed:

> I went to check the ice for safety (because I wanted to go skating). There were many critical people there, but I was sure that the ice would hold me.

After her reflection on this dream, Jessica recognized the critical people as members of her family who are disapproving and demanding. She realized how much life energy she has used defending herself against their probing judgments. She decided to "befriend the giant" and to respond to their critiques with compassion, recognizing the losses and traumas each of them has also experienced.

Jessica affirmed her own resolve to let go of her addiction to perfection and embrace her true masculine, that part of her that is always in the service of her feminine nature. In the dream, she honored her own standpoint. She was sure the ice would hold her. Then, four days later, Jessica dreamed: "A large boy baby kisses me. He does not want to be put to bed." She celebrated the news that her young masculine soul would rather stay awake!

The Lost Children

For many of the women in the group, the tale of "The Raven" also evoked feelings of compassion for the impatient queen who lost her child. Several of the women had children who were ill as infants and inconsolable at night. They remembered their own feelings of desperation and distress, followed by feelings of guilt, wishing they didn't have to put up with these children and could get more rest. If a mother feels this ambivalence, and then something does happen to the child, for example, a serious illness or death, her loss can be profound.

Two of the women in the group had lost young children to death. Having her child die is a major trauma for a woman, and, generally, has a profound impact on her view of herself and her world. All of the assumptions about how life should be are shattered. For the mother, the mourning following her child's death is complicated by questions of who was to blame, how could it have been prevented, and how can she go on living for herself, for her other children, and for her spouse? Letting go of the sadness and grief of her loss is like abandoning a connection to her child forever. The woman may believe that staying in the sadness continues to connect her to the child that she loved and lost.[162]

One of the women who had lost her baby at birth, found it very difficult to allow herself to experience deep joy. After her work on this tale, she realized that it was time to let her child go. She wrote a story about him, and shared it with her other children who had not known him. Together, they had a ritual to celebrate his life as part of their family. After this, the woman experienced profound peace. She had let her child go to his rest. And now, she could rest as well. The image of her son no longer came in her dreams.

For the second woman, symptoms of depression were the sign of her continued mourning for a young daughter who had died suddenly and violently. She had recurring dreams about her lost child locked in a basement room, unable to escape. Gradually, the dream images changed, and the child appeared in other parts of the house. Through her active imagination dialogues with the dream images of her daughter, the woman was able to weep with regret for what she wished she could have done for her child. She was finally able let go of feelings of guilt that, somehow, she was responsible for her child's death. She was then able to say good-bye to her daughter and thank her for being part of her life. The image of her daughter did not come into her dreams again. The woman was then able to move on with her own life.

Even those women in the group who were not able, for various reasons, to have children of their own were able to relate to the weeping mother whose child had flown away. Some had reconciled themselves to the loss of motherhood, and others still struggled with their pain. One woman felt that she still carried a daughter waiting to be born.

Reclaiming the Estranged Feminine Spirit

Several of the women in the group, after reflecting on the tale of "The Raven," associated the bewitched raven-daughter with their estrangement from their own creative feminine spirit. A few days after working on the tale, Alexis had the following dream:

> A friendly little bird was pecking at the window. I let him in. He showed up again in my car. I stopped to open the blind that was covering the rear window, and I saw him on the floor, looking for crumbs. Estelle was in the back seat. She was nursing a baby. Then I was driving a car downhill on an earth road full of bumps. The brakes were not working. I had to use the hand brake, which also failed to work. Fortunately, a pothole on the road stopped the car.

In this dream, we see an image of her feminine spirit (the little bird) trying to enter Alexis's life space. When she opened the blind covering her rear window (which she associated with an opening to her unconscious shadow), Alexis realized that the bird was looking for crumbs on the floor. Her spirit was seeking nourishment and attention from Alexis, but there are only crumbs available. Alexis acknowledged that she had been neglecting her creative life. Another aspect of her feminine, however (the image of Estelle), is in the back seat, nursing a child. Alexis associated Estelle with that part of herself that is able to claim her creativity. However, the newborn creative energy being nourished is in the "back seat" of Alexis's life!

Then the dream shifted to a scene of an impending disaster. Alexis could not stop her car. She had no brakes on her life. The dream illustrated to Alexis that her life was certainly going "downhill." Her redemption was in a *pothole*, a break in her path, which forced her to stop. Alexis saw the image of the pothole as similar to the rut in which she felt caught. The saving grace that the rut offers Alexis is that it gets her attention and prevents her from crashing. Alexis heard the warning in the dream. She wrote:

Wake up and feed your creative spirit more than crumbs, or you will find yourself in danger. Get the brakes fixed on your life, slow down, and get a focus on your own destiny!

Alexis recognized that she was in danger of "wishing away" what she most valued because she had gotten into a rut. Her creative work had become a burden, just as the daughter in the tale had become a burden to the queen mother. Alexis also acknowledged that the feathered old woman in the tale was challenging her to keep moving so that she would *finally* recognize the danger in which she had placed herself. Often, we have to get stuck before we can recognize the destructive pattern or spell under which we have been living.

Four Years Later

When we reflected as a group on this tale, four years later, Alexis echoed the words of the bewitched daughter, "Alas for me, who was born a king's daughter!" She now understood the curse that goes with being overprotected and special. Alexis felt that the tale forced her to address the ways she needed to escape from the insecurities her mother transferred onto her, and to reclaim her own voice.

Estelle found the tale a challenge to her inner masculine to stay awake and to seize the opportunities that were presenting themselves to her to be truly and freely herself.

Michaela, Emily, and Rita recognized how their early trauma of losing their mothers' love had profoundly affected their lives and their perceptions of their self-worth.

Four years after we first explored the tale of "The Raven," Jessica was able to identify with the lost daughter turned into a raven. In her response to the mother who wished her away, Jessica wrote:

> You gave me up because I was too needy, but I didn't need what you had to give. My godmother gave me another way to be. There was another trap. She wanted me all to herself. She was the sorceress. But I have freed myself from the cage. I have come home to myself.

Claire saw the glass mountain, four years later, as the place of spiritual transformation. Through her active imagination, when she lifted the bell jar off the little evergreen tree, she discovered a beautifully sculpted bonsai tree!

When we revisited the tale of "The Raven," each woman in the group acknowledged the ways in which she had reclaimed her own life and released herself from the curse of her mother's rejection and neglect. Each recognized how she had come to: define the issues that had kept her captive, differentiate herself from her mother (or stepmother), and make the distinctions necessary to move forward with discipline and determination to claim her own destiny.

Each of the women reclaimed from the robbers what was hers:

- the stick of discrimination that opens any door, so that she is aware of her choices of paths to follow,

- the cloak of clarity and authority that removes the masks she has worn to protect herself and enables her to be more freely visible, and

- the horse of strength, the power of her raw energy to move on with her life, determined to leap over any obstacle in the way.

Lifting the glass bell jar covers off our evergreen souls allows us to breathe in the spirit of life. To be released from the smothering effects of the wound of maternal deprivation requires that we claim the right to live our own unique lives and stay clear and focused on our own paths.

To be abandoned literally means to be "without a call," without a destiny.[163]

We are "kings' daughters"; we have the right to rule over and claim our own physical and emotional lives. We have the right to mourn the traumas and losses that have afflicted our feminine souls and solidified our spirits. We have the right to discover and claim our own destinies.

Reflection Questions:

Chapter VI—Life under Glass: The Tale of the Raven

1. Have there been times in my life when I was invited to "stand and wait," when I didn't have the patience and stamina to stay awake? What has this experience taught me?

2. Have I attempted to escape from the traumas and losses in my life through addictions to food, work, sex, substances, or perfection and pleasing?

3. Are there aspects of my life in which I have felt robbed of:
   - the stick of discrimination that opens any door, so that I could freely chose the direction of my life?
   - the cloak of clarity, so that I no longer have to disguise who I really am behind masks over my true self?
   - the horse of personal strength, to get on with my life and jump over any obstacle in the way?

4. If this is so, how can I now reclaim these stolen treasures for my life now?

CHAPTER VII

IN OUR MOTHER'S MIRROR: THE TALE OF SNOW WHITE

The mirror crack'd from side to side
"The curse is come upon me," cried
The Lady of Shalott.
—Alfred Lord Tennyson

A broken mirror is associated symbolically with an impending dark fate. Many women whose mothers did not experience the value of their own true feminine worth live with split, fragmented, or distorted images of themselves as women. Positive mirroring by their mothers is essential for daughters to be able to recognize their own beauty and goodness. If this does not happen (or happens only partially) a girl child is unable to see herself truly reflected in her mother's eyes. Instead, she may only see her mother's pain and alienation from her own feminine soul. This leaves the girl child lost in the dark forest of life, confused, and struggling to discover her own identity.

The tale of "Snow White" is a story of a daughter whose mother could not love herself enough to truly love her child. Snow White's mother had probably experienced maternal deprivation herself and was also carrying the wound of self-estrangement.[164] Our mother complex, the unconscious layers of positive or negative energy we carry from our experience of being mothered, is not just about our relationship to our own personal mother. It also carries forward what is unresolved in our maternal history, including our grandmothers and great-grandmothers.[165]

In the original version of this Grimm's tale, the mother who longs for the beautiful daughter is also the one who tries to destroy her. After arranging for her death at the hands of the huntsman, the queen asks for the heart of her child so that she can consume it. Subsequent versions changed her request to her child's liver and lungs. The Grimm brothers altered the second edition of the tale, changing the mother to a stepmother. They probably did this to make the story more palatable for children and the mothers who read them the tale.

214

The tale of Snow White is a story about losing one's heart in the face of the devouring energy of the negative mother. In differing ways, each of the women in the group had experienced this loss of heart.

A Synopsis of the Tale of Snow White

In a faraway land in the midst of winter, while the snow is quietly falling, a queen sits working at a palace window framed with black ebony. As she sews, she pricks her finger, and three drops of her blood fall on the white snow. "I hope my little daughter will grow up to have skin as white as snow, cheeks as red as blood, and hair as black as ebony," she says. And so, her little girl grows more beautiful each day, and they call her Snow White. But, sadly, not long afterward, the queen dies. The king then marries a very beautiful woman who cannot bear to have anyone be more beautiful than she is. Each day the new queen consults her magic mirror, "Mirror, mirror on the wall, who is the fairest of them all?" As long as the mirror confirms that she is the fairest in the land, the queen is content.

Then one day, when she consults her magic mirror she receives a different response. This time the mirror replies, "Thou, Queen, may fair and beauteous be, but Snow White is lovelier far than thee." When the queen hears this, she becomes enraged, and turns yellow and green with envy. She orders her huntsman: "Take the child out of my sight and kill her. Then, bring me back Snow White's liver and lungs so that I can consume them." The huntsman takes Snow White to the forest. But when she pleads with him to spare her life and promises that she will run away through the wild woods and never return home again, he takes pity on her. He feels a great weight lift from his heart when he realizes that he does not have to kill her. He expects that the wild animals will do what he doesn't have the courage to do. Then the huntsman kills a wild boar and brings the animal's liver and lungs back to be consumed by the queen.

Snow White runs through the dark forest. Although she hears the sounds of wild beasts, none come near to harm her. Exhausted, she finally arrives at a little cottage where everything inside is neat and tidy. As the table has been set for dinner with seven plates, she eats some food from each plate and drinks some wine from each glass. Since she is exhausted from running through the forest, she tries each of the seven beds and finally falls asleep in the seventh one. When the seven dwarfs, who live there, return home and find her sleeping, they take care not to awaken her.

When Snow White awakes in the morning, she is surprised to see the dwarfs. When she tells them what has happened to her, they agree that if she will keep all things in order in the house and cook and wash and knit and spin for them, she can stay and they will care for her. Snow White responds to their proposal, "O yes,

I would love to!"[166] The dwarfs warn her that, since the queen will try to find her, she should not let anyone into the cottage.

After dining on what she believes to be the liver and lungs of Snow White, the queen consults her magic mirror, "Mirror, mirror on the wall, who is the fairest of them all?" To her horror, the mirror responds:

> Thou Queen are the fairest in all this land,
> But over the hills in the greenwood shade,
> Where the seven dwarfs their dwelling have made
> There Snow White is hiding her head, and she
> Is lovelier far, O Queen than thee!

The queen is enraged. She simply has to be the fairest in the land or envy will give her no rest. So she disguises herself as an old peddler woman and goes to the house of the dwarfs, offering laces and other pretty things. "This woman looks harmless," thinks Snow White, so she lets her into the cottage. The disguised queen shows Snow White some colorful laces that would make her look pretty and offers to tie one for her. The jealous queen ties the lace so tightly that Snow White loses her breath and falls to the floor. When the dwarfs return from mining silver and gold in the mountains, they are dismayed to see their lovely Snow White apparently dead. Then they find the laces that had been tied too tightly and cut them. To their relief, Snow White begins to breathe again. They warn her once more that the queen will try to kill her and that she should let no one into the cottage.

When the queen returns to the castle, she asks her magic mirror, "Who is the fairest in all the land?" and she gets the same reply as before. She knows then that the dwarfs have revived Snow White. The queen is now more determined than ever to destroy Snow White. This time, she disguises herself as another old woman, offering pretty combs for sale. When the queen knocks on the door of the dwarfs' cottage, Snow White replies, "I'm not allowed to let anyone in." The queen responds, "You can look can't you? Why don't you try one of these pretty combs?" Snow White takes a comb and puts it in her hair. As soon as it touches her hair, she falls down as if dead. When the dwarfs came home they find her, once again, senseless on the floor. When they discover the poisoned comb and remove it from her hair, she revives. Once again, they warn her not to open the door to anyone while they are away.

When the queen goes home to her magic mirror, she gets the same reply as before. She trembles with rage. Then she vows, "Snow White must die, even if it costs me my life!" This time, the queen prepares a poisoned apple and disguises herself as an old peasant woman. The red, ripe side of the apple is poisoned and the pale, unripe side is not. When the queen arrives at the dwarfs' cottage, Snow White will not open the door because the dwarfs have forbidden her to do so. So the disguised queen offers the apple to Snow White as a gift, and Snow White opens the window. When she hesitates to take the apple, the queen laughs, and takes a bite out of the pale side to prove that the apple is not poisoned. Then Snow White holds out her hand and takes the poisoned apple from the queen. When she takes the first bite, she falls down dead.

This time, when the queen returns to her magic mirror it confirms that she is once more "the fairest of all the fair." Her envious heart is finally at rest, insofar as an envious heart can ever be at rest!

When the dwarfs come home they cannot revive Snow White, although they comb her hair and wash her with water and wine. This time, they fear she is dead. They mourn her for three days, but they cannot bear to bury her in the dark ground. Instead, they prepare a glass coffin so that they can continue to look on her beauty. Indeed, she appears to be asleep. They write her name on the coffin in gold letters, adding that she is a king's daughter. Then, the dwarfs take turns keeping watch over her. The birds of the air come to visit her: first an owl, then a raven, and lastly, a dove.

Some years later, a prince is hunting in the forest and sees the beautiful Snow White in her glass coffin. He begs the dwarfs to let him have her coffin, offering them money. They reply, "We will not part with her for all the riches in the world!" But the prince is so persistent that eventually, out of pity for him, they agree to give him the coffin. When his servants lift it to carry it away, they stumble over the root of a tree. The core of the poisoned apple that is stuck in Snow White's throat is jarred loose. She sits up, opens the lid of the glass coffin, and asks, "Where am I?" The prince replies, "You are with me." He tells her of his love for her and asks her to marry him. She consents, and a great wedding feast is prepared.

Every one is invited to the wedding, including the jealous queen. After she dresses for the feast, the queen asks her magic mirror, "Who is the fairest in the land?" This time the mirror answers, "Lovelier far is the new-made queen!" When she hears this, the queen becomes enraged. But her curiosity gets the better of her, and she sets out to see this new queen. When she arrives and realizes that the bride is none other than Snow White, whom she has assumed to be dead, she is choked with rage. She steps into a pair of red-hot slippers that have been placed before her and dances until she falls dead.

And the prince and Snow White live and reign happily ever after.[167]

After reading the tale together, I invited each woman in the group to insert herself into the story and reflect on the question, "Who is Snow White in me?" Using the process of active imagination, each woman engaged in dialogues between Snow White and her stepmother, her father, and the other images in the tale. The women also recorded their dreams, as well as their reflections, following our work on the tale in the group.

The Magic Mirror

Emily expressed Snow White's dilemma, which she understood from her own life experience: "Everyone sees that I am beautiful. But I don't have the magic mirror to see it myself."

For the daughter, the magic mirror is the reflection of her own beauty and goodness in her mother's eyes. When this is missing, her young soul is wounded in a profound way. Eventually, the daughter can come to know her own beauty through the reflections of other "mothers," such as mentors, teachers, therapists, and older women friends. But when the initial mirror is cracked, fragmented, or distorted, the daughter's image of herself may take years to repair.

The loss of positive mirroring by her mother, regardless of the reason for its occurrence, is equivalent to the child being deprived of experiencing a basic sense of herself.[168] The daughter who does not experience being accepted and acceptable to her mother as she is feels cut off from a safe haven for developing her feminine identity and value as a woman. She feels adrift in a world in which she perceives herself as insignificant and powerless.

The Canadian poet Moira MacDougall, in an unpublished poem she entitled "Snow White," captured the feelings of alienation of the child who is not reflected by her mother:

> Life became an apple-cranberry crumble, baked
> to a golden symmetry of tart and sweet,
> oatmeal crisp and butter moist, complete
> with a scoop of ice cream melting a white lake
> creating a moat and an island. I would take
> my silver-plated oar and row discretely
> far from our crowded dining room suite
> to bathe and nibble away the ache
> of my mom's neat and apportioned judgments
> of the world, of me, sliced from her ripened breasts:
> the serious, the silly, and the unsaved.
> I hungered to bask in her acceptance

but choked on the dreamy island I'd ingested
as sure as Snow White in her glassy grave.[169]

When her mother does not mirror the beauty and goodness of her daughter, the daughter is left with a distorted image of herself and afflicted with the wound of self-estrangement. Her true self becomes hidden. Who she is, in her essence, is overshadowed by her feelings of abandonment and grief.

One of the first indicators of the presence of the wound of self-estrangement is the daughter's confusion about her ability to know what it means to be loved.[170] She may find herself entering into relationships that she thinks will bring her love, only to be disappointed over and over again.

In the original version of the tale, the queen asks that her daughter's heart be brought to her so that she can consume it. The child who lacks the mirroring of her beauty and goodness from her mother often "loses heart." She is haunted by the unspoken question, "How will I ever know I am loved?" She is not familiar with the signs to look for, the reflections that affirm that she is worthy of unconditional love.

In her response to the tale, Claire wrote a poem about her life choices. Each of the stanzas began with the words, "For the lack of the love of myself."

Claire acknowledged that she had repeatedly made decisions that were not supportive of her own life and that did not bring her the unconditional love she desired. After reflecting on this tale, she experienced a deep stabbing pain in her left arm, which she connected with the energy of her heart. She acknowledged the pain and felt a deep sadness "that it had to be so." Claire recognized that the source of her pain lay in her feelings of alienation and distance from her mother, who carried her own self-abandonment wound. Claire decided to write a letter to her own daughter, reflecting the daughter's beauty and goodness to her, so that the curse would not be passed on to another generation.

A woman who has not been positively reflected by her mother, or early caretakers, may find herself having difficulties with intimate relationships. Unconsciously, she may long for the nourishing and affirming mother she never had and find it difficult to maintain a balance between closeness and separation in her relationships. Sometimes she may demand more closeness than is healthy, and at other times she may distance herself and become aloof.

If a woman with the wound of maternal deprivation is unconscious of the source of her longing, she may choose a friend or partner to take the place of her mother. She may be seeking, as the song goes, "Someone, to watch over me," rather than a true friend or partner. Such relationships are not generally satisfying over time because the other is unconsciously just a stand-in for her mother. The survival of her relationships depends on the woman's ability to become conscious of the ways she is using her friend or partner. She then needs to make the choice to let the other be who she/he is, rather than expecting her/him to serve as a substitute for the mother she didn't have. Sometimes, both parties in the relationship are mother-deprived and unconsciously feed the other's needs. One woman, who was in a crisis in her relationship with her husband, dreamed:

> Vincent and I were climbing up a long hill together. We looked over the edge of the hill. We were looking for two potted mums.

Through her work on the images in her dream, the woman came to see that, although the *mums* referred to in the dream were chrysanthemums, the word *mum* or *mummy* is a Canadian term of endearment for mother. When she was able to accept that both she and her husband were longing for the mothering they had missed, she felt a greater compassion for herself and her partner in their struggle. She had grown beyond needing him to be her mother and wanted a mutual relationship. However, he was not willing to let go of the rage he felt at being abandoned once again by mother. When the woman refused to continue the arrangement, he finally was able to seek a therapeutic relationship to work through his own emotional needs.

Another sign of the wound of self-estrangement is the woman's difficulty in expressing her own feelings. Emotional abandonment creates in the daughter confusion about her emotions. It may be very difficult for her to acknowledge her feelings, let alone express them. She may believe that she has *no right* to feel. While she may appear to others to be functioning well, inside she feels empty.[171]

Estelle had felt alienated from her emotions for many years. She had concluded that feelings, especially anger, were unsafe. Even sadness seemed dangerous. Her mother often sank into periods of depression, from which Estelle felt obligated to save her. Both Estelle and Alexis shared, after working with this tale, that they were expected to positively mirror their mothers, even though their mothers were not able to do the same for them.

When the maternally deprived woman does allow herself to finally express her emotions, the emotions often are manifested in an exaggerated rage, a heightened fear and anxiety, or excessive shame—none of which appear to be in proportion to the reality of her situation. In other words, her emotions are either muted or exaggerated.

We see this phenomenon in the tale of "Snow White." The queen mother's emotions are magnified and extreme, while Snow White's feelings are hardly mentioned. Even after her ordeal of running through the woods hungry and thirsty, Snow White is very considerate. "She doesn't want to eat anyone else's entire meal, so she eats a bit of bread and vegetables from each plate and a sip of wine from each cup."[172]

The wound of self-estrangement, which is precipitated by maternal depriva- tion and rejection, manifests itself in the daughter as fluctuating self-esteem and heightened yearning for acknowledgement and approval from others.[173] It is also seen in the excessive energy the woman devotes to developing her persona, that is, the positive way she wishes to be seen by others.

After reflecting on the tale of "Snow White," Alexis expressed her belief that it was her own life myth. She shared with the group details of a recent theatrical performance (which she had choreographed) in which she kept trying on a series of hats in order to decide which one best suited her. She tried on the hats of the witch, the wild woman, the clown, the seductress, and the good little girl. None quite fit her. The refrain of the song she composed and sang after trying on each hat was, "If only I were free to be me, I would follow my own dream."

Alexis realized that as long as she felt obligated to mirror her mother, who could not mirror her in return, she would not be free to claim her own life and follow her own destiny. She recognized that she felt obligated to live out the role her mother had scripted her to play.

A split occurs in the feminine soul of a woman who is estranged from her true self. Both Snow White and her mother, the queen, carried the wound of self- estrangement, which is often passed from mother to daughter. The queen mani- fested a grandiose reaction to the wound through her envy and rage. Snow White exhibited a depressive response with feelings of anxiety and powerlessness. They both ended up paralyzed, one with burning rage, and the other choked with fear and preserved under glass.

Both grandiose behavior and depression in the maternally deprived woman are defenses against entering into the traumatic pain of the loss of her mother's love. In order for her to move toward healing, she needs to choose to become conscious and to follow the path of individuation, reconnecting with the self that was abandoned.

Envy Would Leave Her No Rest

The queen mother cannot bear the thought that anyone might be more beautiful than she. She simply has to be the fairest in the land or envy will leave her no rest. Envy is a toxic state of rivalry, which includes coveting the goods of another and greedily plotting to possess what the other has. When the queen hears that Snow White is "a thousand times more fair," she turns yellow and green with envy.

Turning yellow would signify an obstruction or disease of the liver, the organ of detoxification associated in ancient myths with the soul. Turning green would indicate that the person was probably poisoned. When we are envious, we are in a psychologically toxic state. We become obsessed with what the other has that we desire and trapped within a fixation that possesses us and consumes our life energies. We are no longer free to think clearly or to choose objectively.

Envy is based on the assumption of scarcity. In her response to the queen in her active imagination, Michaela wrote: "Why are you so threatened by the existence of a beautiful child? Whatever made you think that her beauty diminishes your beauty? There is no scarcity of beauty!"

Jessica expressed compassion for the queen mother. She wrote: "The queen did not believe that she was good enough. Instead of appreciating another's gift, she could only see what was lacking in herself. She thought she could resolve her problem by getting rid of the other. All her energy went into protecting herself."

Jessica made the association with a dream in which she found herself in the bottom of a well while another woman was trying to suffocate her by throwing dirt down on top of her. Jessica realized that the "other woman" was an image of herself that berated her and tried to stifle her creativity. She saw the queen as a part of herself that became paralyzed when she became focused on what was lacking in herself. Jessica acknowledged that her own challenge was to befriend the wicked queen within her so that she didn't continue to terrorize herself with the fear that she wasn't "good enough."

The woman who has been wounded by the deprivation of her mother's love and by the resulting estrangement from her own sense of self believes that love is a scarce commodity and that personal affirmation and admiration are limited resources.

The Tyranny of Needing to be Beautiful

The queen mother believes that she has to be the most beautiful, "the fairest in all the land," or her very existence will be threatened. She is actually willing to destroy her own life in order to kill Snow White and maintain the illusion of her superior beauty.

In her active imagination dialogue, Michaela has Snow White say to the queen Mother:

> I used to be afraid of you, but I'm not anymore! I realize, now, that you must be very fearful and insecure to think that your beauty is all you are!

If how a woman looks defines her intrinsic value, what are the consequences for her life? Psychological research reports a dramatic increase in eating disorders among women over the past four decades.[174] This has become a serious public health concern, with close to 90 percent of North American college-age women reporting that they have been, or are, on diets to become or stay slim. In addition, there is evidence that some women participate in behaviors that they know are dangerous to their health, such as smoking, for purposes of weight control. This is a response to social pressure that associates being slim with being beautiful. When a woman internalizes the norms of a sexist culture, her desire to be beautiful and receive social approval, particularly the admiration of men, may overshadow her consciousness of the consequences to her health. The competition for male attention increases when the number of available princes appears limited. When a woman feels a need to comply with what she perceives to be "what men want," she will develop an image of herself as an object determined by external norms and the judgments of men. This is an especially vulnerable place for a woman who has experienced maternal deprivation and the consequent wound of estrangement from her authentic self. The belief that she must be beautiful, "even if it kills" her, further alienates her from claiming and valuing her own unique existence.

Michaela wrote to the queen in Snow White's voice: "Imagine being willing to die yourself rather than let me live!"

After our work in the group on the tale, Estelle wrote:

> I'm sick of the stress of having to be beautiful. While it made me feel special, I realize now how I always felt trapped. The competition to be beautiful brought the queen no peace. There is never peace where there are comparisons. Of the seven ways to be miserable, comparing myself with others is at the top of the list!

When a woman is caught in having to be thin in order to be admired and considered beautiful, she is a prime candidate for an eating disorder. There is increasing scientific evidence that dieting may lead to disordered eating behaviors. Woodman writes:

> In most eating disorders, the body is sick with the poison of the negative mother. "Take my milk for gall," is the message she receives from her negative mother.[175]

The Three Trials

The queen mother goes into a rage after discovering that the huntsman has deceived her, and that the liver and lungs she has consumed are not those of her daughter. Both of these organs detoxify the body. The liver removes toxins from our blood, and the lungs cleanse the air we breathe. In the ancient world, the liver was considered the seat of the soul, while the lungs were associated with the breath of the spirit. The queen wants to possess the soul and spirit of her young daughter. To accomplish this, she decides to kill Snow White, herself.

The queen mother puts on three disguises of an old woman, an image symbolically associated with one who is wise. This is often the way we are seduced by the dark mother into participating in the destruction of our own souls. She comes in the guise of goodness and appears harmless. In her first disguise as an old peddler woman, she is selling pretty things. Snow White (although warned by the dwarfs to let no one in the house) thinks to herself, "This woman looks so harmless; it must be all right to let her in." Then the wicked queen cuts off Snow White's breath with the pretty silk lace and leaves her for dead.

After the dwarfs revive Snow White, the queen mother comes again, in the guise of another old woman. This time Snow White tells her, "I can't let anyone in." But the queen mother replies, "You can look, can't you?" Again, she seduces Snow White into opening the door and buying the poisoned comb. When Snow White puts it in her hair, she falls into a dead faint. These first two temptations are seductive appeals by the queen to Snow White's vanity. Snow White is not alert to the dangerous power of the negative mother, even though she has been warned repeatedly.

When the dwarfs revive Snow White the second time, the queen "trembles with rage." Then she vows, "Snow White must die, even if it costs me my life." The queen goes to a secret room and makes a very poisonous apple. This time disguised as an old peasant woman, she offers Snow White the apple as a gift. The disguised queen takes a bite out of the side of the apple that is not poisoned to prove that it is safe. The "poisoned apple" is the invitation of the negative mother to taste what is forbidden. The women in the group associated it with swallowing lies.

In the Disney movie version of the tale, Snow White is convinced by the disguised queen's promise that when she tastes the apple what she most wishes will come true—which is, of course, for her prince to come!

This time, the queen assumes that the dwarfs will bury Snow White alive. However, they cannot bring themselves to put her in the dark ground. Instead, they make her a glass coffin, over which they stand guard.

Three times Snow White meets the dark mother in her many disguises. As a group, we examined her three trials in terms of our own lives, exploring the questions:

- What is the lace that cuts off my breath, my spirit?
- What is the poisoned comb I wear that destroys my ability to think clearly and to stay conscious?
- What is the poisoned apple I swallow that chokes off my life? How do I get seduced into toxic love relationships?

Jessica reflected on the times in her life that she felt "paralyzed by the tightening lace cutting off my breath." She saw herself seduced by the promise of the voice of the negative mother within: "Be pretty, be servant, be safe." Then Jessica wrote:

> Snow White feared for her life. She couldn't leave the house for fear of being taken over by the wicked queen mother. But where was her freedom? By choosing to be safe, she was trapped. Perhaps if she had left the safety of the dwarf's world she would have had more resources to help her deal with the wicked queen. In seeking the protection of others, she became sorry for herself and gave naïve excuses: "I'm not allowed," "They won't let me," "I can't." In her state of protection, she was isolated from the real world and not able to use her own capacity for clear judgment. She depended on the dwarfs to protect and save her. She was so busy being protected, and defending herself, that she had no time to be creative.

After her reflection of the three trials of the tale, Estelle acknowledged that when she becomes anxious, she anticipates the coming of the wicked queen and stops breathing. In her bodywork, she discovered that she holds her breath and experiences tightness in her upper body when she is afraid. Estelle recognized the "poisoned comb" as her fear of having her creative work judged and compared with others'. She experienced swallowing the "poisoned apple" as her readiness to please and rescue others.

For Alexis, the "lace" that cuts off her breath and smothers her spirit is her fear of judgment and criticism, and the "poisoned comb" is her belief that she is required "to meet the expectations" of her husband and father. Swallowing the "poisoned apple" for Alexis is about silencing herself and not choosing her own life dream—instead, believing that she must live out her family's scripted role for her life.

She Held out Her Hand and Took the Poison

Snow White holds out her hand to the disguised queen and takes the poisoned apple. The child who is abused emotionally and/or physically wants to believe that it will not happen again. Her hope is that this time it will be different. Her abuser is disguised as a simple peasant woman offering her the polished fruit of the apple tree as a gift. Suspecting nothing, she accepts the poisoned gift.

The queen comes to Snow White while she is in the home of the dwarfs, symbolically in a stunted state of her inner masculine development. She is naive, not able to think for herself or make a sound judgment for her own protection. In spite of the warnings, she repeatedly puts herself in danger. After working with the images of the tale, Emily stated in a painfully clear way: "When you are abused, you repress it. You don't want to remember. You trust again, and again, and you are repeatedly hurt."

Indeed, the evidence in cases of parental child abuse shows that the child will cling to the abuser parent in the hope that the relationship will change and the abuse will stop. Hirgoyen[176] describes the behavior of the abuser as "stalking the soul." The child struggles to understand and adapt to the abuser's demands but only experiences increasing inner chaos when the abuse continues. This leaves her in a state where her very self is diminished. Her own soul is wounded, and she questions the worth of her existence. If the child/woman asserts her own right to exist and resists the abuse, she may then be accused of being abusive to her own abuser.[177]

Rita struggled for years with the question of her own right to exist. Her stepmother's continued negating behavior toward her left her soul fragile, sensitive to rejection and feelings of inadequacy. If she did not defend her stepmother when she was in conflict with her father, Rita was declared an ungrateful and hurtful child. This left Rita confused, doubting her own judgment and feelings.

Emotional and psychological abuse can be insidious in its capacity to destroy the soul. This is particularly true when the abuse occurs when there are no other witnesses. The abuser may appear pleasant and supportive of the child when others are present. When physical abuse is evident, such as we see in the murderous intentions of the queen mother, there is generally a deeper layer underneath of emotional and psychological abuse. The emotional rejection of the child/woman usually precedes physical abuse, which includes any attempt to destroy her life or inflict harm on her body. But regardless of whether or not the abuse includes physical injury, emotional and psychological abuse are sufficient to strike terror into the child's heart and leave her scarred by the trauma.

In her active imagination dialogue as Snow White, Emily responded from her own role as daughter to her stepmother:

> You told me so many times you wished me dead. You threw in my face, "I hate you. I wish I would never have to see you again." You couldn't stand the bright light of the child, the innocence, and the giftedness. You wiped it out whenever you could. There was not enough paper provided to write on, or for painting, or material for sewing. You and your daughter walked around in fine clothes. I was given mostly double hand-me-downs. Your verbal abuse never stopped; there was always a reason to put me down. You did not give me a reason to trust. I could never come to you to be consoled.

Emily yearned for the mother in the beginning of the tale of "Snow White"— the mother who longed for her daughter to be "white as snow, red as blood, and black as ebony." Emily remembered reading the tale as a child and imagining the queen as an ideal mother, one capable of love, and who wanted all that was beautiful for her child. Instead, Emily's experience of her life with her stepmother was like being, as she expressed it, "in a terrorist camp."

Emily continued, after reflecting on the tale and putting herself in the place of Snow White:

> Why did my mother give me her name? Then, shortly after that, she died for me, not physically, but she might as well have. It might have made things easier to accept. Everyone can see that I am beautiful, but I don't know that. I did not have her magic mirror that told me so. I feel my stepmother's hate and envy, but I push it away.

Emily wrote in her active imagination dialogue between Snow White and the queen:

> Do you have any idea of the great longing I had as a child to be mothered, to be loved? To be enfolded in warmth, caring, loving, and holding, to just once feel safe? Do you know what it feels like for a child to never feel safe? Every time you laid eyes on me

you hated me so much your heart turned over in your bosom. You were yellow and green with envy.

Emily then continued her dialogue, addressing her own stepmother:

> I lived in constant fear. You hit me often, punched me down into a little heap of bones, helpless, alone. I remember one time you were hitting me and your own child, my stepsister, told you that you were crazy. She tried to stop you and you turned around and hit her too. You took the prize money for the story that I wrote that was printed in our newspaper. Your reasoning was that I always used up so much paper. My intention, when I sent the story in to the newspaper, was to earn some money. They encouraged me to write more, but no way would you let that happen. I realize now, *that* was the biggest crime you ever committed against me.

The child whose spirit is crushed by the negative mother may find herself reliving the patterns over and over in her life if she doesn't become conscious. Emily continued in her dialogue with her stepmother:

> I don't hate you for this today. I now have an understanding of where it comes from. Had you known how to value yourself as a woman, you would have known how to love. You would not have chosen my father as a mate. As I write I become aware yet again, like another turn in the spiral of understanding, how much of what you have done to me, I have done to myself. I can now see that your threatened ego could not allow me to be, just as my ego now gives me so much trouble in allowing my own soul to shine through.

When a woman endures the ravages of the negative mother when she is young, she may come to the conclusion that somehow it was her own fault. Perhaps if she could have been different, behaved more appropriately, been more beautiful, or even been a boy, then perhaps, her mother would have loved her.

After working with the tale, Claire recalled a dream she associated with the tale of Snow White:

There was huge, rounded three-story house way up in the Arctic Mountains. A man-and-wife team of scientists and their one daughter lived there. I was being shown through the house. There were many old clay figurines of tigers, elephants, and lots of clay animals everywhere. The whole place was unique, with spectacular nooks and cubbyholes to explore. Then a woman murdered the three of them. First she got them into the girl's bedroom. Then she sucked the lifeblood out of the man first, while the wife and child watched. Then she did the same thing to the wife as the child watched, and then the child. I was horrified. They had done nothing wrong. They were exceptional people, living in a desolate place.

In her reflections on the dream, Claire was struck by the powerful images of animal life frozen in clay. The tigers and elephants had no life in them. The house in the dream reminded Claire of a castle with many "nooks and cubbyholes" to be explored. However, it was occupied by a negative feminine energy that sucked the life force out of the occupants one after another, starting with the father. These murders all occurred in the bedroom of the daughter, the place where she engaged with the unconscious in her dreams.

When she worked with this dream, Claire remembered an earlier dream she had had when we were reflecting on the tale of "The Handless Maiden." In that dream, the child told her mother and father, "We all need to go into treatment." Claire realized that her own mother and father both carried the wound of the negative mother. Both were estranged from their own mothers and from themselves and had passed the curse on to her.

In Claire's current dream, the negative feminine sucked the life force out of the daughter and her parents. All of them were innocent. It was clear to Claire that this fate was not their fault. This is a *very* important message for the woman caught in the vortex of the negative mother complex. *It is not her fault.* Snow White does not bring her mother's destructive behavior upon herself.

In Claire's dream castle there are other forces of powerful instinctual energy, namely, clay images of tigers and elephants. Claire recognized that the focused energy of the tiger and the faithful strength of the elephant needed to be brought to life again within her. She associated both of these magnificent animal images with the positive mother, who is devoted to protecting her offspring.

The traumatic effects of physical and emotional abuse suck the life force out of the child and leave her disheartened and disconnected from her own soul. For some of the women in the group, the abuse was more overt and involved physical abandonment. For others, it was more subversive and took the form of emotional distancing by the mother because of her own wound of self-estrangement.

To stay alive, each of the women had (initially unconsciously and later consciously) distanced herself from her mother's grasp and from her mother's desire to consume her daughter's heart, liver, and lungs. These three organs, which are necessary for sustaining life, are associated with our capacity to be in loving relationships, our ability to care for our own souls, and our willingness to honor the creative spirit within us. Each of the women had, in differing ways, "run away through the wild woods, never to return home again."

The Five Faces of the Masculine

There are two feminine images that appear in this tale: Snow White and the wicked queen mother. With them are five masculine images: the cowardly huntsman, the absent king, the industrious dwarfs, the persistent prince, and the stumbling servants. As a group, we explored the parts of our own masculine energy that each of these five images represented.

The Cowardly Huntsman

The first masculine image to appear in the tale is the huntsman servant of the queen. She orders him to "take the child out of my sight and kill her."

When we explored the role of the huntsman in the tale, the women named him the "obedient coward." We looked at which part of the masculine energy within each of us he could possibly represent. What we identified was that part of ourselves that would take the easy way out—even be willing to sacrifice what is beautiful and creative in our lives—in order to maintain our personal position and the approval of authority. The huntsman within us obeys the orders of the negative mother but is saved from committing soul murder by banishing our young feminine to the wild woods (where she is sure to be devoured).

In the tale, the huntsman responds with pity when Snow White pleads for her life and promises to live in exile and never come home again. But his pity is not true compassion. He makes no plans to find a safe place for her to hide. He is a coward who expects that the wild beasts will do the job that he now doesn't have to do. He is relieved for *himself*, "A great weight lifted from his heart when he didn't have to kill her." The huntsman has the potential to be courageous. Instead, he is weak and fearful. He is in the service of the dark queen. However, he only pretends to do her bidding, as he has no true masculine courage to do otherwise.

In order to save her life, Snow White promises to "run away through the wild woods and never come home again." As we worked on this tale, Michaela remembered, with tears, reciting this line from the fairy tale when she was about five years old. She experienced feelings of fear and sadness as she recalled the memory. She realized now that it was her young child's way of attempting to claim her own power in an environment where she felt she was not valued as a girl. As we were completing our work on the tale, Michaela was trying to decide whether or not to return to the small town where she had grown up and where most of her family still lived. Just thinking about the possibility of returning home left her in a state of panic, even though there didn't appear to be any external reason for her to be afraid. Michaela recognized, through her work on this tale, how much the old fears of not feeling safe at home still haunted her.

Emily ran away from home several times when she was young. When she was returned, she was severely punished. After Emily reflected on the tale, she wrote:

> I too, ran away from home. I did so twice. I was grateful for each place I was able to stay on my journey. It was better than the hate I received at home. My stepmother had a free hand in letting her hatred reign, so, in a way, to run into the deep forest was not more threatening. Now, imagining going into the woods creates fear in me, I don't know what I will meet. Still, I know I have to go or I will die.

Emily continued, affirming her choice to stay alive:

> I have courage. In order to save my life I had to run through the wild forest. I am still running through the wild forest, still trying to protect myself even though the danger has passed. But still I experience myself in the forest, feeling overwhelmed, looking at all the leaves, looking at all of life, not knowing what to do, feeling so lost, feeling like running but not knowing where to go, or to whom, wishing for a safe little house deep in the forest to rest from all the struggle.

The child/woman, who carries the wound of self-estrangement because of the lack of maternal mirroring of her beauty and goodness, yearns for a protector, a father who will save her from the devouring negative mother.

The Absent Father

In this tale, the father/king is absent and without a voice. Snow White is a king's daughter, according to the sign on her coffin. But the masculine energy of a true king (symbolically, one who holds and acts on conscious truth) was not there for her.

When the daughter has a father without a voice, she has no model for beginning to develop her own true masculine, that part of her that can claim a purpose and direction for her life and have the discipline and courage to move toward her own destiny. Her mother may feel disappointed that the man she married didn't turn out to be the prince for whom she hoped. Instead, the dark side of the masculine, which is rigid and alienated from loving relationships, appears in the mother, as we see in this tale. The mother becomes possessed by her own need to have power and control in her life and acts this out with those over whom she can have the most power, her own children.

The absent and voiceless father/king leaves fertile ground for the development of the negative masculine in the disappointed mother/queen. The only mention of the king in the tale is that, after Snow White is born and the first queen dies, he takes a second wife. From then on, he remains absent and silent. He never comes to the defense of his daughter and therefore, colludes in her destruction by the queen. Even in her lost state, there is no mention in the tale of his attempting to find her and bring her safely home again. In some earlier versions of this tale, her father is the one who leaves her in the woods, at the queen's insistence. Like the huntsman in later tales, he doesn't kill Snow White but leaves her in the wild woods to die.

Jessica wrote in her active imagination between Snow White and the father/king: "Daddy, where were you when I needed you?" Jessica reread the poem she had written earlier about her own silent father, caught in the cycle of depression.

> Did he love me?
> He never told me
> Can I let it be?

While we were working on this tale, Jessica's father died. At the end of his life, he was finally able to express his love for her. This helped begin to heal the hurt of the years of silence.

Rita had a father who also "took a second wife" and then left her unprotected in her stepmother's care. He did not defend her from her stepmother's rages and negative messages.

Michaela's father was away on a business trip when her mother made the decision to put her in the hospital to protect her baby brother from becoming infected.

Claire's father was primarily absent from her life while he struggled in the depths of his own depression.

Estelle's father was involved in charity work in the community and didn't have time for his daughter.

Alexis's father was preoccupied with his business and with maintaining his status in the community.

When Emily did an active imagination dialogue between Snow White and her absent father, it consisted of only three words, "Where were you?"

Fearful of her mother and disconnected from her father, Snow White escapes into the forest, the place of transformation and renewal.

The Dwarfs

The third masculine image in the tale is that of the dwarfs. There are seven, each with different aspects of the masculine. They are stunted in their growth. However, they do have the capacity to provide a place of safety for the young fragile feminine. They industriously mine silver and gold in the mountain, which is a metaphor for the home of the Great Mother. They have access to treasures of the moon (silver) and sun (gold), which are also symbols of the feminine and masculine. Dwarfs in myths and tales are generally medial creatures who live between two worlds. They can be viewed as a benevolent creative spiritual force, small and in multiple forms, which would mean that this energy is still without unity and focus.[178]

The seven dwarfs are the first encounter Snow White has with positive masculine energy after she escapes the dagger of the huntsman. They are the early manifestation of the multiple faces of her inner positive masculine not yet fully developed. They caution her to be careful about what she lets into her life. However, she ignores the inner voices of her own primitive intuitive wisdom and puts her soul in danger over and over again.

Twice they save her from the disguised dark energy of the queen mother. They unlace her bindings to let her breathe, reviving her spirit. They remove the poison comb from her hair. Even with their warnings, she continues to participate in her own destruction. When it is "too late," when these inner resources are no longer able to rescue her, they break down in despair and grief. Now, all they can do is mourn and gaze upon her paralyzed beauty.

When they come home the third time she is dead. They look to see if they can find anything poisonous. They unlace her, comb her hair, then wash her in water and wine (most likely to be sure no poisonous ointment has been rubbed on her skin), but nothing helps. "The dear child was dead and dead she remained."[179]

They weep and mourn her for three days and decide not to bury her in the black earth (an image of the dark mother). Instead, they put her in a glass coffin on which they write her name, adding that she is a king's daughter. This is reminiscent of the tale of "The Raven," where the abandoned child, also known as "a king's daughter" is held in a glass mountain, her spirit solidified and stifled by her mother's rejection.

The dwarfs put the glass coffin on the hilltop and take turns staying there to guard it. Michaela wrote in her reflections on this tale: "The dwarfs warned her to be on her guard, but no one stayed *then*. They only guarded her when she was dead."

As we saw in the tale of "The Raven," it is often only after it is *too late* that we are able to awaken to new possibilities in our lives. Then, we have to do it the hard way! If we were to rewrite the stories of our own lives, we would recognize the points in time when we might have listened to our inner voices of wisdom and avoided a tragedy. We could rewrite the tale and assign a dwarf to guard her each day so that Snow White would not fall prey to the wiles of the destructive, negative mother. However, that might mean that the tale would end with her still keeping the house, doing the cooking, making the beds, and washing and sewing and knitting, keeping everything neat and clean and having dinner ready when the dwarfs came home.[180]

It is often our mistakes and blunders of judgment that kill off our old ways of being and allow for the beginning of our redemption from the wound of self-estrangement.

After continuing her reflection on this tale, Emily wrote:

> The dwarfs take good care of me and are concerned about my safety. Why are there seven? My birth home had the number seven. The bed I was born in is still there. If only I follow all the rules I will want for nothing. (Wrong!) Have the dinner ready every night. (I did all that!) Again a woman is tempted with an apple, she dies because she tastes it. So what is the connection? Eve must leave the Garden of Eden because she ate of the Tree of the Knowledge of Good and Evil. Snow White dies only to come alive again in the presence of the prince. One must die in order to live again. Is that what I am doing right now in the midst of these feelings of deep depression? Am I dying in order to live?

Three birds come to mourn Snow White: the owl, a sign of wisdom and holder of mysteries; the raven, a sign of the transformational energy of life and death;

and the dove, a symbol of love and peace.[181] All three are associated with the manifestation of the feminine spirit and are connected to images of the Divine Feminine. Their presence suggests that Snow White's death is a passage to a new understanding of her own true nature and marks the beginning of a spiritual transformation.

Enter the Prince

Snow White lies in her coffin for years before the prince arrives. Her beauty is preserved under glass. There is no indication in the tale (Disney's version not withstanding) that the prince has actually ever seen Snow White alive. He falls in love with her preserved, idealized feminine image. She displays no sign of vitality, just frozen beauty.

If a woman longs for an external prince to come and save her "someday," she may keep herself in a state of paralysis in her efforts to remain slender and beautiful so that he will claim her when he finally comes. She may try to mold her feminine body into the image of a Barbie doll and be caught in "the tyranny of slenderness"[182] so that he will be willing to pay anything for her "coffin." She may refuse to feed her body appropriately and become anorexic or bulimic. Or, she may take up smoking, which she knows will be destructive to her health over time, in order to stay thin.[183] She may subject her body to cosmetic surgical makeovers so that the prince will notice her and make her his bride.

The disguised queen mother is able to seduce Snow White into buying the colorful laces and then the poisoned comb by appealing to her need to look pretty. Each of the women in the group could relate to Snow White's desire to look pretty so that she is ready for the arrival of the prince.

After working with this tale, which she saw as a reflection of her own life story, Alexis wrote a fairy tale about a girl raised in a cocoon who couldn't use her wings. This image was painfully reminiscent for Alexis of Blake's poem about being shut in a "golden cage" by the "prince of love," who "... stretches out (her) golden wing/And mocks (her) loss of liberty."[184]

Alexis was well aware of the hazards of dependence on an external prince, no matter how handsome and well positioned, to redeem her from her own glass coffin. She knew she had to claim her own inner masculine resources of clarity and decisive action if she were to be released from the golden cage. She committed herself to move beyond her family myth that required all of the women in the family to be beautiful and to serve men if they wanted to survive.

The Stumbling Servants

As the servants of the prince carry away the glass coffin, "they stumble over the root of a tree." How very appropriate! The foundation of a tree (metaphor for the coming together of heaven and earth) trips the servants and jolts the poisoned core out of Snow White's throat. She sits up, lifts up the glass lid of the coffin, and exclaims, "Where am I?"

Many of the women in the group who had swallowed the poison of the negative mother had a similar experience. Each felt the layers of messages of negation over her sense of self. Emerging out of the glass cocoon of her unconscious state, each was, at first, confused and disoriented. Indeed, *where is she?* This is a defining moment in her life. What if the prince, who has fallen in love with her dead body under glass, wants her to remain in that frozen state of beauty? His appeal to the dwarfs is: "I can't go on living unless I *look at Snow White*. I will honor and cherish her forever."[185] We can well imagine that if he were receiving her in such a preserved state that he expected she would remain so forever. We could also reasonably assume that what he was promising the dwarfs he would "honor and cherish forever" was the dead preserved image of her beauty. Does this mean she will have to remain beautiful in order to be honored and cherished?

Each of the women in the group was quick to notice that, in contrast to the Disney version of the tale (which actually, combines the fairy tales of "Cinderella," "Briar Rose," and "Snow White" into one), the prince does not awaken Snow White with a kiss. The jolt of the coffin, when the servants stumble over the root of the tree, jars loose the core of the poisoned apple that is stuck in Snow White's throat. She sits up, opens the lid of the coffin herself, and asks, "Where am I?"

Because the servants of the prince *stumble*, Snow White is able to cough up the poisoned core that has choked her all those years and kept her preserved under glass. The stumble is the synchronous, seemingly unrelated, accidental event that finally shakes us loose from our negative, mother-poisoned core. It may be an unexpected gift from a friend we haven't seen in years, a new challenging relationship, a startling dream image, a beautiful painting, a poem we find, a passage in a book to which the "library angel" leads us, or a tragic loss we are forced to face. The *stumble* is like a key found to a door that is ready to be opened. We are ready to spit out the poisoned core of the negative mother. We just need one last jarring event to make it happen! For one of the women in the group *the stumble* was her father's death, for another, it was her daughter's courage in claiming her own life, for yet another, it was the decision to move out of a destructive relationship. Many of the women received dream images that affirmed their decision to cough up the poisoned core and to open their eyes to their own inner prince. The release from the deadly paralysis does not happen unless the woman is willing to claim this focused, purposeful masculine energy within her.

Dwarf energy is not sufficient to save the young feminine from the negative mother. She is not yet sufficiently focused, disciplined, or in touch with her own truth to be safe from the vicious, wicked queen. There comes a time when a woman who is struggling to claim her life feels the shift in her energy, from a place that is scattered and without focus to a place of clarity that compels her to move forward. This was evident in lives of many of the women in the group who were able to claim and harness their creative energies with discipline and focus. They no longer felt scattered and confused. Their creative work took on a new depth of maturity and promise. Michaela named the experience clearly in her journal, "Now I know and can see that my inner prince has arrived!"

Healing the Wound of Self-Estrangement

Psychological research indicates that an attachment to a loving mother provides a child not only with protection, but also with the necessary foundation for a secure base of trust, which is the supportive framework for healthy self-confidence and the ability to build and maintain relationships.[186] This foundation is the beginning of the formation of survival conclusions around trust, which the child formulates for herself. Where there is maternal deprivation, there are likely to be extremes in the child's survival strategies, ranging from excessive dependence to exaggerated self-sufficiency. The first strategy is, in effect, a conclusion of impotency, and the second an assumption of omnipotence. Both strategies are evident in this tale. Snow White reflects an image of powerlessness and impotency, evident in her retreat in fear into "the wild forest" of isolation. On the other hand, the queen mother takes on an inflated omnipotent stance, expressed through her self-righteous rage.

The early wound of self-estrangement leaves the child with an internal conflict over issues of trust. She may come to the conclusion, usually by age three, that there is no one in her environment who she can trust to love and cherish her. She may then decide that she can only trust herself, as her mother is not available to hold up the mirror to her unique worth. She may conclude that she has to operate from a position of being all-powerful in order to survive. At her inner core, she knows that she is not *really* omnipotent, but it is the best defense at her disposal. As she grows into adulthood, she may take on too much responsibility, assuming a position of control in order to maintain her illusion of safety. Her unconscious childhood fear is that "to be out of control" means death. She is resistant to knowing her true self because of her underlying fear that acknowledging the trauma of her early abandonment may throw her into a despair from which she fears she may never return.

After exploring the questions related to Snow White's three trials, Michaela had what she called an "I-don't-want-to-know-this headache." Acute pain came down from her head through her body into her lower spine. She experienced waves of heat as the energy was released. Michaela knew her headache was a sign that she was getting into the area of her early survival conclusion around trust. Whenever life situations began to threaten her pseudo-omnipotent stance of "I can trust myself and no one else," Michaela would get a headache. Her early survival strategy was to rule with her head, while energy needed to go into her body (the place where our early messages of trust and belonging are held). Michaela recognized, in the image of the queen mother in the tale, her own "addiction to omnipotence." Michaela had a dialogue in her active imagination between Sophia, the Divine Feminine, and the dark queen. In the dialogue, Sophia consoles the queen, while holding her hands and reassuring her with the words: "You also are loved, even though you are the king's second wife. You are not inferior; you are not secondary because you were second." Sophia's voice also consoles Michaela in her own feelings of being second to her brother, which had precipitated the development of her assumed omnipotence. Michaela continued in her active imagination dialogue with the queen: "I know you now. You are the one who tries to make me unconscious; you are my addiction!"

After her dialogue with the queen, Michaela wrote, "I see now how meeting you is leading me closer to letting go of my illusion of omnipotence."

Early survival conclusions around trust are often fixed in our psyches. My experience as a psychologist has shown me that these conclusions are generally held deep in our unconscious, entrenched not only in our psyches but also in our bodies. In the process of individuation, they are often manifested in the last phases of psychological transformation. These early belief systems have helped the child to survive and are therefore worthy of respect. But if they continue to rule the woman in her adult life, they can become an addiction to a way of thinking and responding that is destructive of the soul it once saved.

The meaning of the word *addiction* comes from the ancient practice of being a slave to a deity to whom one committed oneself and by whom one was then possessed.[187] The original commitment was intended to secure a place of safety under the protection of the deity. The consequences of this bargain were only realized later when the one addicted (the *addictus*) was no longer free. When faced and challenged, our addictions force us to either claim our unique worth or to remain enslaved.

The Tooth that Nibbles at the Soul: Reclaiming our Freedom

"Narcotics cannot still the Tooth/That nibbles at the soul."[188] Narcotics are used to deaden pain, alter the reality of our lives, and keep us in a state of semi-consciousness. Our addictions serve the same purpose. They may include external addictions to substances, such as food, alcohol, and chemicals, or to activities, such as excitement, work, or sex. Often our real addictions lie deeply in our psyches in our earliest strategies for survival. My experience as a psychologist has shown me that most external addictions are the psyche's attempt to bring to the surface of consciousness "the tooth that nibbles at the soul." Dealing with external addictions may indeed be the gift needed for the internal addiction to emerge and be acknowledged.

One of the women in the group hid her addiction to alcohol for years because she was ashamed that she "could not control it." Her earliest survival conclusion was one of pseudo-omnipotence, which her thirst for alcohol was challenging. Once she was able to surrender her need for omnipotence to the Divine Mother (who she saw to be truly omnipotent) she was able to go for treatment and to accept the help she needed from others.

Before she entered the treatment program, while we were still working on the tale of Snow White, she had the following dream:

> I was in a basement or some kind of underground hall. Several times I passed the furnace room, and each time I noticed a small fire outside the furnace. I did not try to put it out or to get anyone to help, until it became quite large. Then, I was outside on a small hillside. I was supposed to care for four cows belonging to an old woman. When she came back we went to the field to see the cows. Each had a container for water, but the water was frozen. As soon as I saw them, I realized that I had forgotten all about giving them water. The old woman was furious, as one of the cows was almost dead.

After reflecting on the images in this dream, the woman wrote:

> It seems pretty obvious that this dream is telling me that I am ignoring danger, until it becomes a big problem. Cows are nurturing animals, which give milk, (mother-nourishment), which I need for my body and soul to be healthy. I neglect my own physical and emotional health by staying unconscious.

Then the woman remembered that the night she had the dream, she had had four cocktails before going to bed. She recognized the connection between choosing to feed her addiction four times and not attending to the healthy nourishment the old woman offered her in the image of the four cows. She saw the old woman as Sophia, an image of the Divine Feminine for her. The woman identified the out-of-control-fire as the rage of the queen mother within herself. She acknowledged how her addiction to alcohol challenged her early omnipotent survival conclusion.

In her inner conflict around issues of trust, the daughter with the wound of self-estrangement may, on the other hand, come to the conclusion that she is impotent or powerless. In the tale, Snow White is naive. She takes in what others say as truth without examining it for herself. In order to survive, she decides to please and serve. We hear this in the tale when she responds to the list of duties she will have in the house of the dwarfs in exchange for a place of safety and security. In the original tale, when Snow White meets the dwarfs, their only request was that she cooks their meals in exchange for shelter. In later versions, their demands increased to, "If you will keep the house for us, do the cooking, make the beds, wash, sew, knit, and keep everything neat and clean, you can stay with us and not want for anything." To all of this Snow White replies, "I'd love to."[189] Many of the women in the group recognized this bargain of service in exchange for safety. For Jessica, the message she heard and swallowed as her destiny was, "serve and be safe." As she worked with this tale, Jessica felt rage rise within her as she recognized all the ways she had allowed her creative feminine soul to remain in exile, while she kept the bargain of cooking and cleaning in exchange for security in the face of her fears.

Jessica remembered a dream she had of a female seal bottling up from the depths and then submerging again under the water, out of sight. She recognized the seal as an image of herself that primarily stayed hidden. She felt like Snow White, unconscious under glass, unable to breathe deeply of her own authentic existence. Jessica lived in the emotional watery realm of the depths of grief and despair, held in the tragedies of her maternal history. She saw herself as addicted to perfection and, as a consequence, becoming very anxious if she perceived that she "didn't get it right."

The tale indicates that Snow White stays and keeps the house in order, and in the morning the dwarfs go off to the mountains to look for silver and gold (that is, leave for work to make money). In the evening they come home again, and dinner has to be ready. Snow White is a prisoner in the house of the dwarfs (her own stunted and undeveloped masculine side). Their way of protecting her is to isolate her. She is caught in the survival conclusion of pseudo-impotence. The woman who takes on this strategy for survival finds herself in a series of situations where she feels isolated and alone. The demands on her are *serve to survive*. In the process she has no time or energy left to use her own creative gifts.

Reflecting on the issues of trust that were evoked for her by the tale, Emily wrote:

> It feels like not being able to trust (or not being sure what trust is), and out of that place of uncertainty making choices that are not always positive. Just as Snow White again and again trusted the old woman who came to her door. The mirror held up to my face was always that of a bad person. So the child inside feels it is bad, unworthy, unsure. But it still needs to be liked. So it tries to project a good image outward, but still not really believing it, always fearing that it will be taken away. My soul feels encased right now. I am not able to find Self in all this darkness. Everything seems outwardly projected and imagined. I need to face the darkness to fully know it and own it. What of this is mine, and what was projected onto me that I have accepted?

In Emily's reflection, we clearly hear the third alternative that the child may choose around the issue of trust. Fluctuating back and forth, between trusting only herself and trusting only others, the child/woman finds herself on the razor's edge of despair. This is a precarious balance point that continues to reinforce her estrangement from her inner self.

Emily continued her written reflection:

> It is within the outer structure that I have functioned. It gave me a sense of security. Also, it has been out of that outer structure, and not my core structure, that I have made most of my decisions. So when my partner says I have to have things my way, it comes out of those outer layers that are not real. I need structure in order not to feel threatened and collapse.

It was clear to Emily that her struggle with trust went back to her early abandonment. She could not allow herself to feel vulnerable and stay alive, so she built defensive walls around herself that have made her feel even more isolated and alone. She wrote:

> How great the threat on my life must have been to build walls like the walls of Jericho. I need to go back, to allow myself to be

vulnerable again, to be open. Will I ever get there? I need to trust in the fact that in order for the darkness to exist there has to be light.

Healing the wound of self-estrangement precipitated by the experience of maternal deprivation is a long process that requires a commitment to consciousness, openness to new relationships, and a celebration of our unique beauty and destiny. For this to happen, we need new mirrors to be held up to our beauty. We need to be affirmed in our right to exist. We need our lives to be honored and cherished. We need to claim our own true masculine energy, the prince within, who will not desert us if we remain faithful to the process of our own individuation. All of this requires choosing to live our own lives, not the ones assigned to us, or the ones we take on in order to survive. This choice requires re-inhabiting our own souls.

The Red-hot Shoes

The queen mother is invited to the wedding of the daughter whose life she thinks she has destroyed. When she recognizes Snow White, she becomes paralyzed with rage. "But two iron slippers have already been put into the glowing coals, and they are set down in front of her. She is forced to step into the red-hot shoes and dance until she falls to the floor, dead."[190] The dance of the destructive rage of envy annihilates her.

The ending of this tale is similar to the original version of "Briar Rose," in which the jealous mother-in-law tries to destroy her son's wife. Instead, "the queen mother is thrown into the pit of snakes and vipers"[191] which she had designed to kill Briar Rose. If anger and rage, resulting from a compulsion to be in a position of superiority, are our standpoint in life, they will eventually destroy us.

Jessica reported, after her active imagination with the queen mother, that she felt deep compassion for the queen. She saw her as so unconscious in her neediness that in her desperation she wasted her life and extinguished the light of her own life force. Jessica recognized the destructive energy of the consuming flame of anger within herself and affirmed her commitment to staying conscious. She wrote:

> The queen didn't believe she was beautiful. She had to keep comparing herself in the mirror. She was not enough as she was. She had to have it all to be good enough.

Once we claim our own inner prince, we then have the courage to face our negative mother complex. The dark queen comes to witness the coming together of the masculine and feminine at the wedding. The hot iron shoes in which she is forced to dance disintegrate her. Our feet are our roots, our connection with the earth. They symbolize our capacity to take a stance in life, to step forward on the path of our own destiny. Red-hot shoes are put to the roots of the negative mother complex so that the energy can be released and transformed.

Four Years Later

After revisiting the tale four years later, Claire shared with the group the fact that she was finally able to accept the china dishes and silverware her mother had been offering her for years. No longer attached to the negative mother image that she had previously associated with the acceptance of these gifts, Claire was now able to receive them freely and thank her mother. Then she dreamed: "My mother is trying to get back in my house. She is trying to get in through the back (the dark side) of the mirror." Claire remembered her active imagination response to the absent mother in the tale of "Rumpelstilskin." She had pleaded with the absent mother, "If only you would have been there to reflect me."

On revisiting the tale, Estelle became conscious of the fact that she no longer holds her breath. She recognized the "pretty laces" of the wicked queen as the ways she "takes on too much pleasing." She declared: "I am a king's daughter! Now, I can stand on my own two feet and even kayak on my own. I have a choice about the direction my life takes."

Four years later, Emily recognized the ways she still gets caught in being obedient to others and silencing her own voice. She made a commitment to an active imagination dialogue each week with her birth mother who abandoned her and who has since died. Emily longed to reconnect and to get to know her. Then, she dreamed:

> I was offered a cup of poison by my stepmother and father. At first I felt like I had no choice—I must drink it, as I am not worthy enough to live. Then, I realized that it was *not true,* and I refused to swallow it. I flushed it down the toilet.

Emily reconfirmed her resolve not to swallow the toxic messages of her stepmother and father and to honor her own choice to recognize her true worth and make her own life choices.

Revisiting the tale of "Snow White" four years later left Alexis with a sense of "too-lateness," a victimized state of hovering over that which was dead, and even idealizing death. The tale reminded Alexis of her struggle with her own internal wicked queen who comes in various disguises to undermine her confidence in herself. She declared that the good news is that she has moved away from submission to men, from vulnerability to their criticism, and from her feeling of inadequacy in front of them. She no longer feels obliged to fulfill their expectations.

Alexis wrote:

> Being pushed to paint another way, I discovered with clarity who
> I was as an artist. I found out who I was through staying with the
> resistance and not simply complying.

After revisiting the tale of "Snow White," Michaela decided to move back to her hometown. She recognized that she no longer needed to be afraid that home was not safe.

Another woman in the group described how she now felt free "to wear pink," which she had not been able to do since her rape as a young child. It had not felt safe to be pretty, so she had estranged herself from all that she associated with the feminine side of herself. She told the other women in the group, "I'm finally able to claim my own body again, which I didn't even realize I had lost."

Who Will Hold the Mirror?

> Who shows the child just as it is? Who places it within its constellation
> And puts the measure of distance in its hand? [192]

When we revisited the tale four years later, each of the women in the group looked into her mother's mirror. What each woman saw reflected back was the extent to which her mother had been estranged from her own feminine soul.

The rope around her mother's throat silenced Jessica's mother. Each of the women in the family subsequently inherited the noose of silence.

Alexis's mother lived with the profound anxiety that she always had to measure up to what was expected of the women in her family tradition.

Estelle's mother felt rejected and set aside as unworthy compared to her sister. She had also experienced the early traumatic loss of having to suddenly leave her home.

Claire's mother felt pressured by the responsibilities of her career and had very little time for her children.

Michaela's mother experienced the loss of her own family and culture when her marriage meant leaving it all behind and moving to another country.

For two of the women, Emily and Rita, there were double reflections: the images of their birth mothers as well as the images of their stepmothers.

Rita's mother disappeared from the mirror of her life with her sudden death. Emily's mother made the choice to leave the little daughter she had named after herself. Emily indicated that she would never know all the constraints that pushed her mother to that choice. The mirrored images of their stepmothers, for both Rita and Emily, were dark with negation and soul destruction.

For each of the women in the group, in differing ways, the original mirror of her mother was not able to reflect the beauty of her true self. Finding the mirror of her own reflection, and honoring her feminine soul in its unique beauty and goodness, involved the pain of her feet being put to the fire (as happened in the tale to the wicked queen mother). The image of the new mother that emerges is a surprise. She is not white as snow, but black as ebony! Marion Woodman sees the Black Madonna as "the awakened positive mother who is constellated after the purging of the negative mother complex." She is black because "she has literally or figuratively been through the fire and emerged with an immense capacity for love and understanding."[193]

Each of the women emerged from the transforming fire of self-estrangement with an expanded capacity for love and understanding. Despite their different histories, all of the women were able to mirror beauty to one another with compassion.

It was in Einseidlin, Switzerland, the home of the Black Madonna that the inspiration came to me to invite the seven women to reflect on fairy tales as a healing process. Years later, I realized that we had come full circle.

> The daughter who can come out from under the skin of the negative mother will not perpetuate her, but redeem her. The Black Madonna is the patron saint of abandoned daughters who rejoice in their outcast state and can use it to renew the world.[194]

Reflection Questions:

Chapter VII—In Our Mother's Mirror: The Tale of Snow White

1. What survival conclusions around trust have ruled my life:
   - Pseudo-omnipotence, believing that I always have to be in control or be "the best" in order to survive (the queen)? or
   - Pseudo-impotence, believing that I have to please and serve others in order to be "safe" (Snow White)?

2. Are there times/situations when I choose one survival conclusion and other situations where I choose another? What new decisions can I make with this awareness?

3. What addictions rule my life? What are the ways in which they expand my awareness of the "tooth that nibbles at my soul?" How are my early survival conclusions related to my addictions?

4. Who holds the mirror of my unique worth now in my life?

5. How am I the mirror of another's beauty to them?

CHAPTER VIII

THE THREADS REWOVEN

Stories of women breaking bread
at the altar of courage.
portraits of shadows with arms
outstretched
beckoning, striving
to caress our hearts,
to rip away the leathery bindings
squeezing us closed.
Shadows of strangers
nudging
scare the wits out of us.
The Zulu Woman stays planted
as we gallop like deer
dodging behind trees,
afraid to trust.
From a distance we gaze at her form:
Can we trust?
Can we come out from behind props
to test the waters
can we believe that you're real,
that your arms will open
and receive us
without judgment and blame?
Have we reason to believe that you
will give us life?
Our shame falls away like
showers of autumn leaves.
Little by little we savor every
glimmer of hope.
Salty tears like balm for the wound

Naked, vulnerable, milking trust
Sharing the gold coins
buried deep in the well
we bring life to the surface.
Lovingly we cry, we laugh, we touch,
we dance, and we nourish each other
into life.

(Jessica, *Poem in Honor of Zulu Woman*)

For the women in the group, the image of the Black Madonna was that of a Zulu woman. She first appeared in Estelle's dream shortly after we finished our work on the seven fairy tales. She spoke no words. Her power was in her presence.

The image of the Zulu woman became a symbol of the women's commitment to steadfastly claim their own personal power as women. She represented the Divine Mother, the Black Madonna, whose commitment, strength, and courage would never falter. She was, to them, a mother of all mothers, one who would never abandon her children. The image of the Zulu woman also symbolized their ability to confront any dilemma with courage, while honoring their own innate wisdom.

One of the women painted her image. In the painting, the horns of the ancient Great Goddess, surrounded with the colored feathers of a healing shaman, crown her head. An amulet, symbolizing the third eye of inner wisdom, hangs from her neck. Her ears are open to listen and her eyes are focused and steady.

According to Jung, "the principal aim of psychoanalysis is to acquire steadfastness," the quality of faithful and unwavering commitment to follow through on what we know to be true.[195] Throughout our work together, each woman grappled with her own negative mothering experience and its impact on her understanding and valuing of herself as a woman. We discover what it means to be a woman from our relationships with our mothers (or other feminine caretakers), and what it means to be valued as a woman from our fathers (or other masculine figures in our life). When we carry a negative mother complex, we eventually need to become reconciled to the ways we may have rejected and despised our feminine natures, particularly our own bodies, as well as our ability to be creative and generative. As long as the negative mother complex rules us from within, we are not free to fully claim our feminine value and, consequently, our worth as human persons.

> Letting go of the dream of *ever* having a good (enough) mother
> is the healing of the negative mother complex. This is the sacri-
> fice. Next comes the lesson of mothering oneself.[196]

For this reason, it was important that I consciously avoid robbing the women of the opportunity to learn to mother themselves by becoming *too good* a mother to them. Each of the women in the group struggled with facing the reality of learning to honestly mother herself. She had to let go of seeking others to mother her. As well, she had to recognize any temptation to become a mother to others in the hope of being cared for in return.

Six years after we began our work on the seven fairy tales, we came together to celebrate the transformation in each woman's life. It was a powerful time filled with tears, laughter, and dancing. As we had done the first year, after our initial work on the tales, each woman shared the threads of her story from the time our work began to the new rewoven patterns in her present life. She then designed a ritual to celebrate the transformation that had occurred in her life and in her relationships with others.

Estelle began by sharing an image of a starving buffalo, buried alive, which had appeared in her dream just before we began our work together. She reflected on her new awareness of reclaiming her own personal power as a woman (no longer starving and buried alive). New dream images were coming to her now. One image of an opening flower she viewed as a sign of her own opening to the light of her femininity and creative potential. She described another dream of a flag, with a red and black yin/yang symbol, flying on a bridge over a deep canyon. Estelle understood this image to be a sign of her increased willingness to balance the masculine and feminine energies in her life. Estelle recognized that she was being invited to cross the bridge over the deep canyon of despair, which she related to the early loss of her mother's love. She wrote her own fairy tale (which she read to the group) in which she asked the mother who withdrew her love when she had another child: "Why did you go away? What did I do wrong? Wasn't I good enough to make you happy?"

One of the most difficult dilemmas for the sensitive child to face is her mother's silent pain.[197] Estelle recognized that no matter what she did, her mother's sadness did not go away. Estelle had become a mother to her own mother when she was only three years old. This was a role that she understood, even if at times she felt inadequate as a mother. Facing her own children leaving home was very painful for Estelle. She reported that the morning her second daughter left for college, she had the following dream: "I went outside to see the sunrise. The question that came to me as the light dawned on the horizon was: who am I if I am not a mother?"

The answer came to her several days later, through a dream image of another beautiful Zulu woman. When Estelle did an active imagination dialogue with the dream image, asking the question, "Who are you?" the Zulu woman replied:

> I'm on my own. I know the way because I trust in my own inner wisdom. I'm black and you are white, but sometimes I'm white and you are black. Accept the beauty of both the shadow and the light in your life. Move forward in confidence and trust in your own creativity. Allow yourself to make music from your heart.

Then a dream followed for Estelle in which she was clearly the leader of an important creative event. It was her responsibility in the dream to be "out front," encouraging others to claim their creative gifts. This image astonished Estelle, since she had never before considered herself to be a leader (because she had been too busy taking care of others' needs). Several days after the dream, as she continued taking on too many obligations in order to please others, Estelle fell down the stairs and broke her ankle. She saw this as a warning to find her balance, move forward with clarity, and claim her role as a leader. Then she dreamed of a shaman sitting in a lotus flower. He instructed her: "You need to slow down, get off the collective runaway train you are on. Step aside, look within."

Estelle then dreamed of a beautiful little girl who was proud of her creative gifts and felt confident in sharing them with others. She recognized the dream image as an aspect of herself, seeking her soul's desire through sharing her music.

The threads of Estelle's early loss had come full circle. She was now free to live from the spontaneous, creative, young feminine self she had left behind in order to care for her mother's wound. For her ritual, she prepared an image of her young, confident, and creative little girl and invited each of the women in the group to decorate her as a way of celebrating her being alive. This image of Estelle's life now, focused and yet spontaneous, was vibrant with joy at being rediscovered and honored.

Jessica, in her celebration of transformation, recalled one of the first symbols she had worked with from her dreams, "Peter Rabbit hiding under a basket." In this image, she recognized her early struggle with being invisible and not wanting to be seen. She shared with the group:

As we completed our time together a year after our work on the fairy tales, I got in touch with the Zulu woman within myself. I had been shaken to the core after seeing Alexis's black and white mask of the two sides of the feminine. I recognized that my struggle was to live in the light and not the dark. It was the first time I realized that I really didn't know what it meant to be joyful.

Jessica reported that, after that time, she had a "breakthrough dream" in which she encountered her grandmother and heard her voice. Jessica examined her own desire to keep the family secret about her grandmother's suicide. Now she knew she had to give voice to her story. She remembered the image of the bull penned up at the Winter Fair that had come in her dream when we first explored the tale of "Rumpelstilskin." Then, she had seen the horns of her dilemma (of whether or not to share her grandmother's story) to be either to "flaunt it or bury it." But now, she recognized that the resolution was in neither of these choices. The invitation she was being offered now was to celebrate her gift as a writer. Jessica then dreamed:

> I am walking through the rough cut in a mountain. I am amazed that I am able to get through. I thought it was going to be more difficult.

This dream gave Jessica the courage to send her first novel to a publisher. She was able to experience joy when it was accepted.

One of the significant shifts in Jessica's life over the six years occurred when she wrote the story of her young son's death and placed a tombstone on his grave. She was finally able to weave this loose thread of pain and loss back into the fabric of her life. She then felt at peace and could let her child go.

Jessica recalled a powerful dream she had had while we were working on the tale of "The Handless Maiden." She had dreamed of a woman tied to a stake in the ocean, with her hands behind her back. The woman would have drowned when the tide rose had she not been set free by two children. Jessica felt that her own feminine soul had finally been set free from the curse of the family secret, although she continued to get messages from her family that "she should leave well enough alone, or she would do more harm than good."

Just prior to our coming together, six years after beginning our work on the fairy tales, Jessica dreamed there was a parade in her hometown to celebrate the publication of her mother's story. Each of the women in the group committed herself to being part of that parade the day it was published.

As part of her ritual to celebrate her life rewoven, Jessica invited each of the women to choose something that they would be willing to bring to the parade. She shared a quote, which she felt expressed her own life struggle, "[My] deepest fear is not that [I am] inadequate. [My] deepest fear is that [I am] powerful beyond measure."[198]

Jessica finished her ritual with a poem she composed entitled "Dancing Faces."

> Standing in the shadows, beneath the arches
> Of this sacred place I find her
> A black stranger adorned in flowers
> Dancing to the rhythm of the drum.
> Her pulse makes music.
>
> No critical voices inside her head telling her
> She is not good enough.
> Her being radiates compassion.
> I am me and you are you
> No right or wrong way to be.
>
> With her head up and eyes open she beckons.
> I grapple with my failing.
> Longing to live urges me into the open,
> Reassured by her presence.
>
> She does not see my awkwardness or my
> Feeble attempts to be good.
> Her fingers find my pulse LUB DUB
> LUB DUB the beat of life.
> No need to look outside myself.
> I am enough! We dance.

Michaela opened her reflections on the celebration of her transformation, six years after we had begun to work together, by recalling our first session on the tale of "Rumpelstilskin." She remembered the anger and rage she had felt after working with the tale, and the cardiac arrhythmia that she had experienced. She recalled the defensiveness within her that the tale had evoked. She also remembered the series of dreams she had had at that time, of an adolescent masculine figure shackled and enraged. She recognized this dream image as an aspect of herself that was searching for hope and the promise of liberation from her fears.

After our initial work on the fairy tales, Michaela had made an image of a clown, which allowed her to finally break through her serious nature and permit herself to laugh. She stated: "The clown turned my world upside down so that I could see my life from another perspective. I'm actually no longer dizzy when I put my head down, as I have been in the past."

A year after our initial work together, Michaela had a dream in which the mask of a bear (that she had made in her early work) howled in anguish. The dream initially frightened her. When she did an active imagination dialogue with the mask of the bear, a memory she had repressed of being sexually assaulted while hospitalized as a child flooded her with anger and grief. Finally she understood the meaning of earlier dreams from which she would awaken in terror with the image of a male intruder at the foot of her bed. Throughout her earlier psychotherapy work Michaela recognized that something had happened to her in her early years, but she had no memory of any incident that might have elicited these reactions in her dreams. She carried a fear that perhaps something happened with her father, which was unimaginable to her. When the howl of the bear brought the memory of her sexual assault to the surface, she went into a deep rage against her feelings of powerlessness. Michaela then understood the rage of the young masculine figure in her dreams, helpless in his confinement. She expressed her relief that her abuser was not her father or anyone in her family, but a stranger without a face. Michaela shared with the group: "I now understand how the wound of my early sexual assault shaped my resistance to relationships."

After the memory of her sexual assault surfaced, Michaela invited the women in the group to participate in a healing ritual with her. After the ritual, Michaela declared, "I feel now like a plug has been unleashed from my pelvis, and cleansing, living waters are now gushing up within me."

As we celebrated the transformation in her life, Michaela shared:

> I feel now like I'm giving birth to myself. I'm in labor and learning when to breathe and when to push. I'm going back to learn to trust. I can now give thanks for my anger, my fears, and my addictions that kept me on the journey of discovery. Now, I am free to be with others on their journey.

She closed her ritual of transformation with a beautiful song entitled "Now Is the Time."[199] The words of the chorus, which Michaela sang with a clear voice, honored her commitment to celebrating her womanhood. We all rejoiced with

Michaela that she could finally weave her feminine power into a new understanding of herself and her life purpose as a teacher of other women.

Emily initiated her celebration of transformation by honestly acknowledging that she had triple-booked the time that been set aside for our group gathering. She acknowledged that she "wanted it all." She admitted, "In my neediness to be mothered, I seek mothering everywhere."

For her celebration, she invited the spirit of her birth mother to be present, with the sound of a flute. She then put her mother's photograph in the middle of the circle with the words, "I have compassion now for a stranger that I see carrying pain in her eyes."

Emily then shared verses from David Whyte's poem, "Waking Up,"[200] which ends with a strong admonition to let go of pain and get on with life. Emily recognized the conflict within herself to stay in the pain or to move on. A year before our gathering, she had started a journal to get to know her birth mother. She displayed a photograph of her mother and used the process of active imagination to dialogue with her mother's image. She sought information from her birth mother's family and others who had known her. Emily reported that, at times, she still felt anger at having to go on this journey of healing, and at the painful memories it has evoked for her. She stated: "I have lost connection to any God of my past. But, I have found a connection to a God without a name."

Because she was given the same name as her birth mother, Emily admitted that she had been going through the process of deciding whether or not to change her name. Just after she shared this with the group, eight birds appeared in the trees under which we were sitting. When they began to sing, their song was remarkably like the sound of her name! Emily began to laugh. She recalled that family members had told her that her mother often cared for birds and other injured creatures.

Emily felt that she was gradually moving beyond the negative judgment that she had placed on her birth mother. She then shared a recent dream:

> I was out on the wing of an airplane. It was a narrow wing. To keep me safe a skin was put over me—it was as if it were knit out of Ariadne's thread (or like the garment that Joan of Arc wore). It reminded me of threads of life. Then I heard the words, "It is your powerful life story. It is your body knit."

Emily realized that her dream was giving her a message of healing. The two feminine images that appeared in her dream are Ariadne, whose thread of love saved Theseus from the devouring Minotaur, [201] and Joan of Arc, who liberated her people from destruction. Emily recognized both as images of her strong, courageous feminine soul. Her powerful life story is in her body, knit with the threads of love and with the courage to pursue freedom from a life of fear. The story of her abandonment is knit into the fabric of her body. However, now she is being given wings, with which to fly above and beyond her rage at her perceived powerlessness and her fear of another abandonment.

Emily's stepmother's birthday had been several days before our gathering. Emily admitted to the group:

> There is still a band around my heart of white-hot rage about how my stepmother treated me. But I know that Snow White would not have met her prince if she hadn't had a wicked stepmother.

Emily then shared:

> I feel that I am settling more and more into myself, opening the third eye of inner wisdom, trusting myself; meeting myself for the first time. I recognize that there is a force of resistance in me that wants to swallow me up as I move on the journey of self-realization. I feel a sense of contentment, in coming home to myself. I recognize that I am deserving of coming home. I have come such a long, long way. I will never be the same.

After these reflections, Emily shared a recent dream which she had entitled "The Silence."

> I was looking over a stone wall. It had been whitewashed and some worn spots were evident. There was an atmosphere of incredible silence and a feeling of peace.

Emily can now see over the stone wall of the obstacles she has had to face in the past. The wall is not gone, but it is no longer insurmountable. It is now whitewashed, that is, its ugliness is covered, although there are worn spots that are still showing. Despite the wall of her abandonment wound, Emily can now see beyond it. It will never go away; it will always be a part of the fabric of her life, but it no longer dominates the newly woven pattern of her existence.

Emily concluded the celebration of the transformation of her life by sharing the following reflection:

How much can I maintain balance and close the chapter of my being ruled by the wounded child? My hands are free again to be creative. My heart is open to potential surprises. I am determined now to "live my life in ever widening circles."[202]

Just as Emily finished her celebration ritual, a flock of brightly colored birds began to sing over the circle where we were sitting; among them were rose-breasted grosbeaks, purple finch, and yellow canaries. According to mythological lore, the rose-breasted grosbeak is associated with "the healing of the family heart; it can teach us to heal all of the old wounds and hurts of family origin." The canary is part of the finch family and is connected, mythically, with the "awakening of the throat and heart centers of the body."[203]

We all rejoiced with Emily that the natural world, with which she had such a deep and abiding relationship, had come to sing and celebrate the transformation of her life from threads of darkness into newly woven patterns of color, light, and sound.

Claire based her celebration, six years after beginning our work together in the group, on a series of poems that told the story of the transformation of her life. Just two months earlier, she had found a book of poetry by the Sufi mystic, Hafiz. The book was entitled, *The Gift*. Indeed, it proved to be so for her life!

The first poem, which she felt was reflective of her life now, was called, "Tired of Speaking Sweetly." The lines that struck her were: "Break all your teacup talk of God" and "… rip to shreds/All your erroneous notions of truth."[204]

Claire recognized the false beliefs that she had to let go of in order to be free to live her own life. She no longer chose to please others or to live up to their expectations in order to survive. The second poem she read was one with which many of the women in the group were familiar:

Many are called.
But most are frozen,
in corporate or collective cold.
These are the stalled,
who choose not to be chosen,
but rather, to be bought and sold.[205]

After reading this poem, Claire shared her belief that she now appreciated that she had indeed left the "collective cold." As a child, she had never felt she quite belonged to the ordinary world in which most people in her family and community found themselves. She experienced herself struggling to get into that world where others seemed to feel comfortable in their routines of everyday life. Then she had several dreams in which she was dismembered, taken apart piece by piece. Claire felt torn by the realization that she could not go back to the unconscious "collective cold," even if she wanted to! She decided to honor her own wisdom. She recognized that now that she was conscious in so many aspects of her life, she could never go back to leading an unconscious life, no matter how safe and comfortable it appeared.

Mary Oliver's poem, "The Journey," was the third poem Claire chose for her celebration.[206] She asked herself the questions: "Whose life am I saving? Does this mean an external change or an internal shift?" Claire acknowledged that for her it meant *both* letting go of how she might be rescuing others and an inner commitment to honoring her own soul.

Then Claire shared several poems by Hafiz that had helped her renew and sustain her commitment to live her own life more fully and to let go of the anxiety that robs her of sleep and peace. One poem, "We Have Not Come to Take Prisoners,"[207] reminded Claire "to run from anything/that may not strengthen [her] precious budding wings."

Claire recognized that the most profound shift in her transformation was in the deepening of her spiritual life. She felt as if she were one of the Israelites wandering the desert for forty years looking for the Promised Land. She found herself meditating on the phrase, "There in the wilderness is a highway for your God."[208] Claire acknowledged that, although she had been on all kinds of wilderness adventures, "This is a wilderness I did not choose."

Claire realized that in her process of transformation she had experienced what felt like an amputation, a cutting away of what was toxic within her. Then she made a commitment:

- to refuse to just survive,
- to relinquish her need to live through others, and
- to never give up her authenticity.

She stated, "I have decided that there is no self-sacrifice in the script of my life." She concluded her ritual with the question, "What can I celebrate?" The words of Hafiz came to her:

> You carry all the ingredients
> To turn your existence into joy.[209]

Claire affirmed, "Today, I have decided to mix them!"

Alexis began her celebration of transformation with the metaphor of the flow of energy. She declared to the group, "I want to align my personal axis of energy flow with the *axis mundi*, the energy of the world." She expressed her longing to find balance in her yearning for a spiritual center so that she could move more consciously from grandiose expectations to grounding in her intention. She then shared:

> I have always had a burning desire to create. Art is my calling. Painting is my way of healing others and myself. The Divine Feminine for me is no longer the idealized Madonna but *veriditas*, the greening creative energy of life.

Alexis recognized the shift that had occurred within her as she separated herself from her mother's insecurity and made the choice to stand on her own two feet. She recalled the images from her dreams associated with our work on the fairy tales: the witch who came as Mother Hulda to show her the way to the place where she could find nourishment; the bat that became a large, black bird attacking her hand; and her transformation into a gargoyle on the walls of the Cathedral of Notre Dame. Alexis recognized in this last image the ways in which she becomes inflated, needing to be "the honored one to do the healing work."

Alexis reported that she had become keenly aware of the fact that whenever she got caught in grandiose expectations of herself, she became emotionally paralyzed and found herself in a creative desert. Through her transformation work, she made the choice to face her fear of not being/having enough and her reluctance to claim her own independence.

Alexis reported a recent dream that helped her reclaim her energy for her own transformation: "I saw a snake that had one eye. I had to blow on it before it blew on me."

She recalled a myth of a snake with a head at both ends. She reported that according to the myth:

> You must face him. If you don't he will cause you to spin, lonely and afraid. Stand firm when you see him. Each head must see his face. Then, he will bless you with magic. Your truth will be found behind your own eyes, and you will not lose it again.

Alexis interpreted this mythical image to mean that when she is able to face her fears and stand firm she will be able to articulate her own truth more clearly and to access her own hidden power more readily.

She described another dream in which an image of a shaman from one of her paintings came to her. In the dream, she found a stick. The shaman directed her to put it beside a boulder, and she obeyed his instructions. When she returned, a tree had blossomed from the planted stick. She interpreted this dream as a message of affirmation from her inner spiritual healer.

Alexis realized that her body was actually a divining rod. If she were faithful in attending to the shifts of energy within herself, she would be able to live from a healthier, creative place. She committed herself to surrendering to the source of all life, going into the depths, and finding the inner wisdom with which she has been gifted. Alexis acknowledged that she has to leave behind her fears and all the ways she has sabotaged her own creativity in the past. She shared a dream with the group that reinforced her commitment to claim her own personal power:

> I have crossed a large body of water in a canoe. I have to go back the same way. I am confident that I can. I don't belong there anymore.

We celebrated with Alexis her determination to keep "paddling her own canoe," a metaphor for the process of her own individuation. We rejoiced in the confidence she was now able to claim, for honoring her own life and leaving behind old ways of feeling and thinking that robbed her of her personal power and peace.

Rita had moved to another city and was not able to join the group for the celebration of transformation six years after we began our work on the fairy tales. However, her life had continued to blossom with promise once she decided to claim her own destiny, honor her creative gifts as an artist, and experience more deeply the loving relationships within her family.

As we reviewed in Chapter 1, the psychotherapeutic literature describes observable signs that a person is moving beyond a traumatic loss. These include:

- the development of healthy trusting relationships,
- the ability to share information about the effects of the loss and the experience of grief and mourning,
- the willingness to recall the trauma in a safe environment and deal with the feelings that are evoked by the memory, and

- the restructuring of one's thinking so that the trauma can be integrated with meaning into one's life and view of the world.[210]

All seven of the women exhibited signs of transformation following trauma. Each one was able to acknowledge a significant increase in her:

- self-reliance,
- sensitivity to others,
- compassion for herself and others,
- positive self-perception,
- openness to self-disclosure,
- appreciation of the role of suffering in her process of transformation,
- resilience in the face of pain and loss, and
- spiritual growth in her search for meaning.[211]

I felt a deep sense of profound privilege for having been midwife/witness of the process of transformation in each of these courageous women.

Nine years after beginning our work together, Michaela commented that she now realized that she and each of her sister Spinsters had found her own unique way out of her deepest wound to contribute to the healing of others.

Michaela had been wounded in her thinking, falsely believing that being a girl meant being without worth and value. From a woman unable to appreciate her own feminine beauty, she became a teacher of other women, encouraging the unfolding of their journeys and inviting them to discover the truth and beauty of their own lives.

Claire, whose young body had been violated, joined one of the medical professions and committed herself to assisting others in reclaiming the health and integrity of their bodies.

Emily, who had been hungry for love and affirmation, became a holistic healer, using natural remedies from the earth, which had become her mother.

Rita, who had needed to achieve in the external world to prove her worth and right to exist, became an artist focusing on the splendors of the natural world and its inner beauty.

Jessica, whose maternal wound was in being silenced and forbidden to tell the truth, became a writer, uncovering what was hidden so that the unspoken story could be heard and understood.

Alexis, wounded in not being affirmed for her creative gifts, became an artist and teacher, inviting her students to claim their inner spiritual power through their art.

Estelle, wounded in her ability to express her emotions, became a famous musician and teacher, sought after because of her capacity to connect spirituality with the creative expressive power of tone and the blending of sounds.

Each of the women had chosen, in her own way, to re-spin the fragments of her life into new threads that could hold the tension of the trauma of her early loss of a nurturing mother. Each had decided, "to come out from under the image of the negative mother" and find the energy "to rejoice in her outcast state and use it to renew the world."[212]

.

EPILOGUE

The seven little girls who had no mothers grew up to be seven wise women.

The first wise woman moved beyond her corporate career to reclaim her creative gifts as an artist. She developed educational programs to encourage and inspire other women to also claim and share their creative gifts. As a mother and a grandmother, she continues to honor and celebrate the love present in her life.

The second wise woman developed her gifts as a healer. She dedicated her energies to bringing others to the realization that they had the power within themselves to choose a healthy lifestyle. Moving beyond the pervasive despair that had enveloped her early years, she immersed herself in the beauty of the natural world of the Divine Mother who nourished her soul and gave her the courage to fully claim her own body as precious.

The third wise woman rediscovered the positive qualities of the mother she had abandoned when she thought her mother had abandoned her. She triumphed through her struggles, and was finally able to believe in and honor her own beauty as a woman. Her spiritual experience was transformed by a relationship with the Divine Feminine image of Sophia, the Wisdom of God. Through her own liberation from the restrictions of a patriarchal world, she released other women with whom she worked to reclaim their own feminine beauty and power.

The fourth wise woman embraced the pain and losses in her life and focused her life energy as a healer of those who struggled to bring their own pain and loss to a place of transformation. Moving out of self-doubt and despair, she discovered a deeply felt conviction of her true power and worth as a creative woman. Her courage and commitment to life continue to inspire others to claim their own choices for a healthy life.

The fifth wise woman reclaimed her own life in its dark, as well as its light, aspects. She released herself from her need to be the good daughter who reflected a positive image of her mother. No longer afraid of her own shadow, she now celebrates who she is in her own essence. She is a gifted, creative artist and facilitator of the creative gifts of others; her energy flows out like a refreshing spring of life to those who are thirsty.

The sixth wise woman let go of her unhealthy, codependent relationship with her mother. She released herself with conscious compassion to live her own life, setting both her mother and herself free. She also released her daughter from the potential of reliving the relationship she had had with her own mother. Her mother and her daughter both claimed their own lives and pursued the expression of their own creative energies. She has dedicated her life to facilitating a deeper understanding of the relationship between the spiritual and creative worlds in her own work and that of her students.

The seventh wise woman broke the silence of the secret of her maternal history and released her mother from the dark shame of her lost heritage. In the process, a new chapter of life opened for her, for her mother, and for all the members of her family. A deep pride in her roots emerged out of the well of despair. Using her creative gifts and honoring the truth of who she is, she reclaimed her right, and that of her family, to come out from under the pall of shame and death and to experience joy.

ABOUT THE AUTHOR

Marcella Hannon Shields, PhD, is a native of New York City. She has practiced as a psychologist in a variety of clinical and counseling settings in the United States and Canada for more than thirty years. She is the cofounder, with her husband, Eldon, of the Hannon-Shields Centre for Leadership and Peace in Toronto, where the work for this book began. The main purpose of the Centre is the promotion of compassion and peace for persons, communities, and the earth. Out of this commitment, the Children's Peace Theatre was born and continues to serve the community of the city of Toronto. Dr. Shields believes that global peace will only be possible when personal peace and a sense of hope for the future are restored, particularly for our children.

Over the past twenty-five years, Dr. Shields has primarily focused her practice on the healthy psychological development of women. Her practice has been strongly influenced by her study of Carl Jung and her work with Jungian analyst and author Marion Woodman, and a group of women Jungian psychotherapists in Toronto. Having lectured and led workshops in the United States, Canada, and New Zealand, Dr. Shields is now in private practice in the Pocono Mountain area of Pennsylvania, where she resides with her husband.

APPENDIX

A. Reflection Questions by Chapter for Mothers of Daughters:

I. What are the positive threads of your own experience of being mothered? What are the negative experiences that you don't want to repeat with your own daughter?

II. What was your relationship to your father? Did he expect you to achieve for him? What did you have to do to make him proud of you? Do you feel that your daughter has to "get the gold" (and if so, for whom)?

III. What was the atmosphere in your home when you were growing up? Were there hard times that you remember? Did you feel that love and resources were scarce? How did this affect you? What creative gifts can you acknowledge as your own? Can you make the distinction between your own hands (your own way of being creative in the world) and "silver hands" fashioned by a partner or spouse as a substitute for what you may have lost at the hands of your parents?

IV. Did you see yourself as your mother or father's favorite? How did this influence your life? Is one of your daughters your favorite? What are the consequences of this for her and for you?

V. What is your experience of benevolent, hostile, and/or ambivalent sexism? What do you see to be your daughter's experience? What are you teaching your daughter about how to respond to each of these forms of sexism?

VI. How do you deal with the demands, challenges, and irritations of daily life with your daughter? Have you found the balance between discipline and withholding love?

VII. Are you aware of ways in which your daughter might be competing with you for her father's attention? Do you feel competitive with her? How would you know? What choices do you have to share the attention you both need?

B. Reflection Questions by Chapter for Stepmothers of Daughters:

I. What are the positive threads of your own experience of being mothered? What are the negative experiences you don't want to repeat with your stepdaughter(s)? Did you have a stepmother when you were growing up? What was the experience like for you to have a substitute mother?

II. What was your relationship with your father? Did he expect you to achieve for him? What did you have to do to make him proud of you? Did you have a stepfather? What was that experience like for you? Are there men in your life that you find yourself trying to impress with your achievements?

III. What was the atmosphere in your home when you were growing up? Were there hard times that you remember? Were resources and love scarce? How did this affect you? What are the creative gifts that you can acknowledge as your own? Can you make the distinction between your own hands (your own way of being creative in the world) and "silver hands" fashioned by a partner or spouse as a substitute for what you may have lost at the hands of your parents or stepparents?

IV. Did you see yourself as your mother or father's favorite, or did you feel another one of your siblings was her or his favorite? How has this influenced your life? How would you know? Is one of your daughters or stepdaughters your favorite? What are the consequences of this for her and for you? If you have your own daughters, as well as stepdaughters, how do you respond to each of them?

V. What is your experience of benevolent, hostile, and/or ambivalent sexism? What do you see to be your daughter's experience? What are you teaching your daughter/stepdaughter about how to respond to each of these forms of sexism?

VI. How do you deal with the demands, challenges, and irritations of daily life with your stepdaughter? Have you found the balance between discipline and withholding love? How do you handle comments about not being her real mother?

VII. Are you aware of ways in which your stepdaughter might be competing with you for her father's attention? Do you feel competitive with her? How would you know? What choices do you have to share the attention you both need?

C. Reflection Questions by Chapter for Grandmothers of Granddaughters:

I. As you look back over your life, what are the threads of the value of being a woman that you inherited from the women in your family? What threads of your maternal heritage have remained intact and important to you, and which ones have you discarded? What do you want to tell your granddaughter about the true value of being a woman?

II. What painful experiences have you had in raising your own children that you don't want to repeat with your granddaughter? What would make you most proud of her? How can you communicate this to her?

III. Have you ever worn the "silver hands" that kept you from expressing your true creative potential? What bargains have you made in your life that you would not want your granddaughter to repeat?

IV. What does it mean for you to be a good enough grandmother? How can you hold your granddaughter in love without trying to possess her or make demands on her? How will you know if this is happening?

V. What is your own experience of benevolent and hostile sexism? How have you dealt with it in your life? What would you want to share with your granddaughter?

VI. Have there been times when you have tried to avoid or escape the traumas and losses in your life through addictions—including needing to be perfect or having to always please others in order to survive? What has this taught you that you can share with your granddaughter?

VII. How can you truly mirror your granddaughter's beauty to her? In what ways can you affirm her strengths and encourage her to face her future with hope?

D. Reflection Questions by Chapter for Fathers Raising Daughters Without a Consistent Maternal Presence:

I. What do you remember as the positive threads of your relationship with your mother and the other women in your family? What were you taught about the differences between boys and girls and men and women? What are the ten most valuable characteristics of a woman that you still hold to be true? How have you shared this with your daughter?

II. Does your daughter feel that she has to do what Daddy wants, even if she may have other choices she would like to make? How would you know if this were happening? Do you have a dream for your daughter to achieve beyond that which you feel you have been able to achieve? Do you expect her to "get the gold" for you? How do you know?

III. Do you expect your daughter to sacrifice herself for the good of the family? What is your daughter's dream for her own life? Are there ways in which she may feel handicapped by her loyalty to you? Is her creative life her own, or have you made her "silver hands"? What would be the signs that this has happened?

IV. If you have more than one child, do you have a favorite daughter? What signs would be evident if this were true? What are the consequences for her and for you?

V. What is your understanding of the difference between benevolent sexism, hostile sexism, and ambivalent sexism? Do you fit the description of the benevolent father, trying to protect your daughter from the world? Or, do you find yourself fitting the sexist category of hostile or ambivalent? How does this affect your relationship with your daughter?

VI. Are you an "absent" father, either emotionally or physically? How present are you to the healthy development of your daughter? How do you know?

VII. What do you see to be the qualities of a beautiful girl/woman? How are these reflected in your daughter? If you are in relationships with women, how does this affect your daughter (or is there competition between these women and your daughter)? What would be the signs that this is happening? How do you mirror your daughter's beauty back to her?

NOTES

Introduction

1   Kathrin Asper, *Rumpelstilskin and the Voice of the Patriarchy*. Conference Notes. Einsiedlin, Switzerland, June 1994.

2   Sybille Birkhauser-Oeri, *The Mother: Archetypal Image in Fairy Tales*. (Toronto: Inner City Press, 1988), 9.

3   Carl G. Jung, *The Collected Works of Carl G. Jung*, trans. R. F. C. Hull, Bollingen Series XX, Vol. 9. (Princeton, N.J.: Princeton University Press, 1971), 5-6.

4   Max. Luthi, *Volksmarchen and Volkssagen*, 2nd ed. (Bern and Munich: Franck Verlag, l966).

5   Jack Zipes, ed., *Don't Bet On the Prince* (New York: Routledge, 1989).

6   Maria M. Tatar, *The Hard Facts of the Grimm's Fairy Tales* (Princeton, N.J.: Princeton University Press, 1987), 29.

7   Kathrin Asper, *The Abandoned Child Within: On Losing and Regaining Self Worth* (New York: Fromm, 1993), 5.

8   Marie Louise Von Franz, *The Cat: A Tale of Feminine Redemption* (Toronto: Inner City Books, 1999), 9.

9   J. D. Salinger, *Raise High the Roof Beams Carpenters & Seymour: An Introduction* (Boston: Little, Brown & Co., 1963), 160-161.

10 "The Rock Will Wear Away," Lyrics by Holly Near, Music by Meg Christian, Hereford Music/Thumbelina Music, 1977.

Chapter I—Spinning Threads That Hold

11 J. and W. Grimm, *Grimm's Tales for Young and Old: The Complete Stories*, trans. Ralph Mannheim (Garden City: Doubleday, 1977).

12 Marina Warner, *From the Beast to the Blonde: On Fairy Tales and Their Tellers* (New York: Farrar, Strauss and Giroux, 1994), 124-128.

13   Ibid.

14   Ibid., 169.

15   Gertrude M. Nelson, *Here All Dwell Free* (New York: Fawcett Columbine, 1991), 230.

16   Carl G. Jung, "Psychological Aspects of the Mother Archetype, The Archetypes and the Collective Unconscious" in *Collected Works*, 9i, 184+.

17   Berkhauser-Oeri, *The Mother*, 116.

18   G. W. Brown, O. Bifulco, and L. Bridge, "Life Stress, Chronic Sub-Clinical Symptoms and Vulnerability to Clinical Depression," *Journal of Affective Disorders* 11 (1986), 1-19.

19   L. Y. Abramson, G. L. Metalsky, and L. B. Alloy, "Hopelessness Depression: A Theory Based Subtype of Depression," *Psychological Review* 96 (1989), 358-372.

20   D. Jack, "Silencing the Self: The Power of Social Imperatives in Female Depression" in R. Fornasek and A. Gurian, eds., *Women and Depression: A Lifespan Perspective* (New York: Springer, 1987), 161-181.

21   C. G. Jung, *Collected Works*, 9i, 184+.

22   Ellen McGrath, et al., *Women and Depression, Risk Factors and Treatment Issues* (Washington, D.C.: APA Books, 1990), 16-18.

23   Claire, untitled poem, 1996.

24   MacGrath, et al., *Women and Depression*, 19.

25   S. Nolen-Hocksema, 1987, *Psychological Bulletin*, 101, 259-282.

26   Robert Johnson, *Inner Work: Using Dreams and Active Imagination for Personal Growth* (New York: Harper and Row, 1986), 24.

27   McGrath, et al., *Women and Depression*, 18-19.

28   Bruno Bettleheim, *The Uses of Enchantment: The Meaning and Importance of Fairy Tales* (New York: Alfred A. Knopf, 1977).

29   Berkauser-Oeri, *The Mother*, 116.

30   Johnson, *Inner Work*, 21.

31   Adrienne Rich, *Of Woman Born: Motherhood as Experience and Institution* (New York: Norton, 1986), 220.

32   Theresa Rando, Conference Notes, "Therapeutic Interventions in Grief and Mourning," 2003.

33   McGrath, et al., *Women and Depression*, 19.

34   Asper, *The Abandoned Child Within*, 31.

35   Ibid., 25, 28.

36   D. W. Winnicott, *Maturational Processes and the Facilitating Environment* (New York: International Universities Press, 1980).

37   Rando, "Therapeutic Interventions," 2003.

38   J. and W. Grimm, *Grimm's Tales for Young and Old, #55*

39   Ibid., A variation of "The Tale of the Three Spinners," #14.

40   Ibid., #31.

41   Ibid., #24.

42   Ibid., #50.

43   Ibid., #93.

44   Ibid., #53.

45   Diane Fassel, "The Dream," unpublished poem, 1995.

46   Claire, untitled poem, 1996.

Chapter II—In the Name of the Father: The Tale of Rumplestilskin

47   J. and W. Grimm, *Childhood and Household Tales*, 1810.

48   Iona and Peter Opie, *The Classic Fairy Tales* (London: Oxford University Press, 1974), 195.

49   This synopsis is based on the text from *German Popular Stories*, translated from *Kinder und Haus Marchen, Collected by M. M. Grimm from Oral Tradition* (London: C. Baldwyn, 1823). This was the first printing of the story in English, ref. Opie, *Classic Fairy Tales*, 197-198.

50   C. G. Jung, *Memories, Dreams, Reflections* (New York: Vintage Books, 1965), 117, 124.

51   *The Bible*, The Book of Judith, 13: 4-9.

52   J. and W. Grimm, *Grimm's Tales for Young and Old*, # 55.

53   Von Franz, *The Cat: A Tale of Feminine Redemption*, 88.

54   Marie Louise Von Franz, *The Problem of the Feminine in Fairy Tales* (Dallas, Tex.: Spring Publications, 1972), 58.

55   I. and P. Opie, *The Classic Fairy Tales*, 196.

56   J. Bowlby, *Attachment and Loss* (New York: Basic Books, 1976, 1980, 1983), Vol. 1, 379; Vol. 2, Chap. 2; Vol. 3, 368ff.

57   Ibid.

58   Robert Kegan, *The Evolving Self: Problems and Process in Human Development* (Cambridge, Mass.: Harvard University Press, 1982), 100,107,191.

59   Carl G. Jung, ed. Sonu Shamdasani, *The Psychology of Kundalini Yoga: Notes of Seminar in 1932*, Bollingen Series, XCIX (Princeton, N.J.: Princeton University Press, 1996), 28-29.

60   Mario Jacoby, *The Longing for Paradise: Psychological Perspectives on an Archetype* (Boston: Sigo Press, 1985).

61   I. and P. Opie, *The Classic Fairy Tales*, 198.

62   Edward F. Edinger, *The Creation of Consciousness* (Toronto: Inner City Books, 1984).

63   Tatar, *The Hard Facts of the Grimm's Fairy Tales*, 128.

64   J. and W. Grimm, *The Grimm's Tales for Young and Old*, #14.

65   Estelle's song, 1996.

Chapter III—Emancipation from Servitude: The Tale of the Handless Maiden

66   This synopsis of the tale of "The Handless Maiden" is based on the early Grimm's tale entitled "The Girl Without Hands." For a complete version of the story see Nelson, *Here All Dwell Free*, 11-27.

67   Nelson, *Here All Dwell Free*, 14.

68   Tatar, *The Hard Facts of the Grimm's Fairy Tales*, 80, 149.

69   Von Franz, *The Feminine in Fairy Tales*, 42.

70   Nelson, *Here All Dwell Free*, 11.

71   Gloria Steinhem, *Revolution from Within: A Book of Self Esteem* (Boston: Little, Brown & Co., 1992), 228. See also: Jean Goodwin and Reina Attiasr, "Eating Disorders in Victims of Multi-modal Childhood Abuse," *Festschrift for Cornelia Wilbur*, ed. Richard Kluft, n.d.

72   Mary Oliver, "The Journey," poem in *New and Selected Poems* (Boston: Beacon Press, 1992), 114.

73   Von Franz, *The Problem of the Feminine in Fairy Tales*, 81.

74   Ted Andrews, *Animal Speak* (St. Paul, Minn.: Llewellyn Publishing, 1997), 248.

75   L. F. Baum, *The Wizard of Oz*, 1900.

76 Tatar, *The Hard Facts of the Grimm's Fairy Tales*, 80,149.

77 Andrews, *Animal Speak*, 363.

78 Von Franz, *The Problem of the Feminine in Fairy Tales*, 83.

79 *Bible*, 1 John 4:18.

80 Nelson, *Here All Dwell Free*, 336-341.

81 Tatar, *The Hard Facts of the Grimm's Fairy Tales*, 80.

82 Ibid.

83 Nelson, *Here All Dwell Free*, 22.

84 J. and W. Grimm, *Grimm's Tales*, #31.

85 Von Franz, *The Problem of the Feminine in Fairy Tales*, 57.

86 Nelson, *Here all Dwell Free*, 27.

87 Von Franz, *The Problem of the Feminine in Fairy Tales*, 88.

88 Andrews, *Animal Speak*, 337.

89 Oliver, "The Journey," 114-115.

Chapter IV—Rising from the Well of Grief: The Tale of Mother Hulda

90 J. and W. Grimm, *Grimm's Tales for Young and Old*, #24.

91 Nor Hall, *The Moon and the Virgin: Reflections on the Archetypal Feminine* (New York: Harper and Row, 1980), 207.

92 Ibid., 211-213.

93 Jacob Grimm, *Teutonic Mythology*, trans. James Steven Stallybrass (New York: Dover, 1966).

94 The original title of this tale in Grimm's 1812 edition of *Kinder und Haus Marchen* was "Mother Holle." This synopsis is based on the 1857 version of the tale in which the widow-mother became a stepmother (ref. Tatar, *The Hard Facts of the Grimm's Fairy Tales*, 28.) For a source of the complete tale see *Household Stories from the Collection of the Brothers Grimm*, trans. Lucy Crane (New York: Dover Publications, 1963).

95 Carl G. Jung, ed. Sonu Shamdasani, *The Psychology of Kundalini Yoga. Notes of Seminar in 1932*, Bollingen Series, XCIX (Princeton, N.J., Princeton University Press, 1996), 28-29.

96 *Bible*, Gospel of Mark 8:35.

97   D. W. Winnicott, *Maturational Processes and the Facilitating Environment*, 6th ed. (New York, International University Press, 1980), 49.

98   Ibid., 58.

99   J. and W. Grimm, *Grimm's Tales for Young and Old*, #24.

100 Asper, *The Abandoned Child Within*, 144-145.

101 Marion Woodman & Robert Bly, *The Maiden King* (New York: Henry Holt & Co., 1998), 149-150.

102 Robert A. Johnson, *Owning Your Own Shadow* (New York: Harper Collins, 1991), 8.

103 Asper, *The Abandoned Child Within*, 186-187.

104 I. and P. Opie, *The Classic Fairy Tales*, 98-102.

105 Ibid.

106 Asper, *The Abandoned Child Within*, 186.

107 Edward C. Whitmount, "The Evolution of the Shadow" in *Meeting the Shadow*, ed. C. Zweig and J. Abrams (Jeremy P. Tarcher/Perigee Books, 1991), 12.

108 J. and W. Grimm, *Grimm's Tales for Young and Old*, #24.

109 Ibid.

110 J. M. Barrie, *Peter Pan and Wendy* (New York: Orchard Books, 2004).

Chapter V—Waking from the Sleep of Ages: The Tale of Briar Rose

111 Woodman and Bly, *The Maiden King*, 1998.

112 Caitlin Matthews, *Sophia, Goddess of Wisdom*, (London: Thorsons, 1992).

113 Madonna Kolbenschlag, *Kiss Sleeping Beauty Goodbye: Breaking the Spell of Feminine Myths and Models* (New York: Doubleday and Co, 1979).

114 I. and P. Opie, *The Classic Fairy Tales*, 81.

115 J. and W. Grimm, *Grimm's Tales for Young and Old*, #50.

116 I. and P. Opie, *The Classic Fairy Tales*, 89-93.

117 This synopsis is based on the version of the tale in *German Popular Stories, Translated from the Kinder und Haus Marchen, Collected by M. M. Grimm, from Oral Tradition* (London: C. Baldwyn, 1823). For a full version of the tale see *The Grimm's Tales for Young and Old*, #50.

118 Bettlehiem, *The Uses of Enchantment*, 235.

119 Hall, *The Moon and the Virgin*, 197.

120 Ibid., 191.

121 P. Glick, et al. "Ambivalent Sexism and Attitudes toward Wife Abuse in Turkey and Brazil," *Psychology of Women Quarterly* (December 26, 2002), 292-297.

122 Ibid.

123 Ibid.

124 Ibid.

125 P. Glick and S. T. Fiske, "An Ambivalent Alliance: Hostile and Benevolent Sexism as Complementary Justifications for Gender Inequality," *American Psychologist* (February 2001), 109-118.

126 Ibid.

127 J. and W. Grimm, *Grimm's Tales for Young and Old*, #50.

128 D. Prentice and C. Carranza, "What Women and Men Should Be, Shouldn't Be, Are Allowed to Be, and Don't Have to Be: The Context of Prescriptive Gender Stereotypes," *Psychology of Women Quarterly* (December 2002), 269-281.

129 James Hollis, *The Eden Project: In Search of the Magical Other* (Toronto: Inner City Books, 1998).

130 Ibid.

131 J. and W. Grimm, *Grimm's Tales for Young and Old*, #50.

132 Marge Piercy, "The judgment," part of the poem "Laying Down the Tower" in *Circles on the Water* (New York: Alfred A. Knopf, 1982), 135.

133 Virginia Woolfe, *A Room of One's Own* (New York: Harcourt, Brace and Jovanovich, 1929, republished 1981).

134 C. G. Jung, *Collected Works*, 9i, P 184+.

135 I. and P. Opie, *The Classic Fairy Tales*, 86.

136 Asper, *The Abandoned Child Within*, 82.

137 Marion Woodman, *The Owl Was a Baker's Daughter* (Toronto: Inner City Books, 1980), 79.

138 Nelson, *Here All Dwell Free*, 205.

139 I. and P. Opie, *The Classic Fairy Tales*, 92.

140 Nelson, *Here All Dwell Free*, 211.

141 Woolfe, *A Room of One's Own.*

Chapter VI—Life Under Glass: The Tale of the Raven

142 This is a synopsis of the version of the Grimm's tale of "The Raven" that we used in the group. The original Grimm's tale of "The Raven," was published in *Kinder und Haus Marchen, Childhood and Household Tales.* A later version of the tale can be found in *Grimm's Tales for Young and Old,* #93.

143 Birkhauser-Oeri, *The Mother,* 64.

144 Asper, *The Abandoned Child Within,* 146.

145 Andrews, *Animal Speak,* 187.

146 F. H. Burnett, *The Secret Garden* (New York: Harper Collins, 1911).

147 Marion Woodman, *Bone: Dying into Life* (New York: Penguin Press, 2000), 164.

148 Jung, *Collected Works,* 13, 262.

149 Birkhauser-Oeri, *The Mother,* 65.

150 Andrews, *Animal Speak,* 241.

151 Ibid., 315.

152 Ibid., 283.

153 Ibid., 69.

154 Woodman and Bly, *The Maiden King,* 1998.

155 Hall, *The Moon and the Virgin,* 210-211.

156 Birkhauser-Oeri, *The Mother,* 64.

157 Theresa Rando, *Treatment of Complicated Bereavement* (Champaign, Ill.: Research Press, 1993).

158 ———, "Therapeutic Interventions in Grief and Mourning," Conference Notes, July 2003.

159 John Bowlby, *Attachment and Loss,* 1976, 1980, 1983.

160 Rando, Conference Notes, 2003, ref. to Moore and Fine, 1990, 199.

161 Karen Horney, *Neurosis and Human Growth: The Struggle toward Self-Realization* (New York: W. W. Norton, 1950), 64-65.

162 Theresa Rando, ed., *Parental Loss of a Child* (Champaign, Ill.: Research Press, 1986).

163 Woodman, *The Pregnant Virgin,* 34.

Chapter VII—In Our Mother's Mirror: The Tale of Snow White

164 Asper, *The Abandoned Child Within*, 19.

165 Woodman and Bly, *The Maiden King*, 149.

166 J. and W. Grimm, *Grimm's Tales for Young and Old*, #53.

167 This synopsis of the tale of "Snow White" is based on the text of the tale published under its original title, "Snow Drop," in *German Popular Stories, Translated from Kinder und Haus Marchen, Collected by M. M. Grimm from Oral Tradition* (London: C. Baldwyn, 1823). [Ref. Opie, *The Classic Fairy Tales*, 175-182.]

168 Asper, *The Abandoned Child Within*, 140-142.

169 Moira MacDougall, "Snow White," unpublished poem, 1998.

170 Asper, *The Abandoned Child Within*, 67.

171 Ibid., 30.

172 J. and W. Grimm, *Grimm's Tales for Young and Old*, #53.

173 Asper, *The Abandoned Child Within*, 30.

174 S. Lyubomirsky, et al., "What Triggers Abnormal Eating in Bulimic and Non-Bulimic Women," *Psychology of Women Quarterly* (2001), 25, 223-232.

175 Woodman, *The Pregnant Virgin*, 119.

176 M. F. Hirgoyen, *Stalking the Soul: Emotional Abuse and the Erosion of Identity* (New York: Helen Marx Books, 2000).

177 Ibid.

178 Birkhauser-Oeri, *The Mother*, 36.

179 J. and W. Grimm, *Grimm's Tales*, #53.

180 Ibid., 186.

181 Andrews, *Animal Speak*, 172, 187, 133.

182 A. N. Zucker, et al., "Smoking in College Women: The Role of Thinness Pressures, Media Exposure, and Critical Consciousness," *Psychology of Women Quarterly* (2001), 25, 233-241.

183 Ibid.

184 William Blake, Song VIII in *The Complete Poetry and Prose of William Blake*, ed. D. V. Erdman (Berkeley: University of California Press, 1982).

185 J. and W. Grimm, *Grimm's Tales*, #53.

186 John Bowlby, *The Making and Breaking of Affectional Bonds*, 1979, 103; *Attachment and Loss*, Vol. 2, 1976, 322ff.

187 Sylvia Brinton-Perea, *Celtic Queen Maeve and Addictions* (York Beach, Maine: Nicholas-Hays, 2001), 117.

188 Emily Dickinson, "The World Is Not Conclusive," in *Norton Anthology of American Literature*, Vol. 1, 2458.

189 J. and W. Grimm, *Grimm's Tales*, #53.

190 I. and P. Opie, *The Classic Fairy Tales*, 175.

191 Ibid., 92.

192 R. M. Rilke, *Duino Elegies*, No. 4, trans. David Young (New York: W.W. Norton, 1978).

193 Woodman, *The Pregnant Virgin*, 100.

194 Ibid., 122.

Chapter VIII—The Threads Rewoven

195 Carl G. Jung, *Collected Works*, Vol. 16, 185-186.

196 C. Moreau, Jungian Winter Seminar Notes, "Shadow and Healing, Suffering and Meaning," Zurich, Switzerland, January 1997.

197 Woodman, *The Pregnant Virgin*, 108.

198 Marianne Williamson, *Return To Love: Reflections on the Principles of A Course in Miracles* (New York: Harper Collins, 1992), 190-191.

199 C. Fulmer, "Now Is the Time," musical composition, 1994.

200 David Whyte, "Waking Up," poem in *Where Many Rivers Meet* (Langley, Washington: Many Rivers Press, 1993), 236-237.

201 B. P. Powell, ed., "The Tale of Ariadne and Theseus," in *Classical Myth* (Saddle River, N.J.: Prentice Hall, 2001), 429.

202 R. M. Rilke, "I am living my life in circles expanding," in *The Book of Hours*, trans. A. L. Peck (London: Hogarth Press, 1961), 45.

203 Andrews, *Animal Speak*, 148, 123.

204 Daniel Ladinsky, *The Gift: Poems by Hafiz, the Great Sufi Master* (New York: Penguin Press, 1999), 187.

205 L. Pieper, "Many Are Called," unpublished poem, 1982.

206 Mary Oliver, "The Journey," in *New and Selected Poems*, 114.

207 Ladinsky, *The Gift*, 28.

208 *Bible*, Isaiah 40: 3.

209 Ladinsky, *The Gift*, 48.

210 Rando, *Treatment of Complicated Bereavement*, 1993.

211 ———, Conference Notes, "Therapeutic Interventions in Grief and Mourning," July 2003.

212 Woodman, *The Pregnant Virgin*, 100.

GLOSSARY

Active Imagination: The process of engaging images from dreams in a dialogue recorded by the dreamer in order to discover the meaning and message of the image.

Addictions: Repeated patterns of behavior that ultimately never satisfy.

Amplification: The process of achieving a deeper understanding of symbols as they appear in dreams, fairy tales, and myths, usually through spontaneous associations with the image to gain an appreciation of their personal meaning.

Archetype: Universal images and motifs that occur over and over in dreams, fairy tales, and myths across cultures and time.

Baba Yaga: The old woman of fairy tales and myths who challenges heroes and heroines to stay true to their own destiny.

Consciousness: That which is in our awareness and, consequently, can be acted upon if we choose to do so.

Defenses: Unconscious strategies that we develop in order to avoid what we perceive to be unpleasant or aversive.

Fate: The belief that we have no choice over our own lives and destinies because it has been predetermined for us by others or by the circumstances of our birth or status in society.

Feminine/Masculine: The yin and yang of our lives as women and men; two aspects of ourselves as human persons.

Individuation: The process by which we come to claim our true identities; the path to self-realization.

Metaphor: A symbolic bridge to expanding our understanding of images.

Mother Complex: Unconscious layers of memory of our relationships with our mothers (or other maternal caretakers) that are charged with meaning. These layers will often rise to the surface when events in our lives evoke the memories of what remains unfinished in our relationships with our mothers (or other maternal caretakers).

Mother Abandonment Wound: The residual effects of maternal deprivation that are carried into our adult lives and continue to affect our perception of ourselves and our relationships with others.

Patriarch: The word means master or ruler with sovereign power. The expression *patriarchal world* refers to one in which the father/king has ultimate power. This may be experienced as a benevolent, protective relationship, or a demanding, tyrannical one.

Persona: Our way of presenting ourselves and wanting to be seen by others. The word was originally associated with an actor's mask.

Puer/Puella: Men/women who refuse to grow up and take responsibility for their own lives. They do not develop mature relationships with others. Instead, they expect that others will care for them in the way that they desire.

Self: An image of the Divine within the human person, the totality of the human personality. (In contrast, the self with a small *s* refers to the human ego.)

Soul: An image of our life principle, which has as its essential characteristic the capacity to animate and be animated.

Shadow: Those aspects of ourselves that we deny and which are, therefore, hidden from our awareness. Our shadow includes both the positive and negative attributes that we do not acknowledge as our own but generally readily identify in others.

Tribe: A connection to our families and cultural heritage.

Trauma: A life event over which we have no control that affects us deeply (generally, both physically and emotionally). It can occur as a result of a physical external event such as a natural disaster, a human-generated disaster (such as war, genocide), or a dramatic personal loss such as abandonment or the sudden death of a loved one. This latter is referred to as a relational trauma.

Unconscious: The personal unconscious refers to that which remains hidden from our individual awareness. The collective unconscious includes the universal qualities of the human psyche that are outside of our awareness and not restricted to our individual personality.

BIBLIOGRAPHY

Andrews, T. *Animal Speak*, St. Paul, Minn.: Llewellyn, 1997.

Asper, K. *The Abandoned Child Within: On Losing and Regaining Self Worth*. New York: Fromm, 1993.

Bettleheim, B. *The Uses of Enchantment: The Meaning and Importance of Fairy Tales*. New York: Alfred A. Knopf, 1977.

Birkhauser-Oeri, S. *The Mother: Archetypal Images in Fairy Tales*, Toronto: Inner City Books, 1988.

Bowlby, J. *The Making and Breaking of Affectional Bonds*. London : Routledge & Kegan Paul, 1979.

———. *Attachment and Loss*. Vol. 1, 2nd ed. New York: Basic Books, 1983.

———. *Attachment and Loss*, Vol. 2 and Vol.3. New York: Basic Books, 1976, 1980.

Carlson, K. *In Her Image: The Unhealed Daughter's Search for Her Mother*. Boston: Shambhala, 1990.

Edinger, E. F. *The Creation of Consciousness*. Toronto: Inner City Books, 1984.

Edelman, H. *Motherless Daughters: The Legacy of Loss*. New York: Addison-Wesley, 1994.

Fromm, E. *The Forgotten Language: An Introduction to the Understanding of Dreams, Fairy Tales, and Myths*. New York: Holt, Rinehart, and Winston, 1951.

Grimm, J. and W. *Grimm's Tales for Young and Old: The Complete Stories*. Trans. Ralph Manheim. Garden City, N.Y.: Doubleday, 1977.

————. *The Penguin Selected Tales of the Brothers Grimm*. London: Claremont Books, 1995.

Hall, N. *The Moon and the Virgin: Reflections on the Archetypal Feminine*. New York: Harper and Row, 1980.

Hirgoyen, M. F. *Stalking the Soul: Emotional Abuse and the Erosion of Identity*. New York: Helen Marx Books, 2000.

Hollis, J. *The Eden Project: In Search of the Magical Other*. Toronto: Inner City Books, l998.

Jacoby, M. *The Longing for Paradise: Psychological Perspectives on an Archetype*, Boston, Mass.: Sigo Press, 1985.

Johnson, R. *Inner Work: Using Dreams and Active Imagination for Personal Growth*. New York: Harper and Row, 1986.

————. *Owning Your Own Shadow: Understanding the Dark Side of the Psyche*. New York: Harper Collins, 1993.

Jung, C. G. *Collected Works*. Ed. Gerhard Adler et al., Bollingen Series XX. Princeton, N.J.: Princeton University Press, 1954.

————. *The Psychology of Kundalini Yoga*. Notes of Seminar in 1932 Bollingen Series, XCIX. Ed. Sonu Shamdasani. Princeton, N.J.: Princeton University Press, 1996.

————. *Memories, Dreams, Reflections*. Ed. Aniela Jaffe, trans. Richard and Clara Winston. New York: Random House, 1961.

Kegan, R. *The Evolving Self: Problem and Process in Human Development*. Cambridge, Mass.: Harvard University Press, 1982.

————. *In Over Our Heads: The Mental Demands of Modern Life*. Cambridge, Mass.: Harvard University Press, 1994.

Kolbenschlag, M. *Kiss Sleeping Beauty Goodbye: Breaking the Spell of Feminine Myths and Models*. New York: Doubleday, 1979.

Luthi, M. *Once Upon A Time: On the Nature of Fairy Tales.* Trans. L. Chadeayne and P. Gottwald. Bloomington: Indiana University Press, 1976.

McGrath, E., et al. *Women and Depression, Risk Factors and Treatment Issues.* Washington, D.C.: American Psychological Association Books, 1990.

Miller, A. *Breaking Down the Wall of Silence.* New York: Dutton, 1991.

Nelson, G. M. *Here All Dwell Free: Stories to Heal the Wounded Feminine.* New York: Ballantine Books, 1991.

Opie, I. and P. *The Classic Fairy Tales.* London: Oxford Press, 1974.

Perera, S. B. *Celtic Queen Maeve and Addictions.* York Beach, Maine: Nicholas-Hays, 2001.

————. *The Scapegoat Complex: Toward a Mythology of Shadow and Guilt.* Toronto: Inner City Books, 1993.

Rando, T. A., Ed. *Parental Loss of a Child,* Champaign, Ill.: Research Press, 1986.

————. *Treatment of Complicated Bereavement,* Champaign, Ill.: Research Press, 1993.

Rich, A. *Of Woman Born: Motherhood as Experience and Institution.* New York: Norton, 1986.

Steinem, G. *Revolution from Within: A Book of Self Esteem.* Boston: Little, Brown, 1992.

Tatar, M. *The Hard Facts of the Grimm's Fairy Tales.* Princeton, N.J.: Princeton University Press, 1987.

Von Franz, M. *The Problem of the Feminine in Fairy Tales.* Dallas, Tex.: Spring, 1972.

————. *An Introduction to the Interpretation of Fairy Tales.* Dallas, Tex.: Spring, 1978.

———. *The Cat: A Tale of Feminine Redemption*. Toronto: Inner City Books, 1999.

Warner, M. *From the Beast to the Blonde: On Fairy Tales and Their Tellers*. New York: Farrar, Strauss and Giroux, 1994.

Winnicott, D. W. *Maturational Processes and the Facilitating Environment*. 6th ed. New York: International University Press, 1980.

Woodman, M. *The Owl Was a Baker's Daughter*. Toronto: Inner City Books, 1980.

———. *The Pregnant Virgin*. Toronto: Inner City Books, 1985.

Woodman, M., et al. *Leaving My Father's House: A Journey to Conscious Femininity*. Boston: Shambhala, 1993.

Woodman, M., and R. Bly. *The Maiden King: The Reunion of the Masculine and Feminine*. New York: Henry Holt, 1998.

Woolfe, V. *A Room of One's Own*. 1929. New York: Harcourt, Brace, and Jovanovich, 1981.

978-0-595-46106-6
0-595-46106-9

Printed in the United States
120960LV00008B/4/P